Who Goes There

Who Goes There

(Travels through Strangest Britain, in Search of The Doctor)

Nick Griffiths

Legend Press
Independent Book Publisher

Legend Press Ltd
The Old Fire Station, 140 Tabernacle Street,
London EC2A 4SD
info@legendpress.co.uk
www.legendpress.co.uk

www.whogoesthere.org.uk
www.nickgriffiths.co.uk

*All characters, other than those clearly in the public domain, and
place names, other than those well-established such as towns and
cities, are fictitious and any resemblance is purely coincidental.*

Set in Times
Printed by Lightning Source, UK

Cover designed by Gudrun Jobst
www.yellowoftheegg.co.uk

Legend Press

Independent Book Publisher

Also by Nick Griffiths:

Dalek I Loved You

(Gollancz)

In the Footsteps of Harrison Dextrose

(Legend Press)

For Dad

FOREWORD

When I wrote my *Doctor Who* memoir, *Dalek I Loved You*, it was all about transferring memories to paper while sitting down. Why not, I thought afterwards, go several steps further: actually become a part of the programme? Travel to the very locations they had filmed in, occupy perhaps the same spot that the Doctor himself had once commanded. Even if the actors and production crew had left the scene up to 37 years earlier.

It didn't matter – they had still *been* there.

Doctor Who is a very odd programme, set in time and space, on alien worlds and future Earths. When I set out to visit several of its choicest locations, soak up the nostalgia, imagine myself in the adventures, it hadn't occurred to me that the places I'd be visiting might be downright weird. Old Baal Clay Pit, anyone? Dungeness nuclear power station? Binnegar Heath Sand Pit?

As the strangeness became apparent, I found myself hooked. By following a route dictated by inspired location managers down the decades, I was being treated to some of Britain's most obscure, eye-opening, regularly bonkers corners.

I don't even like travelling. At least not the getting-from-A-to-B bit. Loathe it. All that inhaling other people's teeny bits of dead skin; having to hold on to a handrail just to wee; the mindless tedium; being pestered by government scientists for a saliva sample, so they can harvest my developing halitosis to experiment and eventually produce the world's most hideous chemical weapon. Can't be doing with it.

But another beauty of *Doctor Who* was that they endeavoured not to stray too far from London – their base, and indeed mine – cost and speed being of the essence. So I could start in the capital, conveniently home; yet as the bug gripped me, I found myself venturing further and further out: Kent, Surrey, Dorset, Oxfordshire, Buckinghamshire, Wiltshire. Wales.

Somehow, it all felt painless (Ealing notwithstanding; see inside), all that travelling to distant worlds.

The locations, I chose from memory and through research. There are certain *Doctor Who* scenes, particularly from childhood, that are seared into my subconscious. In *Day of the Daleks*, for instance, where the Daleks and Ogrons emerge, supposedly from another planet, onto Earth via a tunnel beneath a small bridge. That's actually Bulls Bridge, on the Grand Union Canal in Southall. I had to go there.

Or the village scenes in *The Android Invasion*. All that sunshine and green, not a soul around, somehow so terribly English. (East Hagbourne, Oxfordshire. Went there, too.) Or the churchyard in *The Daemons*, where the UNIT bod fires at the leering, demented gargoyle, Bok. (St Michael's Church, Aldbourne, Wiltshire. Ditto.)

Other locations slammed a tattooed fist on a table and demanded to be included. How could I not visit the Dalek planet of Skaro, for instance? (Binnegar Heath Sandpit or Winspit Quarry, each in Dorset, Betchworth Quarry in Surrey… depends on which *Who* story you go by. It's amazing that anyone in southern England is still alive, such has been the pepperpot activity there.)

And I used the truly fabulous website, www.doctorwholocations.net, trawling the lists of stories, seeking anything that stuck.

Finally, I brought the whole thing up-to-date by hitting Wales, where so much of the new *Doctor Who* is filmed. Had to be some juicy madness among that lot. As indeed proved the case.

So this is a travel book with a television programme at its core, which just happened to become also about quaint, obscure, eccentric Britain. You can follow its progress on the companion website:

www.whogoesthere.org.uk

There, you'll find photographs from the trips, Google Maps of the locations, miscellaneous links and info on the nearest boozer. (Fear not, those unconnected to the internet: I describe every photograph here so, though access to the website would enhance your reading pleasure, it isn't imperative.)

So come with me on a journey through time and space. Admittedly involving several quarries…

AUTHOR'S NOTES

* I'd be very happy if this book inspired people to visit the same locations I went to. However, some – noted in the relevant chapters – might be dangerous, certainly unsuitable for children. Please don't go there. I also got carried away and (cough) trespassed a few times, and I would definitely not advocate anyone doing the same. And please don't hassle the bloke at Stargrove Manor. Seriously. It's not open to the public.

* There's also an 'easter egg' on the website. A point that links to a cod-mythical online-only Hidden Chapter. I'll add a clue to finding it at the end of the book.

* Finally, I did the minimum research before heading out on my location trips, so all the background information here was collated at the time of writing. I wanted to have to discover these places for myself. As you will read, I sometimes missed. But that was all part of the adventure. Like *Doctor Who* itself, that is what I wanted these trips to be: not a methodical exercise – an adventure.

TRIP 1

Friday, 30 November 2007

Spearhead from Space

High Street, Ealing

It's Friday morning on the last day of November 2007. Tomorrow the Advent calendar countdown begins. For myself, aged 42, there is no sense of expectation, yet something residual hangs around my being, reminding me of the 'good old days' (which is no cliché, it's just fact).

That inner child never dies, though I had assumed it would. Surely old people can't remember back through the decades, to a time of hoops-with-sticks for toys and chipped knees? But it turns out they can.

My mum once penned a little biography, hand-written on ruled paper, a dozen pages of A5, which I sent off to a magazine for old folks, and which they disgracefully never printed. As a little girl – try picturing your mother as a child; why is it so difficult? – she would sit at the kitchen table and pretend to play the piano with her fingers, because few parents of that era could afford an actual piano. Plink plonk plink ker-*chung* etc.

It seemed to me the lamest of games, yet utterly charming.

A child's idea of perfect fun, circa the 1930s.

Forty years later, she would try to impart a sense of wonderment to me by hanging an advent calendar above the breakfast bar, come the beginning of December. Those illustrations. That glitter. Those Christmas staples: Santa, robin, snow, reindeer, sleigh, Christmas tree – a child's shorthand for cosiness and gifts.

I'd clamber atop a kitchen stool to reach calendar height and immediately trace out the route of the days. There's 1… where's 2? There! And so on, until 24. Ah, 24 – often *double* doors! Twice the mystery. What could anything that size possibly be? (Usually a crib scene, which for the budding atheist proved something of a disappointment, swiftly trounced by the knowledge that tomorrow Santa would arrive.)

My favourite ever advent calendar had a Christmas tree as its centrepiece, containing five doors up the length of its unseen trunk. At the base, 20, up to 24 at the very top. So it offered the standard countdown – *plus* an extra-special last-five-days via the magical tree. Boy, did those 20s take on an added significance. Extra manipulation for a child who really needed no manipulating.

What do children get these days? Something branded – Disney, *Doctor Who* (very wrong, though only in this circumstance), Bratz, Power Rangers – with chocolate, like today's youth need more calories and less soul. Worse, the doors tend to be in uniform rows and columns, so the fun of seeking out the numbers is painfully diminished.

Inside, the nadir arrives. A shaped pool of crap brown, which has to be pushed out from the back, often dislodging chocolates for a later date, which then rattle around in the packaging, and you turn it over and – oh – it's an indistinct Santa. Or perhaps a reindeer with dysentery?

Finally, the child tries to peer through the clear plastic mould to catch the black-and-white line drawing within, when they would be better off trying to peer into their hearts to find an artery unclogged by commercialism. I pity them, I really do, for they know no different.

I have tried, in vain, to find an advent calendar for my son Dylan that didn't contain confectionery, like those back in my day, when opening a glitter-encrusted flap of cardboard to discover a tiny painting of a beachball-plus-teddy meant nothing and everything. It's impossible to describe that 'Christmas feeling' because it's all about endorphins, memory and expectation – try getting a handle on those – but it's simply special.

Maybe kids today feel the same, and I'm doing them a disservice; I just don't believe you should be scoffing down chocolate at seven in the morning. Eat your sodding breakfast! yes, even if they are coco pops! Don't get smart with me YOU LITTLE...

So it's Friday morning and my mate Andy is down from Stourbridge. I have kept very few friends from those university days. Why? Partly it's mutual and partly it's because most of my lecture-mates were gits, but also because I don't believe one needs a surfeit of mates. The politics get cluttered. Gossip's fun the moment it hits, but then everyone throws in their penn'orth and the diluted tale becomes less enticing than a night in with the *New Statesman*. Or indeed *a* new statesman, someone buck-toothed with whinny, possibly a LibDem.

And here's another Bad Thing about These Days. Owing to the likes of Facebook and MySpace, everyone is obliged to collect 'friends', like I used to collect bubblegum cards. Anyone caught on Facebook with fewer than 87 'friends' becomes the runt of the litter, deemed a sad-sack with the social skills of a camel. The one with the tongue bacteria.

It's like Nazi Germany, only not quite that bad. I've been caught up in it, too. I have 58 Facebook 'friends' – the majority of whom I rarely talk to – and one of them I have met just once, briefly, which my wife had to remind me of. At least I know today that said Jamie B 'is a fan of Radio El'Boss in Obourg'. If only I knew what that meant. Or indeed cared.

Why did I accept Jamie B's friend request, when I didn't know him from Adam, or even from Jamies A, C or D? Because it added 1 to my number of Facebook 'friends'. At any age above 12, how sad is that?

Andy from Stourbridge, to his voluminous credit, is yet to succumb to the paranoia of Facebook. So we email each other, occasionally actually talk to each other on the telephone, and a few times a year get on a train and physically visit each other. It's marvelously old-fashioned.

Andy, it transpires, is a genuine, solid human being, almost six-foot-tall, and if I cut him he surely would bleed.

Memo to self: be careful with knives around Andy.

We like the same stuff: quizzes, beer/cider, pool (table not swimming, though we did that once, by mistake). Equally, he's one of the few people I know who will sit through something like *Doctor Who*'s *The Talons of Weng-Chiang*, starring Tom Baker, all six episodes and 150 minutes of it, not only failing to complain but actively engrossed. In fact, having already seen the story umpteen times, *I* would be the one who became occasionally distracted by the resonant ping of an arriving email upstairs.

Our plan is to visit five *Doctor Who* locations over the next two days, working across London from west to east. These are they:

* The Marks & Spencer (formerly John Sanders Ltd) on High Street, Ealing, where the Auton shop dummies smashed their way out of their window display, in 1970's *Spearhead from Space*, to massacre passing Ealing types.

* The NCP car park – I know, it's all glamour – on Midland Road, near St Pancras, which doubled as UNIT HQ in the same story. Whether this still exists, since the development of the Eurostar terminal at King's Cross, remains to be seen.

* The Favourite Doll Factory just off Holloway Road, the interior of which became the doll factory used by the Nestene Consciousness (also in *Spearhead*) to manufacture its plastic Autons. During the programme, dolls are seen on the production line: dolls with eyes that blink, permed hair that shines, jointed only at the shoulders and hips. Since dolls these days are expected to say "Fuck off" in three languages, perform oral sex, smoke crack and litter willfully, one can only hope that the Favourite Doll Factory has moved with the times, or its existence too must be in doubt.

* Clink Street in Southwark, where, in 1977's *The Talons of Weng-Chiang*, the Doctor and Leela rush to aid a Cockney geezer being attacked by Chinese gang members.

* Wapping Old Stairs East, leading down to the Thames in the East End. A Victorian bobby, also in *Talons*, pulls a body from the water here. Handily, it's next to the Town of Ramsgate pub.

Two *Who* stories, then, both of which I own on DVD (and video; cough) – and which I have watched more times than feels necessary.

Since we really need to get going, having risen late after a night of gigging and unfortunately successful late-booze-seeking, there is only time to watch one fully through; we shall have to fast-forward through the other to the locations of relevance, for purposes of recognition.

I offer the guest the choice, so it's Andy who picks *The Talons of Weng-Chiang*.

It's an undeniable work of genius, from the typewriter of classic *Doctor Who*'s greatest writer, Robert Holmes. The late

Holmes was also responsible for the likes of: *Spearhead from Space*, *Terror of the Autons, The Ark in Space, The Brain of Morbius, The Deadly Assassin, The Caves of Androzani* – as well as *The Two Doctors*, but everyone's allowed to become jaded.

If those titles mean nothing to you, just study them and *imagine*. *The Brain* of *Morbius*! Who's this Morbius and why is his brain being talked about as a separate entity? *Terror* of the *Autons*! The *who*? And why are they so terrifying? (*The Deadly Assassin* might have slipped through the net, as any assassin who isn't 'deadly' is frankly a bit shit.)

Russell T Davies, the man behind the new *Who* revival and no dialogue slouch himself, said this after Holmes' death: "Take *The Talons of Weng-Chiang*, for example. Watch episode one. It's the best dialogue ever written. It's up there with Dennis Potter." Rest assured that he's not exaggerating.

So I lay on one sofa, Andy lay on the other, we ate Eccles cakes and Wine Pastilles for breakfast – which, as adults, we have every right to do – while the Walthamstow morning spread its gloom over the outside of the house, and we cosseted ourselves in Holmes' Victoriana.

Essentially, the story is this: the Doctor (Tom Baker) and companion Leela (a savage plucked from another planet, played by Louise Jameson) land in Victorian London. There's a mutated nutter in the basement of a theatre, sucking the lifeforce from women kidnapped by his Oriental accomplice, the magician Li H'sen-Chang. The Doctor is aided by theatre impresario Henry Gordon Jago, a coward, however with a literally loquacious line in alliteration, and the estimable proper doctor, Professor Lightfoot.

The story contains the wonderfully sinister Mr Sin, the Peking Homunculus, an Eastern-garbed ventriloquist's dummy with eyes that move, limbs that work and a sharp knife – and one of the most rubbish *Who* monsters ever: the giant rat, which I described in *Dalek I Loved You* as resembling 'stock doing a runner from Carpet World'.

Here is one dialogue exchange, to give you an essence of the piece:

Lightfoot: Forgive us, ma'am.
Leela (a savage, remember): For what?
Lightfoot: For being so indelicate in the presence of a lady of refinement.
Leela (to the Doctor): Does he mean me?

Oh, go on, here's another:

Lightfoot (discussing sugar in tea): And then, for example, I would say, 'One lump or two, Miss Leela?' To which you reply 'One will suffice, thank you.' Now do you follow?
Leela: Supposing I want two?
Lightfoot: Oh no no no. One lump for ladies!
Leela: Then why do you ask me?

That's Bob Holmes there, taking the pee out of social etiquette and sexism – *in 1977*. Back when young women wearing outer clothing that dropped below their gusset were ridiculed in the street and forced into service with the WI, laden with jam-making equipment, and ladies in bikinis were used to advertise anything from cars to fridge-freezers and beer-making kits. Oh, and blokes had perms.

Frankly, it's going to be a pleasure to follow in the sphere-prints of the man's mind's eye. But time waits for no man, the December daylight is impatient to depart and we have another DVD to watch. *Spearhead from Space*, starring Jon Pertwee in his debut as the Doctor, and co-starring the Autons, feature-lite plastic monsters in denim suits, looking suspiciously like shop dummies who might today inhabit Mr Byrite's window, with snap-down wrists concealing guns that kill.

That was my first-ever *Doctor Who* story, back when I was four-and-a-bit, and to say I have watched it several times since is an understatement. I'm actually quite relieved that we only have time to fast-forward to the relevant locations: the doll factory, that car park, and the iconic scene in which the Autons come to life, like Madonna in her *Vogue* promo, only less breasty, in a department store window.

We make notes of landmarks to watch out for – that church spire in Ealing, rising above the shops of 1970, looks particularly useful – and plan the route of our first day. Yep, we'll be going again tomorrow. I told you Andy would be easily cajoled.

One location stands out as some kind of *Who*-related Holy Grail: the Autons at M&S, so the route plans itself: east to west, Ealing first, then the car park off Euston Road, before travelling downwards and outwards to Clink Street near London Bridge. This leaves the doll factory and Wapping for tomorrow. With mice unavailable, these are the best-laid plans of men alone. Surely nothing can go wrong?

There is just one potential spanner in the works. We are both lovers of a genuine *olde worlde* boozer, something from London's past, unfettered by chrome, un-bored by loud-voiced arrogance in suits, with honest stains on walls and ceiling and an atmosphere that harks back through the ages. Andy, ever keen, has pre-researched these (on the embarrassingly useful www.fancyapint.com) and carries with him a sheath of print-outs, detailing some dozen delightful pubs in the environs of our five locations. And Ealing corresponds very neatly with St Mary's Road's The Red Lion, once Britain's most popular pub name, lately superseded by The Twat & Bling.

So we leave for the tube and deepest West London, Andy enquiring whether he should take an overcoat, as if I am his mother. There is a distinct bite to the air and a sense of anticipation. We are inescapably off.

The journey... well, it goes on forever. It is interminable. It is a ride on a merry-go-round, without the 'merry' and on the first revolution you notice the operator is having a heart attack; come revolution number nine, he's clutching his left arm, mouthing "Help!", you're shouting "Don't you bastard die!" back at him, and it's becoming painfully apparent that you're stuck on the thing.

Perhaps it's not that bad, but put it this way: I used to do a daily Central Line run to White City, when I worked in the *Radio Times* offices, and as I look up on reaching White City, I'm thinking we've been travelling for long enough to reach Slough, let alone Ealing.

White City is noticeably the station at which the underground train begins to go overground. Out there was once a celebrated greyhound track, and before that the stadium for the 1908 Olympics. Then the BBC came along, like an irate god with a television fixation, and clomped great buildings all over it. Dig down beneath that vast complex and you'll probably find an athlete or two sharing a grave with Mick the Miller.

We had left Walthamstow in daylight. It's dusk by the time we reach White City; the heavens are drizzling all over the train windows, forming rivulets of doom. Among too numerous other stations, we still have the Actons to go: East Acton, North Acton, West Acton – don't ask me what happened to South Acton; if you're that bothered, petition Transport for London – it's where traditionally People Who Work at the BBC live. So you imagine a Queen's-English kind of place where stiff-upper-lip types in suits mingle uneasily with crazies in colourful corduroy who suggest programmes about troubled teenagers cooking soup for gibbons in Haiti, and whose youthful idiocy has to be slapped down or we'll all become far

23

too Channel 4. Whatever, I'm glad we're not stopping.

It has become apparent that our timetable isn't working, so after a quick discussion we knock the Midland Road NCP car park off the night's itinerary. Neither of us is gutted.

By the time we reach Ealing Broadway station, I feel like we've gone far enough west to be in sodding Washington. Yet amazingly, as we disembark, loads of other people do too. I think: haven't you got homes to go to? And then I realise: these People Live Here. In Ealing!

A schoolboy barges through a tube barrier and tromps towards us, sodden and demoralised (despite leaving Ealing) and, sure enough, it's tipping down as we exit the station and turn left towards The Mall. Immediately, a familiar sensation hits me: one of *déjà vu*. I'm staring at the pub across the road junction and I'm certain: I have been here before.

I voice this to Andy. "I've sat in that pub before, waiting for someone," I tell him. "I just can't remember why."

Quick as a flash, he's back at me. "Because you like beer."

It feels like wartime spirit: you're cold, you're wet, you're on foreign soil, a grunt on some god-forsaken mission, but your buddy cracks a gag that sparks the lame-ometer into life, spirits are raised and you chortle for Britain. I love that guy.

And it works. The fear lifts and I wonder whether I might not begin to enjoy myself. Although our surroundings are pure commercialism – Coffee Republic (not actually a republic), Sainsbury's Local, Greggs the bakers – the place doesn't feel too homogenised. There is character trying to get out.

Further on the plus side, no one has yet mugged us, Christmas lighting is tingeing the air festive and the rain does seem to be easing off. And with map in hand, we are both aware that our goal – yes, Marks & Spencer in Ealing – is just around the next corner.

You now what? I'm genuinely quite excited. In less than two minutes, we'll be standing outside the (replacement) window that the Autons smashed their way out of, oooh, 37 years earlier.

Let's have a closer look at those scenes...

It's a dull, overcast early morning in Ealing. No vehicles in shot as the camera faces down what is now New Broadway, but was then probably just a continuation of The Broadway. Tall Victorian buildings with shops on their ground-floors, a church with a spire and just one or two indistinct souls, probably waiting for a bus.

The camera begins to pan left, shows the LILLEY & SKINNER department store sign with its crest all proud, its first and second floors boring red brick and uniform rows of windows.

Cross the zebra crossing and we're at John Sanders Ltd, its name in shadows above an entrance lit by strip lighting, and a sign: '*VISIT OUR* CONFECTIONERY DEPARTMENT *GROUND FLOOR*', in a 'jaunty' Sixties typeface. Now we're at the Autons.

The dummy heads glow, such is the lighting in the window, in a shop front that curves as the pavement follows it. The camera pans past, stops at the sheepskin coats and reverses, back to the plastic nasties.

Two old cars pass each other in the window's reflection as the camera comes to a halt, focusing on five non-dudes, in winter overcoats, leather jackets and orange corduroy, with slacks; shirt buttons done up to the top, mostly with ties, boxed shirts at their feet. Five guys you might find discussing interest rates and engine horsepower, while shagging each other's missus.

Their faces are angled slightly upwards, as if they're curious, perhaps sniffing for the scent of blood, sardonic smiles on their mouths, chubby cheeks and dark, hollow eyeholes beneath mop-top wigs.

'Twonnng!' [Spooky synth noise.]

The chap in grey and blue starts; two other heads twitch. All five come to life. It's a genuinely disturbing scene, and beautifully charted out.

The chap in grey and blue clenches and unclenches his left fist. Corduroy chap's fingers drop down to reveal the barrel of a gun.

Cut to: community bobby chatting to capped worker in Nissan hut. What was that he heard? Breaking glass? He runs, flat-footed, to investigate.

The Autons have broken out of John Sanders Ltd – can't blame them, if that's the sort of fashion they were flogging – and are heading down the High Street. The bobby is proceeding at such pace that he almost runs into them.

Focus on his face: horror/disbelief/chinstrap.

He's being attacked by Man at C&A!

Chap in grey and blue fires, a flash from his gun and a plume of orange smoke billows from our bobby's belly. Officer down! Middle-aged woman, looks like she might be a royal housekeeper, screams in close-up.

Now we're back in a different John Sanders Ltd window – there's a large ecclesiastical building in its reflection. A shiny Auton hand on an armchair arm twitches. His head moves, he stands up, nothing behind the eyes. Another Auton, wearing a paisley smoking jacket (or dressing gown, it's hard to tell them apart), price tag 84'0 – 84 shillings! – joins him; then another.

Cut to a queue at a bus stop. Innocent, unsuspecting Ealing folk of various ages. *Behind you! You're being hunted down by aliens wearing paisley!*

You get the idea. Really: fabulous, shocking scenes.

Back in present day Ealing it's properly dark now, so the vast twinkling tree with blue-and-silver star at its top in the church grounds to our right – no doubt our ecclesiastical building in that reflection – is beaming Christmas cheer into the heavens;

there's a Barratts Shoes on the opposite corner of the High Street, where Lilley & Skinner used to be, these days a far less grand operation. And just over our left shoulders, there it is: The Window. And it's full of shop dummies!

"This is it!" I exclaim rather too loudly. "This is the junction!"

Right, let's look at this impassively. I'm in Ealing, the weather's pretty miserable, I'm wrapped up against the cold in a vast anorak – yes, I know – and I'm outside Marks & Spencer's shop window, hoping it can transport me back several decades to a time when BBC cameras shot a small science-fiction show that lit up children's (and their parents') Saturday teatimes.

And somehow, amazingly, it's working. Maybe it's the curve of this street corner, which does feel like it was the actual one in the show I watched earlier today – sure, the shops have changed hands, but you could superimpose this scene over the one in *Spearhead from Space* and find a match, like a telly-DNA detective – but mainly I think it's the M&S dummies. Though these are far more sophisticated than any Auton crew, and all ladies, if you want to find something disconcerting in their expressions, oh, it's there. You stare at them – and they stare back.

And there are five of them! Just like in the show itself. These are all shiny white-skinned, perfectly proportioned – where's the one who secretly binges on Snickers bars and cheese once the children have been packed off to nursery? – in black evening wear, presumably because that's what Ealing ladies prefer of a night out. Their hair-dos are sculpted bobs, their expressions are slightly aloof and they're all clutching a handbag. Far classier than the Auton shower.

Visit, if you can, www.whogoesthere.org.uk, where the accompanying photo albums reside. Hit page 1 in the menu and check out *pic 1.1* – she's the one I stared at first. That plastic shiny woman really does stare back! The blank eyes in shadow, the mean points of her bob, that black-jewelled necklace. If that woman isn't a puppet of some higher consciousness, I don't know who is.

It's the way they're all lined up (*pic 1.2*), like an identity parade at the local nick in which there are no innocents. There is one who doesn't stare back at you, instead focusing on a spot on the pavement outside, flaunting cleavage – yet you just *sense* she has you in the crosshairs of her peripheral vision (*pic 1.3*).

It's weird: there really is a connection to the past, standing in this very spot.

So I ask Andy to take a photograph of me, looking scared, staring into the window. The problem is: how does the amateur actor give off a sense of terror? Why, by holding one's hands up in 'Shock/horror!' and doing the same with one's face – while well-adjusted Ealing shoppers walk past, thinking to themselves: who is that prat and why's he doing that?

To explain to them that I'm trying to recreate a sense of dread from *Doctor Who*'s 1970 serial, *Spearhead from Space*, would only compound my nerdiness, so I shout at Andy in some desperation, "Get a bloody move on!" while he faffs with the shutter button and hangs a finger over the lens.

Two community coppers walk past and I pray they haven't clocked me behaving suspiciously. It would be bad enough to have to explain my actions, without doing it in an official capacity. Thankfully, they keep on going.

Jesus, I feel self-conscious (*pic 1.4*). While planning this trip, I had entertained the idea of contacting the M&S Ealing branch manager, to ask whether I could stand in his/her shop window, pretending to be a mannequin, moving only occasionally, to witness the comedy expressions of passers-by. Realising that I can barely stand *outside* the shop without blushing ten shades redder than Mars itself, I make a mental note to knock that idea on its head until it has descended into a coma.

It's with a sense of satisfaction, which I think Andy shares to a lesser extent (or he wouldn't keep banging on about being hungry), that we wander down the High Street, into Ealing Green, towards the Red Lion. My first location visit, and a genuine sense of the ghosts of *Doctor Who*.

The retail outlets are more independent down this way: Ealing Rug Gallery, As Nature Intended (an organic store, not a honeypot for nudists), Polish Deli and an Oxfam Bookshop. I check the window for signs of *Dalek I Loved You*, am happy to find none, and wonder whether the *Barefoot Doctor*, whose tome is clearly visible at a knockdown price, will ever be able to afford shoes.

The streets are now very dark, even with the festive lights lining Walpole Park at work, and we continue past Ealing Studios, which is smaller than I would have expected, until we reach the pub, where we can plan our visit to Clink Street.

The Red Lion (*pic 1.6, lifted from www.fancapint.com, since I forgot to snap one in my eagerness for cider*) is surprisingly loud and full, for 4.35pm on a Friday. Several of the punters appear to be postal workers. This is a wonderfully homely place, just as we had hoped, amber lit with occasional candles, and photographs crammed along its walls of film and television stars from bygone eras. There's Noele Gordon, formerly of *Crossroads*. And there, Basil Brush – autographed! By whom, one can only wonder.

How did we pass the time in the pub, we two gentlemen with our tankards full of fun? We discuss how porter is made. Andy is actually drinking the stuff, this dark, pungent, tall puddle, which leads us to discuss its manufacturing process. He suspects it's made from stale beer (yum) and promises to check this in his *Good Beer Guide* and get back to me. I hope he forgets.

And we make plans, or rather, break them. After two pints of cider, in this lovely, warm, comforting environment far from home, with further booze available on tap, the idea of trekking back into town, then off to London Bridge and Clink Street, in *that* weather, feels as welcoming as the prospect of filing one's toenails down past the knuckle then trying to shimmy to the toilet without falling over.

So we knock the idea on the head, add Clink Street to tomorrow's schedule and content ourselves with a job well done.

There is one twist in the tale. When we finally drag ourselves out of the pub towards the hideous journey home, we pass a second M&S window that I had previously passed by, in my eagerness to find my primary target, just around the corner from our sinister ladies – the one directly opposite the church. Of course – this must be the window the second set of Autons escaped from! And in that window I spot a junior dummy, in woollens (*pic 1.5*), which frankly out-Autons the Autons themselves.

It is Damien in white. It is Beelzebub's young nephew, wearing its aunt's Christmas gifts. The label says 'Cardigan £12', the eyes say, 'I've got your address, I'm coming round to your house some time after midnight, and I'm going to sit in a chair at the end of your bed, waiting for you to wake with the scream of the demented.'

TRIP 2

Saturday, 1 December 2007

The Talons of Weng-Chiang

Clink Street, Southwark

Another late start. Well, it's the weekend and the first of December to boot.

Since Clink Street was last on our agenda yesterday, it's going first today. Afterwards, we'll head along the river to Wapping and the fight with the Chinese, then up to Holloway Road for the Favourite Doll Factory. Which leaves us perfectly placed for the Victoria Line back to Walthamstow, where we'll be competing in the Film & TV Quiz in the Rose & Crown, before a taxi ride south to the temptingly titled Feeling Gloomy club night at the Islington Academy.

A day's agenda doesn't get much more enticing.

(You'll notice that a location has already been dropped from the weekend's schedule. Clearly, our mice-and-men planning might have been more efficiently executed by mice; however, better to focus the mind than to dilute.)

Southwark is mercifully far closer to Walthamstow than Ealing. Then again, so is Kathmandu. The weather's far more pleasant today, too: one of those bright, clear skies accompanied by a wintry chill, which invigorate the soul, or at least require one to wear a scarf.

I'm really looking forward to this trip. Visiting somewhere that a location manager decided perfectly resembled Victorian Streets, back in 1977, has to be historically stimulating, and it's south of the river (just), a region I rarely encounter.

So we exit the tube at Bank and stroll past the Bank of England, a vast sarcophagus of concrete with no windows at ground level, perhaps to keep robbers out, or just to make bankers, devoid of daylight, look still drearier. Then over London Bridge, where the crosswinds hit, forcing those scarves tighter around the larynx.

At the southern end of the bridge, I am surprised to find a very big church, which turns out to be Southwark Cathedral (*photographed in perfectly moody darkness later that evening, pics 2.1 and 2.2*). So that's where they put it! All windows, spires and grandeur, it comprehensively overshadows the surrounding bustle of contemporary London.

The cathedral is also known as The Cathedral and Collegiate Church of St Saviour and St Mary Overie, which is more of a mouthful and was first mentioned in the Domesday Book of 1086, when it was run by one Bishop Odon of Conteville. Samuel Pepys also mentions the building in his diary, dated 21st July, 1663. And Shakespeare's brother, Edmund, is buried there, a stained-glass window depicting scenes from various of William's plays, William being a better writer than Edmund, who bred ferrets for his only semi-popular Edmund Shakespeare's Ferret Theatre. (Part of that sentence isn't entirely true, which is a shame.)

More importantly, research post-trip reveals that exterior shots of Southwark Cathedral were used in new *Who*'s series three episode, *The Lazarus Experiment*. A double whammy of locations, by pure happenstance.

Andy is keen to visit Borough Market, which shelters in the

lee of the ecclesiastical behemoth, and is a stone's throw – mind those cathedral windows, you young tyke – from Clink Street. Despite 25 years in the capital, I couldn't have told you what the market sold, which I am now pleased to put right.

Borough Market sells fresh produce. Shiny, enticing fresh produce, in an atmosphere that is pure London, dressed up December-style in the trimmings of Christmas. Fish, fruit & veg, chutneys, meat, pies, a shark's head with understandably wonky eye here, an oyster there, cheeses... I am particularly entranced by a series of giant cheeses at Neal's Yard Dairy, so much so that I take a picture of some (*pic 2.3*) and purchase a large wedge of Stichelton. Only afterwards does Andy point out that we are going clubbing later and that most clubbers fail to take cheese with them.

I have no choice but to start eating the cheese and hope that I will have finished it by 11pm. Happily, Andy likes Stichelton, a creamy kind of Stilton, also. If only we had some crackers.

And so to Clink Street, which we approach via Stoney Street to the south. Despite scaffolding to our right, shrouded in tarpaulin, and shops to our left, neither lumpable under 'Victoriana', beneath this steadily blackening sky it just feels right.

The staggerings of gin drinkers and footfalls of pious types on their way to worship are ghost-steps beneath our feet and, as Clink Street grows closer, it's like approaching a time capsule of *Who*vian delights and Victorian underworld. It feels, dare I say it, almost magical.

Then we hit Clink Street itself... and the sensation disappears, as if with the flick of a switch. Maybe it's the Starbuck's before us, draining the vibe with its coffee-flavoured ubiquity, or the aged brick walls painted a hideous 'modern' blue and grey. Perhaps it's all these milling people, tourist visitors to the replica Golden Hinde, Sir Francis Drake's galleon, around the corner, or just wandering aimlessly, wondering how to fill an afternoon. I don't know, but something's disappeared: this just doesn't feel like the street that the Doctor and Leela stalked down, though history records that it is.

Andy is of the same mind, so we decide to tour the environs, seeking out any pocket of authenticity. Heading left towards Bankend, the first discovery is Clink Street Prison, 'The prison that gave its name to all others' ('in the clink' meaning 'in prison', at least on these shores).

A sign notes that it operated from 1106-1780 and that 'beare bayting' (bear-bating) and 'bolle bayting' (bull-bating) – you wonder whether there was any large mammal those ex-Londoners wouldn't have routinely annoyed – took place in arenas nearby.

The area was once rife with prostitutes, many of whom ended up within the prison walls, alongside heretics and debtors. A museum now inhabits the site, monking music drifting up from its entrance. One window offers passers-by a view down into the basement, where a tableau of dummies depicts a blacksmith knocking up chains for an inmate (*pic 2.4*). It's about as realistic as that stock doing a runner from Carpet World.

Ahead of us is a vast, looming red-brick arch, beneath which the cobbles of the street have clearly been renewed, and past that, Vinopolis, er, 'City of Wine' (not so much a city as a big building). This monument to wine-tasting appears to have swallowed up part of Clink Street itself, which can be seen through glass and chrome, inside the entrance hall. Perhaps that's where the authenticity went? Gobbled down like so much plonk?

The only scent of this place as it might have been a century ago, sad to say, comes as we pass a homeless man, slumped in a gutter, giving off a pungent odour of piss.

We perform a lap of Vinopolis, round Bankend and Park Street, back into Stoney Street, and fail even to find the manhole cover through which the Doc and Leela descended into the sewers.

We have sought a portal to poo, and we have failed. Talk about doomed.

But the visit must be recorded for posterity, so it's photograph time. Where best to take it? Beneath the Clink Street road sign! ... And we can't find one of those, either. Instead, I stand in the cobbled street and pull a kung fu pose (*pic 2.5*), in dubious tribute to Weng-Chiang; however, as fearsome-looking as a Chihuahua in a dress.

After M&S Ealing's time-tunnel to the past, this has been a disappointment. Robert Holmes' street scene feels suffocated by modernity.

Well, there was that one moment of recognition, early on, and Borough Market was an unexpected find. Plus, of course, Andy has with him his sheath of pub details – and The Rake, alleged to be London's smallest boozer, happens to be 50 yards away, on Winchester Walk.

It's early evening. Time, once again, has deserted us. The other locations will just have to hit a 'To Do' list.

Squeezed inside The Rake, the drizzle and darkness barred from entry, I discover a cider so orange that it cries out to be photographed (*pic 2.6*), and we lightly souse the afternoon's disappointment while eating cheese.

TRIP 3

Thursday, 27 December 2007

Colony in Space

Trethurgy, Cornwall

Trethurgy – what a great name. It means 'third thurgy' in Cornish. No it doesn't. I've no idea what it means, but there are loads of place names beginning with Tre- in that part of the world, so I really should work it out. Later, maybe.

Cornwall has become my third home, after London and my folks' place in Kent, since I started seeing – and later married – Sinead. Though she was born in North London, her family moved to Cornwall shortly afterwards so she grew up there, in Fowey (pronounced 'Foy'), at the mouth of the River Fowey.

The Hanks family home, a vast collection of cosy rooms, walls lined with books and children's board games, ivy covered and driven into a slope, was bought for a few thousand and is now worth plenty more. Such is the way of property and the increasing kudos of Fowey.

The deep river mouth in summer is lined with yachts manned by braying types; occasionally, sitting in the Hanks' kitchen, you can watch a tanker go past forever through a window, so madly long are they and so accommodating the underwater trench to the mammoth keels.

It's like a summer holiday, for free. I'd happily pay to spend days in Cornwall and indeed had done so, several times pre-Sinead, when it always rained as if I were experiencing the end of days. Since Sinead, the Cornish summers have generally been scorching. A coincidence? She would suggest otherwise.

Readers of *DILY* will know how I usually holidayed just 22 miles from my childhood home in Horndean with my parents, on the Isle of Wight. And how I was too young to consider the journey time anything less than adventurous.

There was one week away, though – we went to Devon. Sorry, *all the way* to Devon. God knows how many miles that was from our then-home of Alton – hundreds, anyway – and what possessed my Dad into such adventuring, I have no idea.

We stayed in Bude, in a rented cottage on the North Devon coast, not terribly far from Cornwall and Fowey. I recall the photographs. Me sitting on a bollard, fishing, catching nothing, looking suitably uninspired (*can't find the pic*). Then me, looking strangely athletic for such an insecure teen, in second-hand Wrangler jeans (I remember the make! Why?) and brown polo neck, aged about 16, standing next to my mother with a lovely-beach backdrop (*pic 3.1*). She wears a slightly irritated expression and has the looks of a woman two-thirds her age. You know, I've never once told my Mum how attractive she was, and indeed still is, despite being 88 with cancer. Stupidly, such a declaration feels incestuous to me. I wish I had told her.

My favourite photo, though, is of me at a distance, lugging a conger eel I'd just caught during a boat trip from Polperro – practically next-door to Fowey – towards the camera (*pic 3.2*). It's my favourite not because of the admittedly amazing haul, but because of the very fat bloke whose spherical belly cannot help but invade the shot, as he clutches a wonderfully dwarfed child's orange fishing net.

That boat trip has stayed with me. I remember getting a

'bird's nest' in the reel (line tangled all ways, for the non-anglers) as I pulled the beast in, and the captain, who was called Chris, helping to untangle it without tutting. And I remember feeling seasick, such was the exertion required, over 20 minutes, to drag the understandably reluctant creature from its undersea hole. (I've made myself feel bad, writing that.)

I am not exaggerating when I recount that said conger was about five-feet-long, as wide as Mike Tyson's arm, featuring malevolent saucer eyes and a disturbing gob of teeth. Even when it had been gutted, it sat up staring at me from a bucket, occasionally lunging with menace at anyone on the boat (I kid you not).

On the way back to the harbour, Chris let me steer his little craft. I adored the responsibility then, craning a neck towards land, hands on the wheel, though it says more to me now. I was 16. Not ten. Yet he could sense my yearning and I was way too uncool to skulk teen-style out of the task.

Thank goodness.

Having done my location research, I'm well aware that there's a *Doctor Who* site tantalisingly close to Fowey, of fabulous vintage. The aforementioned Trethurgy, where, around early 1971, scenes were filmed in the Old Baal Clay Pit for Jon Pertwee's six-part *Colony in Space*.

Rarely did the production team of yore venture hugely far from London, given budgetary constraints and the fact that the equipment weighed more than the average Billy Bunter birthday spread. So Trethurgy must have offered something pretty special. But what?

(Here's a clue: *Colony in Space*'s tagline on the BBC *Who* website runs: 'A sinister alien quarry hides the most powerful weapon in the universe'. A quarry! My first! And might the universe's most powerful weapon still be there? Hmm.)

First, I have to sit through the serial in question, and I use 'have to' and 'sit through' intentionally. Lordy, what a bore.

The story concerns Earth people attempting to colonise the planet Uxarius, but having problems growing crops. Mmm... farming storylines.

It's the first time Jon Pertwee's Doctor has left Earth in his Tardis, having been exiled there by the Time Lords for reasons I cannot recall. Somehow, it's also fair-while companion Jo Grant's first time inside the Police Box.

"I don't believe it!" she exclaims. "It's bigger inside than out!"

Get with the programme, honey!

Katy Manning (who plays the young woman) is very keen on eye-acting, majoring on 'confused' and 'eager'. Shortly after being 'confused' at this being an actual alien landscape, Jo's so 'eager' to study a flower on the Uxaerian surface – like a total girl – that she fails to spot the spear-wielding swamp-weirdo behind her.

Said swamp-weirdo is a Primitive, and only looks like he should belong in a swamp, being green with pondweed for hair, as the planet is dusty and barren. Why is it so barren? I swiftly failed to care.

So you have the colonists on one side, aided by the Doctor (not Jo), the International Mining Corporation on the other, and the Primitives somewhere grey/green in-between, and they talk and they talk and they talk. Thank goodness the Primitives are mute or *Colony in Space* could have gone on for another eight episodes.

Even the appearance of Roger Delgado's Master can't pep up the proceedings. In fact, the only time I got excited was when I spotted Gail Tilsley from *Coronation Street*.

But I'm here for the location and the excellently named Old Baal Clay Pit is practically the star of the piece. It's a quarry playing a quarry, so perfectly cast, and a desolate space of off-white with cliffs. Frankly, I can't wait.

It being the day after Boxing Day, everyone is eager to escape the house, so I pack the Micra with wife, sister-in-law (Alex) and mother-in-law (Ma Hanks), and we head for Old Baal along the A3082, clutching only the most skeletal of directions, my guts whining for a Cornish pasty.

Plenty of shops are shut or are all out of hot snacks, so when I finally track down my meat-filled desire, in Par, it's a forlorn-looking thing with steak-pieces so tough I consider gluing them together and using them as an interesting murder weapon. Foolishly ignoring that idea, I ingest them instead, when they immediately sit in my stomach like hot coals, muttering to each other, making me feel queasy. An inauspicious start.

Our route takes us first past a sign to Tywardreath (pronounced roughly 'Tyre-dreth', not 'Tie-ward-wreath'), where famously the BBC's *It's Not Easy Being Green* was filmed, involving Dick Strawbridge and his hippie-haired family becoming self-sufficient and water-powered, while making viewers feel less smug. It's also, I've just discovered, the setting for Daphne du Maurier's last novel, *House on the Strand*. ('Tywardreath', in Cornish, means – anyone? – 'House on the Strand'.)

The author, who died in 1989, spent much of her time in this area, had properties in Menabilly and Bodinnick – and the locals won't let you forget it. Indeed, Fowey holds an annual Daphne du Maurier Festival of Arts and Literature every May, which my wife once attended while I was in the pub, with the sole intention of ogling visiting newsreader George Alagiah. He cancelled. Ha.

Come the A391, we're in the heart of china clay country. Over fences and across vegetation, you occasionally glimpse pools of luminescent green: abandoned clay pits that have filled with rainwater over the years, which give off a distinctly alien aura. Equally strange is the patently man-made conical mound (*pic 3.3*) to our left as we head away from Scredda – lost, little realising that our quarry, literally, is obscured from view to our right – which Ma Hanks explains is discarded clay waste that has been 'greened' because the locals found it too white, thus an eyesore.

I've never thought of using green as a verb before and am suitably amused at the idea. Memo to self: Consider 'greening' all white objects in house, as may also be eyesores.

It's amazing how important sticky mud can be. Cornwall is famed (lazily, by myself at least) for its pasties, fish, tin, copper, smuggling, Land's End, pixies – or 'piskies' in these parts; I bought a Joan the Wad pendant in Polperro, on that Devon holiday, which I carried around for ages despite considering superstition silly – and Philip Schofield, off the top of my head, as well as its clay.

The county boasts the largest deposits of kaolin, the official name, in the world, which were first discovered in 1746, at Tregonning Hill, by the Quaker potter, William Cookworthy. Kaolin is used to make porcelain… I'm sorry, it's hard to sound passionate about, well, clay, and I'm suddenly reminded of school geography lessons, taught by a man who inhabited a haze of pipe tobacco, as I drifted into an arena of the disinterested somewhere between consciousness and Nod. Those somehow still on tenterhooks for clay fact are referred to Charles Thurlow's mouth-filling *China Clay from Cornwall and Devon: An Illustrated Account of the Modern China Clay Industry*, which is 762,041st in the Amazon Sales Rank at the time of writing, so the author would no doubt be glad of the patronage.

By now we're completely lost. If 'lost' is indeed the right word, since to be lost implies that you know where you're going. I've cobbled a few directions off the internet, which are more vague than the average politician's reply to a pointed question.

Spotting another set of luminously hued chalk pits in the distance, in mild desperation I stop the car in a lay-by, intending to tromp across some marshland to get a better look. Might one of those be Old Baal? However, I'm confronted at a gate by a crappy sign inviting me to piss off (*pic 3.4*) – 'NO ADMITTANCE TO UNAUTHORISED PERSONS' – put there by IMERYS, the French company who bought English China Clays in 1999, for £756 million. Never one to stand up to authority, or indeed to anyone with that size of wallet, or actually to small children with toys that could have someone's eye out, I do as I'm told.

The mood in the car, while remaining patient and helpful, could also be described as 'ripening'. Why, my teasing in-laws wonder aloud, would anyone want to trudge around Cornwall's less salubrious parts in search of somewhere once connected to *Doctor Who*?

Henry Morton Stanley probably encountered a similar sort of thing before he set off to find Livingstone, I imagine, so I assure everyone that everything will be "cool" before reverting to A Quiet Dignity – praying that we chance upon Old Baal at our earliest.

Instead we end up in Scredda. As far as I can tell, Scredda is a hill, featuring two houses and a postbox, in case the residents make a friend and then write to them.

When we do eventually track down Old Baal, it's purely because we have visited everywhere else in Cornwall at least twice, so it was the only place left. (Follow the signs for Trethurgy – that's my tip. Sadly, the word 'Trethurgy' hadn't managed even a supporting role in my scribbled directions.)

It's around 3pm and naturally it's raining. I am faced with a mini-mutiny.

"Why did we come here?"

"*Doctor Who*'s silly."

"I'm not going up there!"

Reasonable points for the non-obsessed, I am obliged to concede. But we're here and I'm reluctantly in charge of the afternoon, even if it's as Captain Bligh. You never know, I point out to my female-heavy crew, you might even enjoy it.

We park in a small area of gravel and litter before a metal gate, the only car here. Passing through the gate, we start up a slope, treading on small crystalline stones, like hailstones, which make a satisfying crunching sound underfoot, while avoiding dogshit. Water trickles past us, downwards, aiming desperately for the sea.

For Sinead, Ma Hanks and Alex, this is simply a barely enticing walk in the country, in the wind and rain. For me, it's the tantalising bit just before the culmination of a quest. Can Old Baal live up to my expectations? Can it actually recreate, here and now, the planet Uxarieus? It's a lot to ask of a quarry, given almost 37 intervening years. But I'm hopeful – after all, how much can a quarry change?

Following the track chicane-style, we reach another sign (*pic 3.5*), this one noticeably more celebratory than the last, flagging up the China Clay Woodland Project, an initiative of IMERYS and Natural England – though it's the government department Defra (Department for Environment, Food and Rural Affairs) who nab biggest billing. The tossers. The £2.5 million project plans to add trees and suchlike to 837 acres of china-clay waste area... 'Greening', by a less interesting description.

Behind the notice, an unofficial pathway up a sharp incline has been made by horses, given the hoofmarks, and by people in boots, suggesting a shortcut. At the top of it, I expect Uxarieus to stretch out before me, where, no doubt, I will be offered a cup of future-tea by Gail Tilsley, while Jo Grant ogles flora.

I stagger upwards, impatient to catch my first glimpse of this alien land – or at the very least my first quarry, from a show noted for its quarry use – my breathing quickly labouring. But inevitably when you're hyped up, reality lets you down.

It's just flat marsh at the top, squishy underfoot, sodden over the ages, so I must leap from one clump of heather to another to avoid sinking. On the plus side, the atmosphere up here is beguilingly strange. Quiet. Deserted. A peak, barely, though with that sense of isolation, of looking down. Behind me, the sea and Carlyon Bay; before me, I'm certain, so close, Old Baal.

Of course, it may be just me. Ma Hanks has become cold and restless and is already heading back towards the car, accompanied by a sympathetic Sinead (*pic 3.6*). Since I have no time for such quitting antics, I make a mental note to prod them towards a gangplank with a curvy sword later. Alex, at least, bitten I hope by the same bug of exploration that gnaws at my own heels, is already striding ahead, towards the source of the mystery.

I practically jog in my eagerness – you try jogging via heather clumps – towards the tangled shrubs, weeds and gorse that line this section of marsh. When I'm there, I peer through twigs and thorny bushes. Downwards, many metres beneath my feet, is one of those flooded clay pits. And this close, it looks fabulous (*pic 3.7*).

That *green*. How, most accurately, to describe it? *Who* fans: remember the colour of the Wirrn larvae in *The Ark in Space*? Add a little white to that and mix, making sure to lose none of the hue. Non-*Who* fans? Remember slime, in a small bucket, the gross but brilliant toy *du jour* of the early Eighties, which never quite went away? Do the same to that, as above. I hope you're all with me.

The rain has stopped but the wind has discovered ire. I wrap my scarf around myself and seek detail. Is this Uxarieus, now flooded? Impossible to tell in its current state; though I can hardly feel disappointed, such is the queerness of the diorama. If it isn't Uxarieus, it blummin' well should be.

Above green-level it's like a building site that's been abandoned by people in JCBs whose purpose was to create geometric shapes in clay that no dictionary could label. Two white huts perch on a slope, forcing you to wonder, who the hell lived or worked there? It feels so... *remote*.

A trackway from the lowest hut leads down to the green; perhaps before the water came, it guided quarrymen to the quarry floor. They might actually have stepped on Uxarieus – and those with a penchant for television history may even have realised it.

Indeed, the clay-folk working here during the early Seventies probably witnessed the filming, with their colleagues manfully taking the piss out of the blokes in rubber suits, then less manfully making sure they were in front of the telly during those six Saturday evenings – assuming they could handle the storyline's pace – nudging the kids, telling them: "That's where I work. I *saw* him!" meaning the Doctor. "Met him, too – *he shook my hand*!" they might have been tempted to porkify.

Alex appears behind me, disturbing my musings, and I ask her to take a photo (*pic 3.8*) of me, freezing, with the location in the background. She's witnessed the same sights, from a different vantage point, and is of the same mind: that this place is like nothing else. A gem in green, but no standard emerald. Something very different.

I itch to get closer. Right down there, at the water's edge.

So does Alex, who takes off, in which direction I fail to notice, as I look for ways to drop down. But the ground at my feet is disturbingly steep, with so much chaos in the way. I turn to call to my sister-in-law, but she's already gone. Surely she can't have vanished from sight in such a short time?

I follow the natural boundary, clockwise around the green. A vague pathway appears, but no sign of Alex, though I can see some way into the distance. She has indeed just disappeared.

So I've lost everyone. Now it's just me up here, accompanied by a distant dog's bark and traffic drone, and bird calls I'd need Bill Oddie to identify. Paranoia grips me. I call Alex's name, and Sinead's, though I know she's likeliest lounging comfortably in the car. (No, I don't call for my mother-in-law, thank you.) Each time, the wind whips my cry away, depositing it somewhere useless.

I know it's daft; it's just a sensation I couldn't shake off, brought on by the atmosphere of the place. I also suddenly worry unduly that I shouldn't really be there, that this might be private property, that uniformed security guards – the Nazi types habitually togged up by *Doctor Who* – might be on my case. That from behind me I'd hear, "Excuse me, sir…"

Eventually cowardice returned me to the Micra. Well, I'd done the *Who* location, which had far exceeded my expectations, and to continue walking might have turned this perfectly reasonable pursuit into a countryside *ramble*. Far too old-couples-with-visible-socks-and-a-ski-pole-despite-the-absence-of-snow.

As I made my way back, I spotted two things of note:

* A quarry to the right, which I had previously missed, and which was dry (*pics 3.9 and 3.10*). It actually looked like Uxaeruis, all stark and boulder-strewn, as seen in *Colony in Space*. But somehow, such had been the thrill of the previous sights, it didn't seem to matter. *That* had been far more alien. *That* had felt right. I'd wager, or at least hope, that Old Baal himself became flooded some years after the filming, and that

Jo Grant's lupin is currently under several feet of green.

   * The world's most over-elaborate bench (*pic 3.11*), halfway along the path down, which I had somehow failed to take in on the way up, having been blinded by zeal. Part Tudor ruin, part crofter's cottage, it must have been someone's idea of an architectural joke. Admittedly, a very good one.

Then I noticed: my trainers were full of water.

Interlude: I'm writing this up at a friend's house in Brighton, shortly after the event. Her six-year-old son, Jake, came into the lounge to inform us, early evening, with a glint of genius in his eye: "I've got a piece of carrot in my mouth. And I'm going to keep it there for four years."

"Why?" I ask, impressed.

Because, he explained, in all sincerity: "In four years, I won't be hungry!"

The idea intrigues on several levels. Why four years? I'd have worked in fives. Why a carrot? I'd have worked in crisps. And why did he imagine he'd be going hungry in early 2012? Did he read the papers and had worried about the developing energy crisis's effect on food stocks?

The way the child's mind works is pure brilliance. To attempt to capture that level of unselfconscious surrealism, I have to work at it, and it hurts. With all their unformed neural pathways – or whatever – it comes naturally to young children. If they only had the word-power, they would write the funniest books *ever*.

As Jake is on his way to bed later, I call after him: "Have you still got the carrot in your mouth?"

"No," he says, bounding up the stairs.

I'll admit I was disappointed.

As I arrive back at the Micra, Sinead is in the driving seat with Ma Hanks in the back. They've been wondering where I was. Now we all wonder where Alex is.

A car has parked to our right. A bloke in a silly, dangly woollen hat is standing outside, talking to a mate in the front seat. I wonder whether they're discussing *Colony in Space* – as if I can't possibly be the only dork in the country prepared to go to some lengths in pursuit of my passion – so I attempt to eavesdrop their conversation from the passenger seat. When it doesn't work, I ask Sinead to wind down her window as subtly as possible.

Still no luck – my ears are broken after years of standing next to speaker stacks at gigs – so I turn my attention to the masses of litter built up here, which flick discarded Vs at the 'Dumping of rubbish is illegal and prohibited' sign on the gate. I spy an empty Clotted Cream carton and am at least assured I'm in Cornwall (in London, we have spent cartridges and supermodels' septums). Such a grotty entrance to a magical site – why does no one clean it up?

When Alex finally appears after a quarter of an hour, having made her way down towards the water before being turned away by signs in red, she's full of the joys of green. A rift develops in the car: those who enjoyed the trip versus those who didn't, which ceases only when the pub is mentioned. The healing powers of the prospect of booze.

It feels traditional already: *Who* trip then pub.

The locals (everyone but me) fire up a plan. Head back down the A391, turn right along the A390 towards St Austell, and hang a small left towards Charlestown. Most picturesque, evidently.

The village of Charlestown, with dock, was planned by local landowner, Charles Rashleigh, who modestly named it after himself. Building work concluded in 1810, whence ships would sally forth under sail, carrying china clay – illuminate lightbulb above head here – and copper to distant shores.

Even now, clay is exported from Charlestown, though in far lesser quantities than during the 19th century. Well, everything's plastic these days.

We stop in the car park at the top of the village, which, despite this being a date to nothing and a brief visit, requires we pay an all-day charge of £2.50 to remain there. Sod that. Sinead briskly moves the Micra.

In the narrow dock that begins a few yards away are some great boats: a vibrantly coloured Search & Rescue vessel and a pair of tall ships, moored and available for hire to movie directors with seafaring scenes in mind.

It's the sort of thing this part of the world revels in, all salt-smelling and floaty. Anyone with a camera who spots it and can walk past failing to take a photograph or two is a less clichéd man than I. (*See pics 3.12* and *3.13*.)

We continue wandering down towards the sea, past sea shells for sale (*pic 3.14*) and lobster nets (*pic 3.15*), as tourists mooch past in couples and families, hoping for something to brighten up their post-Christmas slump. Despite the history, working industry and kitsch on offer, it doesn't for us. Our mood has dipped. After the adrenalin overload, in my case.

As much as I love Cornwall and its idyllic nature, its tourism is a double-edged sword. Take those lobster nets: they're working nets, yet we 'emmets' – as Cornish people call outsiders – regard them as something quaint, from a museum display. I even took a photo of one; actually, I took more than one, but I didn't want to bore you with all five. It's a net.

So the county can't help but live up to its stereotypes, indeed is forced to trade in them for cash. Cream tea, anyone? And they sort of resent it.

'Emmet' in Cornish means 'ant'. All we little ants, milling around annoyingly, spraying our formic acid (cash, in the ant metaphor).

I've been drinking in Fowey, a lot, and one young local said to me recently, "You're alright, because you're with them [meaning Sinead's brothers, who both live and work in the town]," as if I'd required his acceptance. A barperson, whose alehouse I patronise on a regular basis, half-jokingly called me a "bloody emmet" one night while we were chatting all friendly like, and I was rather taken aback. I thought they liked me.

That's Cornwall for you. Lovely, with caveats. (In Devon, everyone else is a 'grockle' – just so you're forewarned.)

Back in Charlestown, I snap the wife *French Lieutenant's Woman*-style on the end of a quay (*pic 3.16*) as the light fades, before we all trudge back up the hill to find a pub. There's one on our left, glass-fronted, where we check out the menu. Prawn sandwich, £6.25. I bet they're not that much at Old Trafford! The indignation briefly raises our spirits as we huff away. Someone mentions the nearby Shipwreck Centre.

"I hate shipwrecks! Everywhere in Cornwall there are shipwrecks!" quips Ma Hanks.

She has a point.

TRIP 4

Saturday, 7 June 2008

The Talons of Weng-Chiang

Wapping Old Stairs East, Wapping, London

You will notice that Trip 4 takes place more than five months after Trip 3. (If you don't believe me, flick back and check for yourself.) In that time, this sequel to *Dalek I Loved You* was On, Off, On, Off and finally On again, and during those periods of indecision my *Who* travels were left in limbo, as if I were Phileas Fogg awaiting a visa.

There was at least no danger of me thumb-twiddling. In the intervening period, everything happened. We moved house; the *DILY* paperback was published; my first novel, *In the Footsteps of Harrison Dextrose*, was published; *Doctor Who* series four began so my *Radio Times* work went roofwards; my wife discovered that she was (indeed still is) pregnant. And my mother died. That hurt to type.

I wish I knew where to start. With *Doctor Who*, I guess – it always was my escape from reality, ever the televisual comfort blanket for a bloke too old to be seen cuddling cotton.

Wapping Old Stairs East, of course, had been on my list for Trip 1, back in late-November of last year. But we, er, hadn't made it there, despite the historic Town of Ramgsate pub being right next-door.

Now Andy's back in London for the weekend, Ma Hanks is in town, too, visiting sons and daughters, and with Sinead and Alex also on the scene, I can treat our one big happy family to the Saturday afternoon of their lives: a trip to Wapping, an area steeped in more than Rupert Murdoch and printers' strikes. *Doctor Who* lore, for a start.

Those are cracking scenes, in *The Talons of Weng-Chiang*, on London's Victorian streets – Chinese chaps with pigtails, bobbies with whistles, Baker in a deerstalker and Jameson in baggy trousers.

It's night-time, an atmosphere of seediness and gloom pervades, and a musty old bint has spotted something untoward at the edge of the Thames. She calls a copper to investigate, being presumably too musty to do so herself. He leans down, fishes around in the river. It's a body. (Dramatic chords.)

That's where we're heading. Will we find a body? I wouldn't put anything past 'Old Father' Thames.

Television crews seeking a historical London are increasingly drawn to the Docklands, as the rest of the city becomes covered in chrome, glass, satellite dishes and cranes. (I saw a documentary on London hosted by Suggs of Madness, some while back, though this anecdote has stayed with me. He recalled being accompanied by a young nephew who asked him, on spotting the myriad cranes across the skyline: "I love London, Uncle Suggs – but when are they going to finish it?")

Though the Docklands, too, is being developed, travel far enough down the river, away from the heart, and tradition remains.

Wapping was all about sailors and their offshoot tradespeople: sailmakers and boat-builders, innkeepers and whores. Captain Kidd, James Whistler, JW Turner, Charles

Dickens: each was familiar with its grimy haunts.

Dickens, for one, most likely trod the same steps as the *Doctor Who* bobby and attached crone: Wapping Old Stairs East, to give them their full, alluring title. Back in the olden days, when men were men and lumps of poo floated in the river, ships' passengers would embark and disembark via those same slabs. The pub next-door was renamed The Town of Ramsgate in 1688 – an alehouse having existed on the site since 1460 – ideally to attract the fishermen from Ramsgate in Kent, who offloaded their catch there.

That's some cool history already. And you can add to that Execution Dock, from which pirates and more-land-based ne'er-do-wells were hanged close to the waterline, to be taken down only after the tide had covered them three times. According to some sources – though not all – that gallows used to be sited near Wapping Old Stairs.

All that – and a sense of *Who*.

We pack five into the Micra, longest at the front, myself in the driving seat, and pootle down through the City from North London, pass the Tower on our right, drop down Thomas More Street, right into Wapping High Street, and there it is before us: The Town of Ramsgate (*pic 4.1*).

Hanging baskets surround the doorway and leaves on stalks spill from window boxes (*pic 4.2*). A sign high up on the wall promises 'WAPPING OLD STAIRS E.' That'll be the alleyway to the right of the boozer. Though I'm tempted to dash down there, that would claim my prize all too soon. Suspense is key.

On the door itself is a plaque (*pic 4.3*) commemorating the death of 'The Hanging Judge. In this place in 1688, following the fall of James II, the infamous Judge Jeffries, who presided over the Bloody Assizes, enjoyed his last moments of freedom before being captured and beaten while waiting for a passage from London. He was taken to the Tower and died the following year.'

Here is my sum knowledge of the Bloody Assizes: it's a track on Julian Cope's *Fried* album, the one with him naked on the cover, wearing a large turtle-shell, playing with a toy lorry. Which is unlikely to get past any scrupulous History examiner. So let's have a look…

Right. Basically, a bunch of blokes in wigs, led by nationally loathed Lord Chief Justice George Jeffries, went around the country sentencing those who took part in the Monmouth Rebellion (against King James II), to death (mainly) or deportation. A sort of travelling-git roadshow.

My favourite tale comes from Wikipedia, of the 'elderly gentlewoman Dame Alice Lisle', who had harboured a couple of traitors. Found guilty of treason by a reluctant jury, she was sentenced to be burned. However, notes the Wikipedia author, 'This was commuted to beheading'.

Are those cries I can hear of, 'Oh thank you, kind sirs!' No.

There is more to the tale than the Ramsgate's plaque offers. It goes that Jeffries, disguised as a sailor, waiting for a boat to France, just couldn't resist one final pint. Inside the pub, he's recognised, duffed up on account of his reputation and thrown into the Tower.

While applying for a pardon – the gall of the man! – he dies a year later, of kidney disease. The judge, it transpires, has been suffering from agonising kidney stones for some time, to which a few ludicrously forgiving souls attribute his boundless temper.

There are further documents inside the pub, but I'm all full up on history by now, so I take photographs of them (*pics 4.4 and 4.5*) rather than reading them. *That's* dumbing down. Now it's *Who* time.

The Town of Ramsgate is a lovely old place, long and thin, in shades of crimson and brown that soothe the soul and request you tarry. The bar to our left offers a tantalising selection of ales and food, and I leave an order with Sinead so I can zip to the beer garden out back (*pic 4.6*), next to Wapping Old Stairs East.

The decking outside raises you up, so you can see over the pub wall to the steps themselves. I spot a couple there, sitting on the top step. They spot me back, look shifty – at least they did to me – and slink away. Were they here for the same reason as me? Are there *Who*-location nerds all over? I genuinely wonder this, though the lure of a view of the Thames might also explain their presence.

Actually, I'm slightly disappointed that I've already spotted my target accidentally, before I had a chance to stand *in situ*. It feels like stumbling across a present pre-Christmas. So I avert my gaze and take a seat at the front of the terrace, overlooking the river.

Tidal waters batter the pub foundations below, frothing over – I can't help looking – the Wapping steps. Splock. Shlsh. Splock. Shlsh. Splock. Shlsh. Occasionally a big one comes in, rises up and disappears in on itself with a Glunk.

The tide is low, though not far enough out to uncover the riverbed and the very bottom steps. (At bbc.co.uk there is, for some reason, a 360-degree view of this same area at the Thames' lowest ebb, which I've linked from my site.)

The water is – there's no other word for it – brown, given the constantly disturbed silt that forms a suspension. However, I am heartened while disappointed that bloated cadavers are noticeably absent from its caress. In fact, there's no litter at all, despite this little inlet offering an ideal collection point for drifting tat.

Not many are aware of this, but London has 11 buried rivers. The Thames is joined by a tributary along every couple of miles or so. The most famous of these is the River Fleet, which ran from springs at Hampstead Heath, through Kentish Town, down through the City, to feed the Thames at Ludgate, wide enough for merchant ships.

Why do I tell you this? Well, the Fleet passed tanneries, cloth dyers and Smithfield's meat market, among many others, inspiring Jonathon Swift to write, in 1711, of storms causing the river to cascade: 'Sweepings from Butchers Stalls, Dung, Guts and Blood, Drown'd Puppies, stinking Sprats, all drench'd in Mud, Dead Cats and Turnip-Tops come tumbling down the Flood.'

Generously, he omitted to mention the swathes of human sewage.

So *that's* what the Thames could have looked like.

A few years later, warming to Swift's theme, Alexander Pope penned this: 'Fleet ditch, with disemboguing streams / Rolls the large tribute of dead dogs to Thames…'

Clearly a show-off, however proof that no one was in a rush to hook out even the decaying pups. (The Fleet is now but a drain, captured in cast-iron pipework, emerging unseen beneath Blackfriars Bridge.)

Come 1878, the pleasure steamer Princess Alice went down near Becton after a collision with another craft; some 600 of the 800 passengers died, and a report into the tragedy noted their demises had been accelerated by the appalling state of the water. By the 1950s, the Thames was effectively dead.

The river had reached its nadir. Yet these days, amazingly, the Thames is one of the world's cleanest metropolitan rivers, given vastly improved sewage systems, litter laws, diversions of industrial waste and oxygenation programmes.

In 1974, salmon returned to the river for the first time in 150 years. Since then, more than 120 different fish species have been recorded in the waters.

Wonderful news for Londoners; bad news for the *Who* devotee craving just the one dead body, which surely isn't asking much?

With pleasure boats cruising before us along this wide stretch of the river, its opposite bank providing support to the huge

Chambers Wharf, trees, miscellaneous buildings and inevitably cranes, we take late luncheon beneath a greying sky. Still I'm putting off walking in *Weng-Chiang*'s bobby's footsteps, building the suspense.

Ma Hanks has devised a foolproof betting system, which she explains to a rapt audience, though it turns out to be just the old 'doubling-up' lark on any losing bet. Alex mentions a cider farm in Brighton, perking my radar, explaining that the area has "cows there and stuff"; such is the material I have to deal with.

Two old blokes beside us, one with bare feet, are discussing cows. I overhear snippets of conversation: "Gelatine"; "That's all fat and things"; "Fry a pig's trotter".

Opposite me is a family. Two small sons have been given Snakes & Ladders to keep them quiet. One starts in the wrong place and clearly has no concept of the significance of the dice, since he rolls it then moves his marker randomly. The lack of respect for the rules of the game appals me and I have to control an urge to barge across and rant at them.

By the time they're loading red and yellow counters *willy-nilly* into Connect 4, I can only turn away.

As I scribble notes, Ma Hanks remembers the Nick-teasing hobby that began in Trethurgy. "He's pretending to everyone he's working!" she announces. Everyone laughs.

Thus spurred on, she (I assume) jokes: "This beautiful woman [Sinead] – married to this weirdo [me]!"

Clearly the time has come to tread those steps.

Back through the pub, instant left to double-back along Wapping Old Stairs E. It's a narrow walkway, high brick on either side, which widens out before the latest chalkboard hoarding advertising the Town of Ramsgate's wares (*pic 4.7, taken facing back towards the road*). The paving slabs are irregular and look authentically old, polished by the soles of literally tens of thousands, my own merely the latest. Dickens,

Jeffries, artists, sailors, whores – all manner of folk passed this same way.

But at this particular moment you can stuff your Dickens. Conrad Asquith, David McKail and Patsy Smart also once commanded these flagstones. That's PC Quick, Sergeant Kyle and 'Ghoul' (as the BBC put it; I still prefer 'musty old bint'), to you and I.

Up five steps then down, towards an opaque Thames (*pic 4.8*). Yes, this was the place.

I've just watched the scene again and it's amazing how little has changed. Alright, ugly wooden fencing has been set in concrete above the wall, fairly recently I suspect, perhaps to provide privacy for the residential dwelling to the right. It also cuts off access to the second, narrower set of steps alongside, at anything above low tide. But railings, as there are here, did inhabit the same spot back in '77, and the layout remains precisely the same, as does the stonework all around (at least the stonework that hasn't been obscured by yet another Town of Ramsgate hoarding, *pic 4.9*).

It was a cracking little *Who* scene, featuring some classic Robert Holmes lines, if plagued by the dreaded exposition.

"Look! There it is!" says the musty old bint, tugging on the good sergeant's arm, pointing at a corpse only a myopic gent dipped in tar then bin-bags might fail to spot. "*It's a floater alright!*"

The PC prods the deceased with a boat hook, at which our MOB is compelled to announce, "You've got it, guv!"

(Imagine living with the woman! Picture a mealtime: "You've picked up some peas with your fork, guv! You've put the peas in your mouth!… And swallowed them, guv! You've picked up a chip with your fork! Now you've put the fork down without eating the chip, guv! You're eyeing me angrily, guv! You've raised your fists and are punching my bastard running-commentary lights out, guv!" Etc, etc.)

Saddled with the necessity for such tedium – since the *Doctor Who* audience of 1977 clearly consisted of children and retards – Holmes retaliates with minor genius.

MOB [eyeing landed corpse]: "On my oath! *You wouldn't want that served with your onions!*"

You wouldn't want that served with your onions.

I ask Andy to take a photograph of me pretending to look for bodies (*pic 4.10*), then take a moment to myself. What sense of *Who* lingers here?

For sure, the recognition factor notches it right up. On the down side, it was night-time when they filmed and this merely clouded sky doesn't quite do the trick; also it was low tide, so the players trod the riverbed, at that time troubled by beached flotsam. I could have checked the Thames tide tables beforehand, but I fear my companions, in their relentless quest for booze, would have ridiculed the idea of delaying until perfect conditions.

What I can say for certain is that Asquith, McKail and Smart – Patsy Smart, who played maids, landladies, characters whose names began Mrs, rarely Miss, and Aunt Mabel in *Rentaghost*, born 1918, Chingford, died New York 1996, barbiturate poisoning – walked where I stand now. Though they're not Tom Baker, those actors helped bring life to the words-on-paper of Bob Holmes' *Talons of Weng-Chiang*. And here I am now, stooping, scouring the froth. Before me, a sense that London exists only at a distance, that this place is a haven, or a watery museum piece. Splock. Shlsh. Splock. Shlsh. Splock. Shlsh.

As he will continue to do so for decades to come, until this part of London disappears under water and residents row/snorkel to work, Old Father Thames buffets the Wapping stone (*pics 4.11 and 4.12*), wearing it down by nanometres, smoothing it until you can't help but touch it, and depositing algae on its surface, slimy and alive.

You've got it, guv.

TRIP 5

Sunday, 8 June 2008

The Claws of Axos

Dungeness, Kent

It's funny. In November and December of 2004, when I was still working as a TV previewer for the *Daily Mail* – back in the days when they could still somehow scrape together the pennies to afford my whopping freelance wage – I was obliged to cast a critical glance at *Blackpool* (the singing/dancing drama, not the karaoke/stumbling place). That was my first sighting of David Tennant, playing a rakish cop who screws his prime suspect's wife, though he had obviously been around for a while. I wondered who he was and where he had come from.

So, if you'd told me back then that, come 2007, I'd have written a book, that the bloke in *Blackpool* would have read it, and that his quote would be on the cover, I'd have been sceptical to say the least. Who? Him? *How*?

Yet pretty much all of life's great changes happen like that. When I was born in Portsmouth, Sinead Hanks wouldn't even have been a twinkle in her parents' eyes (that would have been her sister, Nicola, who is happily ensconced with Tom). As we grew up, hundreds of miles apart, we were blissfully unaware of each other's existence.

Then, in 1995, I started working at the *Radio Times*, where Anne became a friend and colleague. Anne was friends with Michelle, also at the *RT*, who was friends with freelance writer/editor Suzanne, who was friends with (and commissioned by magazine editor) Lucy; so when I split up with Aileen, I somehow ended up going out with Lucy, who was a childhood friend of Janine, who went to college with Sinead, so when I split up with Lucy... All that, over the course of eight years. Predict *that*, Russell Grant! [Drums fingers. Waits for ages. Gives up, leaving Grant blustering about star charts and fish in space.]

Remove any one person from the equation and my life now would be totally different. Weird, innit?

It also feels slightly unreal, the thought that I'm an author. I believe I had two major ambitions when I was a child: to write a book (tick) and to become an astronaut (still awaiting NASA's call). The respectability inherent in the title 'author' also helps to appease my parents, who worry.

The *Dalek I Loved You* paperback came out on 10 April, a photograph of me aged perhaps 12, hair combed, beside my Mum, raincoat, on its cover. I got hold of an early copy on Thursday 27 March and drove to Margate with it, to see her.

She was then in a hospice adjacent to the Queen Elizabeth, the Queen Mother Hospital. Sinead and I had been moving house, exceptionally busy, so I hadn't had a chance to see her in two or three weeks.

She had cancer. First the lung, then it travelled to her brain. On my previous Kent visit, she was just about to have five consecutive days of chemotherapy to control the growth beneath her skull, with just a weekend off in-between.

I didn't really think it through. Despite being aged 88, Mum seemed to be faring better than could be expected: bright, positive, laughing, still eager to contribute to everyday tasks. Of course I only saw her occasionally, when no doubt the lingering wartime spirit of people her age compelled her to put on a brave face.

But: five days of someone bombarding her lovely old head with radiation.

In *DILY* I wrote: '…my Mum is one tough old bird. You could drive a lorry through her house and she'd pop out of the rubble asking what you want for lunch.'

I thought she would cope.

So I enter the hospice. Three old ladies, all volunteers, bless them, are seated at a desk in the reception, chatting. I ask for Mrs Griffiths. My Mum. One of the ladies offers to show me to her ward.

We walk through the corridors of this terribly quiet place, alive with death, until we reach a room of four beds, three of them occupied.

"There she is," says the volunteer lady.

Erm, I think. That's not her.

Oh, my poor Mum. Suddenly so frail, her hair wispy and white. She spots me, smiles. I choke back the shock, sit beside her.

The eyes – still hers. The face, though so much thinner – Mum's. Her hair, I couldn't get past. It said: cancer. It wasn't right. She cared so much about her appearance, yet here she was. Nightgown, pillows.

I'm so glad I was able to hand her that book, with us on the cover. She called over one of the nurses to show her; hilariously, in the circumstances, I felt embarrassed. Actually tried to stop her. [From side of mouth] "Muuuuum…" Just like the old days.

I stayed overnight with my Dad, who also seemed to be bearing up, but who would be the last to give anything away, and we both visited Mum the following morning. She was having a bed-bath behind drawn curtains, so we perched awkwardly on the empty bed next-door until called away by a lady social worker.

She wanted to discuss Mum's options, though there was only one, really, since Dad's failing eyesight precluded him from waiting on such a frail old lady – a nursing home.

While we were talking, huddled around a small table bearing a tray of teas, a terrible cry, of such anguish, came from one of the wards. A man, in such pain, physical, mental or both. And he groaned and he groaned, wouldn't stop: the guttural sound of someone who knows they are dying.

Mum knew death was imminent too, it was obvious, and she had accepted that. Why would anyone want to live in a strange bed for the rest of their life, feeling like a burden, waiting for the next awful diagnosis, fading but clinging – to what? Mostly, I guess, it's the relatives who would keep them alive.

But you know, I just could not bring myself to tell my mum how much I loved her, how much she meant to me, how much I owed her, or ever countenance saying Goodbye. There always had to be another time. One word, that word – Goodbye – would have meant the end. Couldn't ever have said it.

So I didn't. Dad and I sat beside her bed and I could think of nothing to say. It was excruciating. My mother! Surely there was something? But what can you say in that situation if you aren't prepared to confront the facts? Dad held her hand and mostly Mum stared ahead. She knew.

Eventually – this is so Mum – she said, "I don't know what you two are doing here! You might as well go!" She had a point.

So we left, both expecting that there would be another time, another chance to find some words. I was already planning to return, with Sinead, the following weekend, eight days away. See the tough old bird again.

Dad, thankfully, did get that chance. I didn't. I didn't.

I kissed my Mum's cheek and as I was walking away, something made me turn back. She was looking at me. I smiled. She beamed such a smile back, and in that moment she looked just like the younger, healthy Mum I so remembered. Afterwards, when I thought back on that wonderful wordless exchange, I saw her – this is going to sound ridiculous, particularly given my atheism – amid a shining light, a bright glow. I guess that's just how my mind chooses to remember her.

And that was it.

Deep breath.
Doctor Who.
Comfort blanket.

Andy stayed down for the Sunday, with plans for a pub quiz that evening then a Monday morning train to work. We had tentatively mooted a day trip to Dungeness – tentatively because we might have had hangovers. But as we've grown older our hangovers have decreased in severity because we're crapper at drinking. Dungeness, it would be.

While we ate breakfast, I threw on *The Claws of Axos* DVD. It's fabulous stuff, classic Pertwee. How it failed to make the shortlist for my Top Ten *Who* Stories Ever list in *DILY*, I have no idea.

I absolutely, definitely remember watching the story when it was originally transmitted in early 1971, because of those monsters. The Axons. You got two for the price of one.

First, you had the golden, humanoid creatures with the bulging eyes and permed hair, fresh from an over-enthusiastic Seventies' hairdresser's – a form they assumed to go easy on the eye of their new Earth chums – then you had their natural form, the one you'd have seen had you witnessed them shopping on Axos: this shambles, this ambling mess, a monster made of outsized mincemeat with lumps. An incredible creation, of quite bonkers vision.

So the Axon spaceship, looking like a musical wind instrument the Clangers might have chanced upon, lands on the south-east coast of England – Dungeness, as research tells us – where it buries itself in the ground, leaving only a looming, mottled orange entranceway exposed.

Enter a supporting character with the finest name, for a human, in all of *Doctor Who*. Pigbin Josh. That's Pig-bin. A bin for pigs. A tramp, he might have been, but you can bet his mother called him Josh.

Pigbin – taking the funnier option – is seen wandering around a shingle beach, retrieving an old bike from a bunch of rubbish, then riding it into a water-filled ditch, such is his shock on spotting the Axon ship.

Noticeably, this outdoor filming took place on a day of freak weather conditions – covered in the script by a uniformed bod announcing that the Axon arrival has caused "freak weather conditions" – involving snow and dense fog. As if Dungeness didn't look mad enough on-screen already.

I'd like to find Pigbin's ditch, and the alien landing site, though we don't have much to go on. Just some internet blurb mentioning Dengemarsh Road, which Google Maps show running from Lydd on Sea – as opposed to Lydd-on-Sea, which actually is on the sea, nearby – towards a dead end somewhere around the English Channel.

Easier to track down will be the Dungeness A nuclear station (playing *Who*'s Nuton Power Complex), around and inside which later scenes were filmed of mincemeat-style Axons blowing up traditionally useless UNIT soldiers by extruding tentacles at them... Except that, since 9/11, the power station has been off-limits to visitors, for obvious reasons.

So, one target we could see from space, almost, but cannot

access; the others, we should be able to reach easily enough, but we aren't *exactly* sure where they are.

Am I bovvered? On the contrary.

Gentlemen, we have a challenge.

It's a hot day. Hot, hot, hot. Bees melt in mid-air and the summer of '76 peers out from the pages of an old *Whizzer & Chips*, wearing a knotted hankie. We wind down the windows on the Micra and hit the M20 via the Blackwall Tunnel.

Since I'm driving, Andy kindly agrees to make notes of any whimsical nature that drift my way during the journey, which feel worth recording. I'm reading his scribble now and see he's written, 'Tiger – don't see many of them' (we passed a pub called The Tiger and... no, it just doesn't feel quite as important now) and beneath that, 'We're gay as fuck'.

How very mature.

Since I am all out of whimsical nature, we discuss watching Sparks the previous night at the Islington Academy. Andy loves the band; I've seen and heard little of them since the Seventies. But this is why I mention it: they really should have gone into *DILY* among my childhood reminiscences.

Sparks always seemed to be on *Top of the Pops* in the Seventies and that guy – Ron Mael, I now know – used to give me the heebie jeebies. Sitting there behind his keyboard, looking a bit like Hitler, staring at me – and you, if you were around then – out of the corner of his eyes. Then shifting to the other corner. Always staring, never smiling. Brrrrr. (He was yet another of the pop stars Mum considered "silly".)

Ron turns 60 this year. If that makes me feel old, how must he feel? Mind you, Sparks were brilliant. And I saw Ron smile.

The drive's going well, traffic reasonable. We pass a lorry with 'Eat More Chips' emblazoned along its side and drop down into Kent's so-called Garden of England, wondering whether other places in England with gardens feel miffed.

Off the M20 at junction 10, we're through Cheeseman's Green, Hamstreet – where they're holding a 'Country Fayre' – and Snave. Good, solid English names, amid the flattest countryside this side of Norfolk. It already feels weird around here, which can only be a good sign.

A notice at the beginning of the Romney Road suggests that this is an 'Alcohol control area', while the speed limit drops to 20mph. Suppressing any urge to have fun, we drive through Lydd on Sea and via Robin Hood Lane hit Dengemarsh Road. Destination.

So quiet, the silence only enhanced by the pure blue dome above us and the stillness of the heat. Buildings become sporadic then vanish. The road dwindles into sand and stones, pitted with holes better suited to a lunar roving vehicle than a Micra.

Either side of us: barbed wire, gorse and shingle. I've never seen so much shingle, future grains of sand, laid out flat, stretching away as far as the eye can see, topped by heat-haze. And pylons (*pic 5.1*). Super-pylons, like vast exoskeletons clutching skipping ropes, waiting for the game to start. Follow them into the distance, towards the sea, and there it is: Dungeness nuclear power station, a pale grey box-shaped behemoth (*pic 5.2*).

Jesus, this place is mad.

No wonder *Doctor Who* pitched its tent. Suddenly, we feel like we're the only people alive for miles around. Why would anyone else even come here? It really is like nothing I've seen before. And I think Andy's feeling it too: the excitement.

But we have a job to do. A none too easy job, since one patch of shingle looks exactly the same as another. I've taken a few snaps of the screen during *Claws of Axos* on my cameraphone, which show hut-type buildings behind the Axon spaceship. Nothing within eyeshot looks a remote match. Neither are we having any luck finding water and a potential site for Pigbin's tumble.

So we agree to continue to the end of the line, hoping for a spark of recognition, then to retrace our tyre-treads. Driving at a snail's pace, lest the car do a Buckaroo, we finally reach the furthest extent of the Dengemarsh 'Road', which peters out at a shingle dune... where loads of cars are parked!

Which, to say the least, is a surprise.

We aren't the only people here, after all. But why? Where? *Who*?

I find a space, park and we step outside. There's a notice just up ahead (*pic 5.3*), which we crunch towards across the ubiquitous small-stones. Three red-bar 'Stop' signs, three exclamation marks and liberal use of the word 'DANGER'. 'Do not proceed beyond this point when red flags or lamps are displayed'. I think we get the message: up there is a Ministry of Defence Range.

Instead of looking for red flags, my attention is distracted towards the shoreline to our left, which is lined with people fishing. Loads of them. And when we climb the shingle dune for a better view, there are still more visible, lobbing worms at the sea. Men, women, whole families. There must be a hundred of them.

Then I'm thinking: Dungeness nuclear power station is a mile or so down the coast as the crow – a hugely mutated crow, with five eyes, a human leg growing out of its head, going, "Dear God please help me!" rather than "Caw!" – flies. I'm thinking: Blinky, the three-eyed fish from *The Simpsons*. And these folk are *fishing*?*

* Disclaimer: I accept that my perception of nuclear power may be some distance from the reality and that *The Simpsons* is a cartoon. However, under the terms of the Geneva Convention (is this correct?), I maintain my inalienable right to

exaggerate freely, indeed to make stuff up, at least trying to be funny.

On the plus side, no one seems to be catching anything. Indeed, one family has abandoned the rod-based shenanigans altogether and is titteringly taking snaps of the patriarch, who has fallen asleep wearing what looks like a tent.

Can this place get any odder? Yes it can.

Next thing, we're driving back along Dengemarsh Road and pass a group of perhaps a dozen people, who hadn't been there 20 minutes earlier, aiming short telescopes on tripods at the sky.

There is but one possible explanation: twitchers. Bird-watchers. Ornithologists. (As a bloke tracking down *Doctor Who* locations, I accept that I am hardly at the front of the stone-casting queue.)

They seem to have appeared out of nowhere, and I fear I recall hearing tell of networks who receive calls, as if to a Batphone, when a rare bird is sighted, then dash *en masse* to the scene – which must have happened here.

By coincidence, ahead to our right is a set of farm buildings, so I park after the twitchers. Could this also be where the Axon ship was buried? Incidentally, I can see bugger all in the sky, not even a cloud, certainly no birds, so what they are staring at, I have no idea.

Andy takes a photograph of me, facing the same way I feel *Doctor Who*'s cameras may have faced when panned away from the spaceship (*pic 5.4*), towards the dwellings across shingle, then one to our left, of yet more shingle, where we think the spaceship itself might have been sited (Pic 5.5). Since we could be yards or even miles out, it's hard to tap into any authenticity; a sensation readily brushed aside by the fact that the entire area feels like a giant *Who* set.

It would help though if we were enduring a small blizzard,

amid pea soup, rather than the hottest day of the year thus far.

Not ten yards back along the road, remember, a bunch of birdwatchers are gazing intently into the sky, discussing with great sincerity the possibility of the appearance of a – need to think of a silly bird name… – great tit.

Frankly, I suspect we are all great tits and wonder whether we have unwittingly formed the largest concentration of total nerds in Britain at that particular moment in time.

Yet we all seem perfectly happy. Indeed, I'm having a wonderful time.

(Just as we're leaving, a new car pulls up and I overhear the driver telling his fellow twitchers that, "It's disappeared". Whether he was talking about a rare bird or our collective dignity, I couldn't say.)

Actually, before I leave the subject, I've just stumbled across the RSPB's website, which has a page devoted to Dungeness sightings. Let's see.

On May 27: 'A spoonbill and little stint were seen from Makepeace hide yesterday and four hobbies were around.' (A sentence that surely only makes sense to bird-watchers.)

The week beginning 19 May 'was a good week for raptors'. (Insert your own *Jurassic Park*-based joke here.)

And for our day in question, 8 June? Bugger all! (Though a white egret did fly in two days later.)

I didn't even need a telescope to tell them that.

It's time to hit the power station (not literally, security forces). If we aren't allowed in, we can at least stand outside, get a feel of its vastness, try to spot something familiar. It's not every day you're able to come almost within touching distance – using a withered hand, pustuled, glowing green, answering to the name of 'Wotan' – of a nuclear reactor.

So we drive back along Robin Hood Lane, hang a right into

Dungeness Road and head for town (*pic 5.6*). The heat, if not oppressive, is certainly considering forming a dictatorship, and the flatness of the place gets into your system. Not in a bad way; it's just strange.

The late filmmaker, Derek Jarman, used to live here, in Prospect Cottage, painted black with vivid yellow window-frames, chimney and garden of driftwood, borders and gorse.

According to the Dungeness community website, the *New York Times* suggested that, 'If Kent is the Garden of England, Dungeness is the back gate'. I'm not sure whether that's a compliment.

It goes on: the area is home to numerous rare insect species and one third of all plant types in Britain. Nowhere on the homepage does it mention shingle, which is a surprise.

Right, this is more like it. The Dungeness National Nature Reserve site notes that it is 'one of the largest shingle landscapes in the world'. The area has also been designated a National Nature Reserve (NNR), Special Protection Area (SPA) and a Special Area of Conservation (SAC).

Conclusion: it's a special place.

We reach the coast road, long and straight, with quaint wooden cottages spaced apart to our right and beach then sea to our left. There appear to be abandoned boats towards the shore, odd little huts, *stuff*, littering the beach. Compelled to investigate, I park the car. And I'm so glad I did.

Just: wow. *What on earth* is going on here?

It's like the surface of desolate Planet Paraphernalia. Fishing boats left to decay, holed, lonely, peeling, dot the shingle. I find myself jogging towards one, such is my eagerness for a close-up (*pic 5.7*). Sky blue, white keel, room for one. Is that number FE89? It's hard to tell, given the paint damage. Left there, in the middle of this beach, waiting in vain for its master to return.

When I stand before it, gaze into the tiny cabin (*pic 5.8*), it really affects me. That space, weather-ravaged and leaning, once contained a man. A fisherman who presumably loved his boat and his way of life. I can *feel* his presence, the soul of the craft, picture him staring out to sea while the engine thrummed, plotting. If I touched a stethoscope to that salt-cured wood, I wonder, might I detect the faintest of heartbeats?

Where is that fisherman now? What happened to his livelihood? How did he feel when he parked his craft here, for the final time, knowing he would be leaving it behind after all those years of loyalty?

Maybe I'm wrong: maybe he grew to hate the sodding boat, the routine, the dwindling fish stocks, the poor remuneration for his life-risking efforts. But I doubt it. I reckon he turned around, took one last look. And he shook his head and wondered how it had come to this.

It isn't just the boats. There are also these great rusted hunks of cast-iron machinery, cogs and mechanisms (*pic 5.9*). *Slabs*. I try to lift one, realising I have no chance, but not expecting the crushing, dense immovability I encounter.

Wondering what the hell they are, I discover the answer: an oil-blackened machine is propped on a thick DIY bench, crank handle, tubes, canisters, with more intricate workings nestled in its heart (*pic 5.10*). It smells of oil and gives off a heat stronger from a foot away than the blazing sun's feels today. Heath Robinson writ macho.

Trailing from the front of it, heading towards the sea, is a chain. So it must be a winch, used to haul heavy objects from the shoreline: boats, presumably, or catches in crates. And it's been used recently, meaning someone still works this sea. Yet there's no one around.

No one on land here, nothing in the sky, an empty sea. Every now and again, we hear a distant 'Whoo-whoo!', the whistle of a steam train travelling the Romney, Hythe and Dymchurch line.

Ghost beach.

We wander further and I simply have to take a photograph of the next unloved boat (*pic 5.11*). Her name, still visible. 'TINA'. A beautiful wooden creature, planks undulating, but holed repeatedly along the rear, by vandals, or by someone reusing the material. Poor Tina. What story would she tell?

Fishing nets, lengths of rope, some orange plastic tubing, an old tyre, bits of wood, bags... So much crap. It's spread out, so it isn't an eyesore, but... I can't put a finger on how I feel here. Sorrow for lifestyles traumatised? Elated that I'm witnessing such a unique vision, this patchwork scrap museum?

We come across rusted old train tracks, vegetation growing among them as if evidence were required that they had long been disused. Andy starts balancing along one track, the rubbish tightrope walker, and I snap a picture (*pic 5.12*). It's only afterwards, when I study the result, that I notice the hut to his right, a defiantly wonky construction, leaning haphazardly, a symptom of the strange dereliction.

I poke a head inside the partly opened door of the next nearest hut (*pic 5.13*) and think to myself: Jesus. You couldn't put a single foot inside, such is the chaos. More fishing nets, buckets, tubs, an ashtray, wiring, contraptions... Yet there's a workbench along one wall, with drawers in which, once, there must have been tackle and tools carefully filed. Someone, long ago, took a pride in this place, used it as a sanctuary.

There's a story on the Dungeness community website (www.dungeness.org.uk) of Jim Moate, lifelong resident, who had to quit fishing after a back injury and turned instead to smoking others' catch, hauled in off the Kent coast. In his day, he said, everyone in Dungeness was involved in the fishing industry. "Now there are very few left," he added, back in 2003.

Jim learnt his new craft from the old fishermen and from

recipes he found in his 270-year-old Pearl Cottage, and set up The Smokery, selling to locals and passing trade. He became so adept at his art that he noted, "I could cure a fish so you could bury it with a Pharaoh and it would never go bad."

A heartening story, of someone with a little ingenuity and a lot of pride, moving with the times yet remaining locked in tradition.

Scroll up the webpage to January 2008, and The Smokery is no more. Jim Moate has retired, is off to sunnier climes. 'I know it was Jim's desire to have the Smokery continue in business after he left but not to be – but you never know!!!!' writes the author of the news.

Sadly, you kind of do know.

But it's not all desolation and disrepair. Some 200 yards along the beach, I can now see actual whole fishing boats lined up, working craft, several of them. There are people there, too, milling around.

I don't know Dungeness. This is a fleeting visit and I've taken impressions from one small section of the beach. The oddest section, without a doubt. Certainly there's no air of despondency here. Quite the opposite: there's a calmness that's almost magical. So I just don't know.

I take a ride on an old rail cart, which incredibly still runs smoothly (*pic 5.14*), because the boy inside me demands I do, and we head for the power station, bewildered and amazed.

Wherever you are, so vast is Dungeness' nuclear complex, and so flat the land around, that you can't really miss it. The Dungeness A station, where the *Who* crew filmed UNIT soldiers vainly trying to pot Axons, was built in 1965. It covers 225 acres, an acre being roughly the size of a football pitch.

The monsters were shown wandering flying glass walkways and ambling amok outside, against backdrops of cylindrical storage tanks the volume of 10,000 Party Sevens, piping, cranes, huge square buildings like drab uber-offices, more piping, more piping than that, and the odd Seventies van.

The Axons were after power, you see; not of the airy-fairy megalomaniacal variety, but Edison's actually-running-through-wires stuff. And where better to start than a nuclear reactor? (No other options on postcards, thanks.) I won't spoil the ending, though you can guess who (hint) won.

Dungeness B was opened in 1983, and will remain open until at least 2018. Between them, the A and B stations could power the entire South East of England. No longer. Dungeness A produced its last kilowatt on New Year's Eve 2006 and is currently being decommissioned – a process that will take decades.

The station's Visitor Centre first welcomed in members of the public in 1990, keen no doubt to push the idea of nuclear power as a safe alternative to the depleting natural energy resources. Following the 9/11 attacks, Centre Director Haf Morris told the BBC, "The tours used to include parts of the power station themselves and since the terror attacks visitors have plummeted."

Come March 2004, the Visitor Centre was no more. Which is a bugger. No fatalist, I'd have very happily peered into reactor cores for the chance to sniff some residual Axon. Since that isn't going to happen, let's see what comes second-best...

Back in the Micra, we continue following the coast, past artists' homes – one displaying what appears to be jetsam outside – past the Britannia pub, with plans to return, past two lighthouses, until we're as close to Dungeness A and B as we can possibly come.

I park the car beside a building that throbs loudly, but which doesn't appear to be part of the nuclear set-up. Bizarrely, two oldsters are seated on deckchairs, with their car-boot open, before a high wire fence, facing that throbbing building – and admittedly some colourful wild flowers – sunbathing and picnicing!

There's a beach not two minutes walk away!

Concluding that old people can be very odd, I snap a photo when they're not looking (*pic 5.15*) and we walk a short distance to the fenced perimeter of the power station. A sign – and plenty of chain wire – greets us: 'NUCLEAR INSTALLATIONS ACT 1965 – YOU ARE NOW ENTERING A NUCLEAR LICENSED SITE' (*pic 5.16*). Except that we aren't. This is the end of our road.

We could follow the perimeter wire if we wanted; however paranoid that the Dungeness security people might be paranoid, I don't fancy the idea. No doubt they could watch us on CCTV, maybe debate our motivation. Perhaps become suspicious. Investigate on quad bikes. Wearing uniforms. That's genuinely how I felt then, though it seems daft as I describe it now.

Anyway, we have a fine view of the complex as it is. The buildings begin perhaps 100 yards away, all that grey, giant boxiness. The overwhelming sensation – Andy notices it too – is of silence. Given all the power generation in there, all the machinery, not a sound comes from within, at least not audible at this distance. There's not a soul in the grounds. It's as if the entire site is deserted. But it surely isn't.

Axon recognition factor? The vibe is certainly there: the colours, the pipework, the boxes. But the most recognisable aspect of Dungeness A, a circular, fluted construction, readily visible in *The Claws of Axos*, remains unseen from this vantage point.

So we devise a cunning plan.

When we passed the last of the two lighthouses, the black-painted one (*pic 5.17*), its door was open to the public. Climb to the top of that, we'll only have the best view of the power station in all the land!

God, I hate heights.

Between the interior floors in The Old Lighthouse, the winding stone steps built into the wall have just a railing on the 'drop' side. Of course it's perfectly safe, but there's no convincing my head of that.

So I'm following three very small children upwards. They're gaily skipping, I'm pressing my left shoulder into solid wall, being as far from a potential fall through mere gases as I can possibly manage, and closing my right eye so my brain can't even see and therefore register the potential drop.

Each of the five solid floors is pure bliss. A chance to reduce my heartbeat and muscular tension to normal. Also a chance to learn the history of the lighthouse and to witness its workings and lenses.

Which you can stuff up your bottom. Frankly, I'm desperate just to get up, have a peek, get down, get out. So I snap a hasty photograph or two and pick up a leaflet on the way out.

The Old Lighthouse building dates back to 1901, I discover now, safely seated in a house, and was opened by His Royal Majesty the Prince of Wales, later George V, in 1904. It's 150 feet high and comprises three million bricks. It was decommissioned in 1960, decommissioning seemingly being a habit around these parts.

The lenses, the Great Lens at the very top, and the red-and-green Sector Lens (*pic 5.18*) on the second floor, are utterly gorgeous. Marvels of engineering. Concentric circles in glass that trap the light, like fireflies in a jar, and bounce it at precise angles determined by their creators, who undoubtedly wore small spectacles and tall hats.

But I'm here for the summit, which I reach as my anxiety meter threatens to twitch past the red. Up a ludicrously steep set of wooden steps, set foot on the fifth-floor, stoop to crawl through a hatch immediately left, out onto the balcony... Take one glance towards the power station, experience Anxiety Red Alert, sod the Axons, hand camera to Andy, mumble something, return inside and become painfully aware that to get out, one has to go down. Retrace that same terrifying route by which you ascended, all by yourself.

Shoulder to the wall, opposite eye closed. Go!

Such was the tension with which fear had wracked body, as I set foot once again on blessed shingle, my right thigh muscle spasmed and I dropped to the ground like a complete idiot. But I managed to make it to the pub (The Britannia, which did fab fish and chips).

Safely on *terra firma*, I can study Andy's photographs from the top of Old L. There's one facing roughly north (*pic 5.19*), a panorama featuring two vehicles and the odd building, plus possibly an outside loo, amid several square miles of Dungeness. That's how sparse it is.

Exhibit B, the clincher, is of Dungeness nuclear power station itself, under a haze of heat. Thoughts? Weeeeell... You could replicate it easily in giant grey Lego bricks.

Is that distinctive cylindrical fluted building visible? Not as far as I can tell, so I can only assume it's based on the far side of the complex, though the architecture certainly recalls '71 and the attentions of Axons.

But it's OK. I have an exclusive treat lined up. Discussing my trip with friends over an ale, after the event, I chanced upon two who had actually trod the portal to the Visitor Centre, pre-2004, before someone flipped over the Closed sign for good. So I can take you *inside* Dungeness nuclear power station. On Red Nose Day (for those abroad, BBC comedy-based charity, a day during which folk nationwide do occasionally inane things to collect money for good causes)...

Take it away, Lena Corner (via email):

'We showed up at the gates to be greeted by a hairy man dressed up as Miss Piggy, rattling a bucket of coins. Slightly surreal, we thought, but after spending the night in the local pub and being gleefully informed that the whole peninsula was inhabited pretty much by members of just two families, Dungeness was starting to feel like a place where anything could happen. So we dropped a couple of coins into Miss Piggy's bucket – a collection for Red Nose Day – and wandered in.

There were no searches, no questions, no admission fee, just Miss Piggy, his bucket and us. This was the late-1990s, long before the phrase 'War on Terror' had even been invented, but I do remember being struck by how casual the whole process was.

Once inside we immediately got the fear. Aside from the odd worker wandering around in their Red Nose Day costumes, it felt more like an abandoned building than a working power station. We followed Miss Piggy into the huge turbine hall then up and down ladders and along metal walkways, staring in astonishment at the machinery, which to our eyes looked like something that could have existed in darkest Communist Russia, not on the beach in sunny Kent. We wandered about, sniggering about leaking radiation, nuclear fallout and, of course, Chernobyl.

I remember one of the workers telling us that the sea around the power station was among the cleanest in the country, as it had been through the Processor (or something like that) and out the other end. "It's a great little place for a swim," he told us cheerfully. This seemed to be the predominant attitude at the power station – a simple, fairly blasé relationship with the radioactive substances they worked with.

At one point we were asked to slip into some protective clothing. Out came a pair of stiff, dark blue 'cardigans' and we were ushered through a few sets of double doors to somewhere we found even more terrifying than before. This was probably the high point of our tour, but memory seems to have blanked out what we saw. All we could do was look at each other, as if to say, 'What the hell are we doing here, and how do we get out?'

Besides the insight into the insides of the station, what strikes me from Lena's personal take is the divide between the public and professional perception of nuclear power's safety (or otherwise). Given my science-biased educational background – science A-levels and engineering degree – I tend to trust the lab-coats. But I don't believe the public majority has ever been convinced by nuclear power, nor will they ever be, when Chernobyl and Three Mile Island, for two, are in the history books.

Here's Dungeness power station site director Nick Gore, interviewed in December 2006: "We have never had any significant safety event that's either harmed any member of staff or affected the community in any negative way. To be able to generate electricity for 40 years in a nuclear power station without causing any harm to people or the environment is actually a fantastic achievement."

Part of me wants to believe; however his use of "actually a fantastic" as opposed to "frankly the only acceptable" does concern me.

I'm just grateful that Lena's friend, Olivia, had the foresight to take a camera. Her pictures of Miss Piggy alone – a hairy-armed bloke, pulling an unnatural pose, in blonde wig with porcine nose, wearing what looks like a series of pink bath mats, in front of a fuck-off pylon and desolate car park – are beyond wonderful. (*I've added an album of her Dungeness photographs at 5a on my website.*)

Interlude: Brilliantly, I have only just spotted, among the

extras on my *Claws of Axos* DVD, a feature titled, 'Now and Then: A look back at the Dungeness locations used for this story, contrasting them with how they appear today'. Swift cough. A perusal reveals the actual location map from the filming schedules, pinpointing where the scenes were filmed.

For Pigbin, we should have taken a right off Dengemarsh Road – though I don't recall one existing; perhaps it has been blocked off – and the spaceship was buried beside *Dungeness Road*, so we managed to drive past it. The shingle the *Who* crew piled there remains to this day, Katy Manning (Jo Grant) reveals in her commentary.

Though handy to have known, it could hardly have made our day any more memorable. Well, only a bit.

TRIP 6

(Leg 1 of the Mega-Trip)

Thursday, 26 June 2008

The Mutants

Chislehurst Caves, Kent

"I've had a great idea," said Tom the publisher, when we met at a North London pub in early June.

I was all ears.

"I'm going to publish the follow-up to *Dalek I Loved You* in time for Christmas!" he announced.

(It had a working title of A *Who Odyssey* back then, which I wasn't keen on – too non-*Simpsons* Homer. I *did* like *Binnegar Heath Sand Pit or Bust*, which however didn't really explain anything. So we settled on *Who Goes There*, the classic sentry pun, lacking the question mark.)

Tom is the UK's youngest publisher. He's 27, perhaps 28 now, but looks 17. His hair is so spiky, it catches windblown litter and at the end of a blustery day Wombles form a guard of honour and applaud him. He's a whirlwind of ideas, excellent with his authors, and I will always doff a cap to him.

So it must be a great idea, I thought.

But I also have two other books to write: *The Daredevil Book for Dogs* and *The Daredevil Book for Cats*, both humorous takes on pet life, each half the word-count of this – but still books. Both due by September.

"What's my deadline?" I asked Tom.

"September," he said.

"Right," I said.

So it was around now, late June, that I started to panic. The book was taking shape but I had run out of locations already visited. I needed to cover a lot of places in a short space of time. *I needed to embark on a Mega-Trip.* How cool did that sound?

Time Team add an artificial deadline – three days then out of the ditch, my sideburned friend – so why shouldn't I? Ramp up the drama, fill up the Micra, find a friend.

I needed a companion. It's all very well me popping around the country, savouring the *Who* history and our strange Britain, but those would be my thoughts alone. I need someone to bounce off. (When I said 'Andy noticed it too', concerning the silence at Dungeness power station, it was actually he who mentioned it first; I *knew* it was silent, I just hadn't *noticed* it. So when I say 'I need someone to bounce off', what I really mean is: 'I need someone whose ideas I can steal gratuitously'.)

But who in their right mind is going to spend four – being my plan – consecutive days with me, trapped in a tiny car, batting like a lunatic around the country, when the goals involve a large sand pit… actually, two large sand pits, a couple of quarries and, ahem, a railway bridge?

It's obvious, isn't it? Family! The only people in the world who are actively lumbered with you.

I'm sure *Doctor Who* fans down the ages have made great use of their family members in feeding their own addiction. Then we look at flowers or something back. You scratch my sordid itch, I'll scratch yours.

"Er, Sinead... Would you like to take two days off work *plus* spend the following weekend with me, going around loads of *Doctor Who* locations?"

Amazingly, she didn't really have to think twice.

"Dylan, you're coming with me and Sinead at the weekend, around loads of *Doctor Who* locations."

"But Daaaaaad..."

Bless him.

The beauty of this particular *Who*-related formula, which only became apparent to me slowly, is that there really is something in it for everyone. Even 'normal' people. Because though the final destination might be obscure, perhaps even uninspiring on the face of it, there's the getting there too.

And you're visiting places you would never in an eon have considered previously. More than that: you're actually getting off your butt, leaving the house, and actively going someplace. It's a motivation.

You know what? I am really enjoying myself. And on this Mega-Trip, I *really* enjoyed myself. Sinead and Dylan did, too. Or at least, they said they did.

First consideration: where to go? Britain is practically my oyster. Or the bottom half of it is, spreading out from *Doctor Who*'s then London base. (I'll come to new *Who* and Cardiff later.)

By my estimation, I could cover six locations on the Thursday and Friday with a stopover on the Thursday, then three at the weekend, ditto hotel on the Saturday, since Dylan would be a bit less patient. Nine locations.

I could look at the choice two ways: like opening a treasure chest and cherry-picking the nine shiniest objects; or being given a treasure chest full of shiny objects and being told to discard all but nine. There are so many *Who* stories rattling around my subconscious that, when brought to the fore, take me straight back to my childhood. Scenes within them that come alive, featuring locations I've longed to see for real.

I already have my three bankers, as outlined in the Foreword:

* In *Day of the Daleks*, when the Ogrons and Daleks appear from that arch beneath that old tunnel, having travelled through time and space to reach Earth. As a kid that thrilled and fascinated me. Partly because of the Daleks, mainly because of the Ogrons, these menacing ape-like thickies in leather, with bald black pates and guns. They travelled through time and space, and came out *there*. I have to do that too.

That's Bulls Bridge, in what used to be called Middlesex, now demoted to Greater London.

* *The Android Invasion*. The Doctor (Tom Baker) lands the Tardis in a sunny English wood, after which he and Sarah find themselves in a deserted village, with monument and pub, where locals stare like they did in *American Werewolf.* The pure Englishness of that hamlet always struck me. It's another that went instantly onto my mental hit list.

East Hagbourne, Oxfordshire.

* And of course, the Holy Grail for any respectable *Who* fan: Devil's End. Poll your friends; ask them, 'Who *wouldn't* want to visit a place called Devil's End?' Tar and feather the first fucker with their hand up. Bok the gargoyle, "Chap with wings there – five rounds rapid", Pertwee and Bessie, ancient burial mounds, Roger Delgado's Master, Damaris Hayman, Morris dancers and another quintessential slice of England.

Aldbourne, Wiltshire.

The others I chose are no less evocative, just took some

sifting. Chislehurst Caves? They are unique here, because the location came before any memory of the story. I just wanted to see some caves.

I'd done *Who* caves before: Clearwell Caves in Gloucestershire, covering *The Christmas Invasion*, David Tennant's debut, for the *Radio Times*. I wander into this ancient rock-hole, water drips echoing, follow the tunnel, emerge into a chamber – and there's the Tardis! (They had to dismantle then reassemble it.) Later, I watched the Doctor, in pyjamas, confront the Sycorax leader. And there was such an atmosphere. Of sound in hollows and serious age.

But I'd already been there and written about it. So I wanted to experience anew. Internet research led me to Chislehurst.

I *think* I remember watching the six-part *The Mutants* when it originally aired, during April and May of '72, because I seem to recall the Mutants themselves. Or perhaps I've seen one since and am projecting the memory backwards. Certainly, the story didn't stand out; I sense it was boring, as some of those Pertwee six-parters were wont to be.

It may be telling that the BBC, hardly averse to milking the *Who*vian Pound, have never released *The Mutants*, either on video or on DVD...

Hang on! I've just pottered around Amazon's *Who* section – and they did release *The Mutants* on video. Without telling me! They also released *Ambassadors of Death* and *Invasion of the Dinosaurs*, which somehow passed completely beneath my radar. Seems they came out during 2002-2003, long after DVD had taken a grip. What are the chances, I wonder, of them also being released in that format?

However, I have watched *The Mutants* once since 1972, I guess around 1990, as part of my satellite-recorded bootleg collection, of variable quality. My only vague recollections of that are of some rock-faces, Pertwee being sympathetic to a

Mutant and swirling fog. Or maybe that sort of thing sums up my memories in general.

Such was the unwieldy nature of that collection that I binned the lot during one house move, content in the knowledge that I had forked out for official versions of all my favourite stories.

But… Yesterday I struck unbelievably lucky. One-in-a-million. I came across a copy of the Target paperback novelisation, in a miscellaneous sale rack at Blackwell's on Charing Cross Road. For £1!

Non-*Who*-fans might well be thinking: and? Good for you – never subscribe to blind acceptance. Let me explain.

This Target paperback was first published in 1977. I snapped up a third reprint from 1984. It is now 2008. Though I might have paid just the quid for a 'SALE' copy, it was only £1.95 originally.

Chain bookstores simply don't do stock from 1984. Someone must have found that *Who* delight in a forgotten corner of a warehouse, appreciated its significance and saved it from a vigorous pulping. My copy of *The Mutants* has pages the colour of an old lady's made-up skin and smells of stacked comics.

The back cover promises a 'massive shape scuttling out of the darkness and striking the earth Overlord down'. It's a Mutant! ('A huge insectoid creature.')

Let me not fob you off with the blurb's words any longer, because one of the creatures is pictured on the front. And it looks completely brilliant.

How to describe this? Think Frankenstein made of leather elbow patches, hunch-backed, walrus-eyed, wonky mandibles and a mouldy two-fingered claw, performing a John Inman gesture from the Seventies. Told you it was brilliant.

Inside are characters named Ky, Cotton, Stubbs, Jaeger and the Marshal. Residents of the planet Solos are turning into Mutants, known colloquially as Mutts – and no one knows why. Naturally, the Marshal wants all the Mutts dead.

Anyone else detect allegorical undertones? Good old *Who*.

For my purposes, the book doesn't start terribly hopefully: 'It was a planet of jungles…' But flick through to page 44 and you'll find this:

"Where are we?" whispered Jo. "Is it a cave?"

"A man-made cave. It's an abandoned mine, that runs beneath one of our mountains." [Replied Ky.]

And guess what? Chislehurst Caves were man-made. (Admittedly running beneath Kent, which is hardly noted for its mountains.)

An early start is in order – well, 10-ish – with so much to fit in. For these two days, I've knocked together a Fact Pack, involving notes of our destinations, directions and wishlists of what to find. Partly, it's a necessity, partly it's a response to Sinead's habit when we go away anywhere of taking a 'Day Pack', full primarily of lady-items: wet-wipes, moisturiser, water, that kind of thing. Women, I have come to realise, are petrified of drying out.

As *DILY* readers may recall, our system goes like this: I do the driving and hiding, Sinead does the talking to strangers; when no strangers are in evidence, her duties extend to map-reading, which she adores. If Sinead could staple maps to the inside of her eyelids, she would.

Here's the crunch – and I'm already looking over my shoulder as I type, though the wife is safely miles away at work… Though Sinead is indeed very adept at following the routes, she can get a little carried away. Map-aholic. And it doesn't always go right. There, I said it. (There's a knot in my stomach now.)

So it's a gorgeous sunny morning, we have, effectively, a two-day holiday ahead of us – and we're arguing. Heatedly.

Trapped in a one-way system just outside the Blackwall

Tunnel, which Sinead maintains is no fault of her own, the atmosphere has become dark. Actually, she wants to go home. And we've only been gone half-an-hour!

The map's been lobbed into the footwell and I'm going moodily too fast while trying to guess the right direction. Kofi Annan in the back seat has thrown up his arms in despair and is demanding to be let out.

If I'm seeming ungrateful that would be a reasonable conclusion, of which I am well aware and slightly ashamed. It's a heat-of-the-moment thing. The wife and I are strong-willed, competitive souls – a walk up an escalator usually ends in a race – determined to be right. We used to argue a lot, which was tiring; five years and a wedding later, we've managed to reduce that to, well, just during times of map-reading. The trick is to see out the crushing silence, as liquid tension drips from the car roof in shades of doom.

But wait: by chance, a sign to Chislehurst! Then to Chislehurst Caves! And as we drop off the A222 Bromley Road, down, down the steep Old Hill, sunlight dappling the road through overhanging branches, it seems we're going to make it. Good fortune cracks a smile.

Left into Caveside Close, through what looks like a posh small housing estate, and there it is: car park, large shack, 'Chislehurst Caves' – oh, and a school party. Great. That's all we need: shrieking children poking you with their pencils, giggling behind hands and asking things like, "What's a cave?" at the end of the cave tour.

Otherwise, the car park is largely deserted and, hey, it's a weekday, we're away from the desks and the weather loves us. I park the Micra in shade and we approach the single building to investigate.

A blue plaque (*pic 6.1*) outside the entrance notes: 'People came from across London and north west Kent to shelter here during the Blitz. At the height of the bombardment between October 1940 and July 1941 thousands used the cave system each night.' News to me.

I've done no specific research; no sense knowing everything before you can discover it for yourself. So I'm equally surprised to find, immediately inside the door, framed black-and-white photographs depicting a 'Town below ground'. Gas attack procedure from the 1930s; a World War II hospital within the caves; mushrooms growing, carpets of fungi, also below ground. During the spring air-raids of 1941, 8,000 people were living down here.

It's a shade narrow-minded of me, but I hadn't expected this at all. I'd envisioned a barely popular tourist attraction clinging hopefully to its association with *Doctor Who*, 36 years previously.

A quick tour of the reception, with café beneath lengthy Churchill painting and friendly staff, reveals just one link to that past: a photograph of Pertwee in the caves, surrounded by three kow-towing Mutts (*pic 6.2*). His finger is raised as if he's ticking them off.

The caption reads: 'John [sic] Pertwee was filmed at the caves in 1972.'

They haven't even spelt his name right!

I am mildly miffed for the man.

I'd imagined naively that we would be allowed to wander around Chislehurst Caves at our leisure. Instead, booking tickets, I discover that all tours are guided and that the next one doesn't start until noon, 45 minutes away. The school party has thankfully disappeared, presumably having finished their own tour rather than waiting for it to start, and we are the only people here.

We treat ourselves to a cappuccino from the café, supping it outside as clouds roll over and birds tweet, and a chap in old

British Army uniform appears, talking on a mobile.

Please no, don't let them do reconstructions! Am-dram types playing parts for tourists who can handle that sort of thing, enjoy it even, and myself, who feels cringingly self-conscious on the actors' behalves, for no good reason.

Why have my feet gone cold?

Back inside, still killing time, I reacquaint myself with the displays. Shells, gas masks, wartime rations; life-size diorama of ancient cave refugee with small boy; marriage certificate of Henry David Ramshaw, 21, and Pearl Patricia Hull, 19, who gives her residence at the time of the ceremony as 'Chislehurst Caves'; map of the South East showing where Hitler's Doodlebugs dropped in the Summer of 1944, Kent so dotted red that it appears to have the measles.

Though my parents lived through the war, based in Mitchum, Surrey, while my dad worked on the Spitfires as an engineer, I've never really got to grips with what it must have been like. Without the experience of next-door burning down as the neighbours scream and die, while enemy bomber squadrons drone overhead and everywhere is rubble, it's frankly unimaginable.

An aged notice (*pic 6.3*) reads: 'IN COMMEMORATION OF THE TIME THAT THOUSANDS OF MEN, WOMEN AND CHILDREN LIVED IN THESE CAVES, LONDON'S LARGEST PUBLIC AIR RAID SHELTER DURING THE 1939-45 WAR. AND OF JAMES GEARY GARDNER WHO GAVE THEM SHELTER HERE IN THEIR HOUR OF NEED.'

James Geary Gardner, I have just discovered, was the Caves manager, who successfully supported one Pat Evans – aided by Alan, a local greengrocer, and removals man Albert – in setting up a cinema down in the tunnels to entertain the people. Among myriad other noble tasks, no doubt.

As noon approaches, others are starting to appear: a trio of biddies, two family groups, one currently scoffing a snatched early lunch, two blokes with paunches and a staring-eyed chap alone at a café table. Surely they can't all be writing books about *Doctor Who* locations?

I massacre the final remaining minutes until the tour by perusing the souvenirs – including a model of a dragon on a rock (£7), a pewter Reaper on a glass ball (£5), Skeleton Warriors (£35), and assorted gemstones, such is the way of British tourist attractions, offering any spurious tat for sale, in the interests of staying open – and by visiting the loo.

On the way I pass two of the three biddies, silver-haired yet sprightly.

"Oh yes?" one queries the other.

"I got that for £19.99, reduced from £39.99," comes the reply.

"I was going to say…" Sadly, I miss what she was going to say, as a door closes.

While peeing distractedly, I wonder how many other biddies, all over the country, were having that exact same exchange at that very same time.

Back in reception, a door opens in the far wall and a bearded bloke dressed as a miner – or perhaps he *is* a miner; that's the problem with those am-dram segments – is followed out by a like-totally of American students. Aged in their early teens, I guess, all gabbling away.

"Shall I buy a postcard?" one enquires of a friend.

And I think: what hope does she have in life, if she can't decide for herself whether to buy a postcard?

After this, my notes become fairly untidy. Unreadable in parts. Something else I hadn't foreseen: caves can be dark.

Our group, of more than a dozen, including the trio of biddies and others previously outlined, enter the door through which the students emerged and are instantly into a cave. It was there all along. Tunnel-shaped space, gloom distracted by overhead lighting, something interesting off into the distance. Our guide, a young woman named Chrissy, who looks vaguely reminiscent of Billie Piper, hands out one oil lamp between two.

Since Sinead is on camera duty and I am a Man (say that to yourself in a grunting voice) and therefore Hold Fire (ditto), I take ours.

I can feel its heat on my fingers and smell the cloying fuel. As we troop further into the caves, its presence makes me feel authentic.

I'm liking this already.

We pass the old ticket office (*pic 6.4, modelled by the wife*), where those wishing to shelter from the bombs would pay one old penny per night or sixpence for the week. A large board beside it details the rules of Chislehurst Caves, in golden curly writing. It begins:

'1. No admission or re-entry to the Dormitory Section after 9.30.p.m. (or 10.p.m. during *double* Summer Time)…'

And continues until Rule 19 ('Arrive early and stay put'), sounding pragmatic though not unfriendly. 'Double Summer Time' – it makes you realise how little time there seemed to be, in which to defeat Hitler.

We are ushered onwards, the biddies making Oooh-ing noises – I think they might be trouble – until stopping before a giant map (*pic 6.5*) of the underground complex, which looks as if it's been scorched by an iron in places. To our left is a chamber housing the chapel (*pic 6.6*). Rows of wooden seats (liberated from Hyde Park, I read somewhere earlier), two mannequins dressed in Sunday best, and an altar at the far end, lit as if part of a beguiling grotto. The walls, hewn from chalk… Hang on, I'm missing the map lecture.

Chrissy, the only one with a battery torch – visitors are discouraged from bringing their own, lest we damage each others' eyes – shines it over the layout. And it's incredible, like something out of *Dungeons & Dragons*. A honeycomb of tunnels and chambers, running for more than 22 miles. No wonder we needed a guide.

And… Did she just mention 'Druids'? She did! There are three distinct tunnel systems, each dug out during ancient periods: Saxon, Druid and Roman.

Maybe that sounds lifeless on paper, like a snippet of uncoloured tedium from a history book, but down here, as a mild chill whispers in your ear and voices reverberate, with darkness up ahead – Druidic darkness – I'm tingling with anticipation.

I came here to find some Mutants, and it seems I'll find a whole lot more.

We're guided first towards a large alcove to our left, where a pair of World War I sappers (shop dummies in uniform) are guarding ammunition. One of them is smoking a fag and I wonder whether to point out the health-and-safety issues associated with this, to inevitable hilarity, get the biddy trio giggling, but my mind is already sidetracked.

At some point soon I'm going to have to ask about *Doctor Who* and, since everyone else here is a grown-up, self-consciousness is buffing my cheeks in preparation and making my brain pulsate. I'd contemplated addressing someone official about it before the tour started, but decided to wait, procrastination being the safest option.

As we had first entered the tunnels, I was having an urgent whispered conversation with Sinead, who said she'd ask – in front of everyone else, on my behalf, so they'd know I was too pathetic to do my own groundwork – so I had to urge her, "No, *please*, don't!" then lie, "It's OK, I'll do it."

"Are you sure?"

"Yes!"

[*No!*]

I mentioned this in *DILY*, and funnily enough it hasn't gone away in the intervening year or so: my bizarre fear of striking up a conversation with a stranger, of putting myself in the focus of anyone I don't know, particularly several of them. I hate people staring at me, I hate having my photograph taken, I would rather have snails inspect my nostrils than put my hand up in a group of people and have the person at the front point at me and go, "Yes?", so everyone's head turns.

Very strange. I can get past it, of course – I have had my photograph taken; and I'm a journalist, so I do have to converse with strangers – but it takes some mental preparation.

And that's what I need now.

In a few minutes, I shall be compelled to interrupt our guide, Chrissy, to announce, "Er. I'm writing a book…"

Sound too pompous?

"Hello, I'm an author…"

Lordy no, I might as well wear a cravat and wave a cane around.

Frankly, I don't know what to say. I'm just going to have to do what I usually do in such circumstances: trust to spontaneity. Blurt out something poorly constructed.

Yes, that should work.

It's really dark now, each oil lamp a fairy-light glow up ahead, corridors leading off every which way, as we turn another corner and are shown a series of carvings believed to date from the Great War (*pic 6.7*). The skeleton (*pic 6.8*) is easily spotted, and Chrissy says that another one is of nurse Edith Cavell, the Great War heroine who was executed by the Germans in 1915; however, the reliefs are so indistinct they could equally be of Nookie Bear.

(Sorry, I made that rather evocative, weird symbolism from a bygone age of warring feel rather glib.)

Our guide notes that chalk, being a soft material and easily shaped, is ripe for carving, so the tunnels are littered with the markings of the tens of thousands who have passed through them over the centuries. I hold the oil lamp up to a wall behind me, test this theory – and it's true. Cuts, shapes, names, numbers, pit the off-white, a testament to the human desire to leave a mark, no matter how unnoticed it may be.

Heading further into the 'Saxon' zone, our next stop is a deep alcove dug into one wall. Incredibly, it's a stage. Lonnie Donegan played skiffle down here; David Bowie played twice, with his early beat combos, The Konrads and the Manish Boys; The Animals, The Who; Led Zeppelin launched their Swan Song record label down here, a night described as 'a riot of loud music, booze and naked women'… Jimi Hendrix played someone's birthday party here in '66.

Which all sounds terribly cool, but I'm aware that, as we head into the 'Druid' section, where the tunnels become smaller so I duck instinctively, there is far more to Chislehurst Caves than I had anticipated. What if *The Mutants* being filmed here is considered such a teeny blip in the subterranean history that the guide fails even to mention it? What if we have *already passed* where Pertwee once stood surrounded by Mutts?

There's nothing else for it. When we next stop I fail to take in the lecture, because my mind is performing cartwheels…

A brief silence post-lecture. Now! I practically put my hand up.

"Er, I'm writing a book," I offer. (Damn, just what I didn't want to say!) "About *Doctor Who* locations. And this is one. Jon Pertwee's *The Mutants*, from 1972."

(Yeah, give 'em some detail – dig yourself a deeper hole.) My head actually feels heavy, such is the volume of blood pumping into it at an alarming rate. Thank Christ for the gloom.

Everyone now has me pegged as a complete geek. Or have they? Would it really matter if they do? Oh sweet Jesus. (Fear brings out the blasphemy in me.)

Our guide is staring at me. *Everyone's* staring at me. Just brazen it out. *Get it over with*!

"I was wondering where they filmed?"

"I'll show you," says Chrissy. "It's just around the corner."

Now I'm the absolute centre of attention (in my head). If David Icke jumped out and started ranting about lizard men while wearing a shellsuit, they'd still be transfixed by the bloke obsessed with *Doctor Who*.

Another alcove, perhaps 20 feet deep, ten feet high, walls curving towards a blackened ceiling. "This is where the BBC filmed in 1972," Chrissy explains. "You can still see where they painted parts of the walls gold."

We're there! This is the place! (So we hadn't passed it, our guide would no doubt have mentioned it anyway, and I need never have said anything. Great.) And I also now feel that I should be far more interested in it than everyone else. They think that, too.

So I hold up my lamp, cast a critical eye towards the alcove, wondering whether to rub my chin sagely for effect. The patches of *Doctor Who*'s gold are pretty sparse; you really do need to peer. (Trust Seventies *Doctor Who* to come in here with brushes and gold paint! Space-age, innit!) There are a couple of shiny spodges right at the back at roof level, and perhaps one or two more on the left, but it's hard to tell. Age and sightseers have no doubt weathered parts away.

I ask Chrissy whether they filmed elsewhere, but she isn't sure.

So that's my epicentre of *Who* activity and... Well, it's a chalk alcove – but it's a chalk alcove that Jon Pertwee once acted in, and that's as good as it gets.

But the group is in danger of moving on. We haven't lingered long anywhere. The roughly mile-long tour takes only 45 minutes. I have to have my photograph taken in the spot – or as near as I imagine – where the scene took place. That's part of the deal of this book, as the trips are ticked off, the money-shot: to put myself inside the action, surrounded by *Doctor Who*'s ghosts.

I have to stop them leaving.

"Er…"

Heads swivel once again.

"I have to get a photo," I say, the admission echoing until I swear I can hear Romans sniggering in reverb. This is worse even than Marks & Spencer, Ealing.

Head swimming, I climb the short slope to stand only partway into the alcove. I'm not walking any further and dragging this out. Turn around, face the group. Hold up my lamp. Literally grit my teeth through the embarrassment (*pic 6.9*).

The crowd is muttering. A few titters. Those bloody biddies. I *knew* they were trouble.

I say something hopefully funny, try to make a joke of the situation. No one laughs. Can't remember what it was I said. Just remember it echoing.

Take the picture. Take the picture.

We've had problems with the flash. Occasionally, it decides not to work. Sometimes the memory is full. All this runs through my head when I should be savouring the moment.

I make out Sinead before me, camera aloft.

Flash!

Sweet, satisfying, glorious flash.

I practically sprint down that little slope, envelop myself in the welcoming gloom. Breathe.

Job done.

I could go on. Describe the 'Druid' altar where children might once have been sacrificed, the bowl shape where the blood may have collected, tell of the 'Roman' well, which used to be 100 feet deep but has become far shallower thanks to decades of litter being dumped inside, but I came across something rather bemusing while researching this chapter.

You may have noticed that I had started using quotation marks around 'Roman', 'Saxon' and 'Druid'. Because I just don't know any more.

In 1903, one Professor WJ Nichols discovered abandoned mines in Chiselhurst Caves and wrote a scientific paper or two about them, claiming them to be 8,000 years old, with Druidic significance. Other academics, notably, rushed to debunk this.

Re-read the Caves' own 'Miles of Mystery and history beneath your feet' leaflet, from reception, and the wording may take on a new significance: 'First open to the public in 1900 as a showplace, the guides told the Victorian history of the Romans, Druids and Saxons, Smuggling and Murder.'

'...told the Victorian history of...'

Professor Nichols, I shall assume.

I discovered that guides used to point out the fossilised remains of a large Ichthyosaurus in the cave roof, which others reckoned was just a big piece of flint. That wasn't shown to us.

But please. I would hate to put you off visiting Chislehurst Caves. Whichever history you choose to take in – there have been chalk mines here since 1650 at least, I believe to be a fact, and flint mined here was used to spark weapons during the 1800s – all the wartime stories are of course true, and Jon Pertwee was indeed here. The *Who*-lore is enough to require investigation, and frankly we both had a wonderful time simply savouring the atmosphere. Though I was hurried along before I could sufficiently appreciate the thrill, I undoubtedly stepped where Pertwee himself once placed a dandified boot.

And there was more.

Besides the bonkers Seventies Tolkein-esque graffiti painted on the ladies' loo (*pic 6.10*); the bit where we stood in utter darkness and Chrissy banged an old water tank that echoed in our ears like the demons of Hell awakening; the hospital scene featuring old shop dummies, which looked more like a family dancing to Gary Numan (*pic 6.11*); the woman who gave birth in the caves, so called the girl, er, Cavina (who later changed her name and is believed to live in Sidcup); and the further mannequin scene depicting life below during the air raids (*pic 6.12*)... Great sights and stories. Besides all that, there was one point when Chrissy removed our collective breath, and I even forgot to feel residually self-conscious.

We're at a pool. It shimmers turquoise and ends in a wall and rockfall. It's oddly quiet here, evidently (our guide says) the single area of the caves where there is no echo. And there's a ghost.

A young woman murdered by her husband at this point, 300 years ago, supposedly haunts the caves.

The 'Chislehurst Challenge' was devised: five pounds to anyone who could spend 12 hours beside the pool, without running for their life. Only two have ever managed it. People hear strange noises. See things.

In 1958, a local policeman – I scribbled his name down, but it was so dark I then wrote over the top of it – claimed the prize, but only having become so terrified that he spent hours carving a horse image into a nearby wall, distracting his terrible thoughts. When they came to collect him he was reluctant to turn around, having been convinced that he had felt someone's/something's breath on the back of his neck.

On Hallowe'en 1985, two Caves guides tried it. One was so petrified he ran into a wall, knocking himself unconscious for the duration (so he didn't get the fiver – the tightwads). The other suffered some sort of fit, it's suspected, as he was found the next morning in agony with a dislocated shoulder and carted off in an ambulance (but won the fiver).

Thus ended the 'Chislehurst Challenge'.

TRIP 7

(Leg 2 of the Mega-Trip)

Thursday, 26 June 2008

The Seeds of Doom

Athelhampton House, Dorset

Back once again in the Chislehurst Caves car park, eyes squinting, adjusting to the daylight, I check my watch. It's 12.52. Two more locations to go – 150 miles or so away. The next is a house and gardens, Athelhampton House in Dorset, open to the public, and I have no idea what time it closes. If it's any time around 4pm we may be in trouble, depending upon the traffic on the motorways.

(I'm not making this up for drama's sake, by the way. I really am largely clueless. The Fact Pack contains the essentials, not the detail. As I said previously, I like to trust to spontaneity. Why plot meticulously when you can discover your way via adventure? Of course, if the place does shut before teatime, I'm fucked.)

So we depart Caveside Close in a hurry, reluctantly foregoing the chance of a modest livener in the pub beside us, the impressive-looking Bickley Arms, opened in 1870 according to the sign, details of which I have added to my website, for those more leisurely.

Rejoining the A20 we came in on, we hit the M25 and skirt all of South London until linking with the M3 south-westwards at Thorpe Park. Which makes the progress sound far quicker than in reality.

'Travel broadens the mind,' they say. No it doesn't. Getting there then wandering around a bit does.

During a flight to New Zealand I glued my tongue to the head of the man in front, then tried walking to the loo, to see how far it would stretch – just to pass some time. (It ended up passing its elastic limit and now I have to tie it around my waist with a slip-knot, so that little plan backfired.)

During this drive, at least, I'm still partially high on a cave visit that surpassed expectations, and eagerly anticipating the sights to come.

Sinead reads out a newspaper feature on amateur animators bringing missing episodes of classic *Who* back to life, we discuss Robert Mugabe, Sinead reads out a newspaper feature on pop comebacks (Martin Fry, that sort of thing), and we end up arguing – in a jovial manner – about the merits of the Little Chef.

Sinead has a thing about Little Chefs. *Loves* them. I'm no food snob, in fact I can't bear posh restaurants – all that "Would sir care for a dessert?" (no, but one would care for an orphan child in Africa), peas re-branded as 'teeny organic earth-nurtured spheres *au vert*', lamb being 'slaughtered while listening to Enya' and waiters (people who carry food a bit) peering down their noses – but I cannot stand Little Chefs. There's something so very Britishly depressing about them.

So I formulate a plan, then inform Sinead of it. I'm going to have a series of plastic letters – U, N and T – made, in the exact same typeface and of the very same size as the Little Chef ones.

And one night I'm going to drive around, to every Little Chef in the land, replacing their H, E and Fs with my own concoction. That'll show her! And them!

(I'm writing this a week later and, as it turns out, I'm yet to put the plan into action. Haven't even asked for a quote on the lettering.)

Athelhampton House was, I discovered prior to visiting, the place where the *Who* crew filmed *The Seeds of Doom* in 1975, to air between January and March of 1976.

Prior to my visit, I'd opened my double-pack VHS of the story to find both cassettes still in their cellophane. I guess I must have re-watched it on bootleg, still my memories of *The Seeds of Doom* are so very vivid. It's another that should rightfully have found a spot in my *DILY* Top Ten, but that's what happens when a show runs for so long, at such quality.

Here are those abiding memories:

* Scientist in Antarctica, taken over by alien, turns green.
* And continually mutates into this shambling green blob with arms and legs.
* Then wanders out into the snow.
* Back in Blighty, there's a nutter who wears leather gloves.
* He's called Harrison Chase. (Did that name inspire my own *Harrison Dextrose*? You'd have to ask my subconscious.)
* Chase gets his in a giant wood-chipper, or similar, which is fabulously gruesome.
* This alien, the Krynoid – I remember its name well – grows to a ridiculously enormous size.
* And towers over some sort of manor house.

Some sort of manor house. Athelhampton House & Gardens, Athelhampton, Dorset, DT2 7LG.

So I slapped the vids in my old Matsui and watched *Seeds of*

Doom again, revelled in some classic *Who*.

And it was *brilliant*! Honestly, you could stuff your telly of 2008 – *The Apprentice, The Mighty Boosh, Doctor Who, Peep Show* and *River Cottage Spring*, thus far notwithstanding – because, dated as the effects are, that six-parter would fuel a family of four in entertainment well into the winter.

It feels quite grown-up: part *Avengers*, part *Hammer Horror*, lorded over by Tom Baker as *beau* of the ball.

So, what do we have?

The action opens in the Antarctic, where a pair of research scientists unearth, or rather unsnow – ha, my spellcheck took a few seconds to red-underline that, which had me wondering; mind you, it's just red-underlined 'spellcheck' – an ice-encrusted pod. A seedpod, as it turns out, which will germinate under heat into a plant that whips out and infects the nearest human, who subsequently transmogrifies into a Krynoid. I love the opening exchange:

Moberley: Come on, Charlie, we've got enough samples!
[As if research scientists trying to discover new wonders of nature can have 'enough' samples. "No, I'll just put that rare one back. Cupboard's full."]
Winlett: "This is nice…"
[Nice?!]
Winlett: "…This is something else. Have a look."
[The bloke's kneeling next to you – he can't miss it!]
Moberley: What is it?
[Etc.]

I don't mean to scoff; like I said, this is wonderful stuff. I just enjoyed the naivety of their conversation, being so very classic *Who*.

Antarctica itself looks great in close-up, all swirling snow – which gets trapped in Baker's nose-hair at one stage – and cliffs; the model shots of the research base are also impressive, given the standard limitations (budget, time). It's the scenes from a distance that let the side down: people wandering around Antarctica as backdrop, with polystyrene balls whipped up by a wind machine stage-left laid over the top of them, in CSO, so they glow. (According to www.wholocations.net, Antarctica was filmed at Buckland Sand and Silica in Surrey. That's on tomorrow's agenda.)

Another beautifully naïve aspect of the story is the idea that people can drop in on Antarctica willy-nilly. The Doctor and Sarah do it, as later do a pair of Harrison Chase's stooges (including Boycey from *Only Fools and Horses*).

Chase himself is so utterly mad and malevolent – his mission: to protect the plant life of Mother Earth.

To wear black leather gloves and an outrageous tie, while being bonkers, more like.

There's an insane scene in which Chase twiddles the knobs of a synthesiser in his greenhouse, and the racket he's making is quite nauseous. "The Hymn of the Plants," he explains. "I composed it myself. [Pause for effect, while a nation hopes he stops.] I could play all day in my Green Cathedral." Wibble.

The man is several gnomes short of a garden centre; and there's another bewildering scene, after he has photographed the Krynoid at its most giant stage, in which his voice becomes so dreamlike it sounds discomfortingly post-coital.

Anyway, his mansion, as we have established, is Athelhampton House & Gardens – the Gardens part of which is used extensively. There are chases every which way: it's like an episode of *Tom & Jerry*. But one garden looks very much like another, at least to me, so I need landmarks. Stuff to focus on. A hit-list for the Fact Pack:

* Queen Victoria – There's a statue, her in old age, the None More Dour Period, which features in a scene involving John

Challis from *Only Fools* (playing henchman Scobey) and two black-suited paramilitary minions with guns hunting down our heroes, and stopping to confer at Victoria. She's top of my list, being so recognisable.

* Water – Scobey meets his end in a river or somesuch, drowned by living weed. Surely can't be hard to track down.

* Small-tree-lined avenue – Body of minion discovered there. Looks pretty distinctive.

* Tree topiary – A line of trees shaped like stretched pyramids. The Doc and Sarah leg it past these.

* Cottage – The fledgling Krynoid (actually an actor in a hideous green bodysuit) is put to bed here by Chase and his butler. That's in the grounds.

* The house itself – Can't really miss it.

…Not even from the A35, because it's very well signposted. There are some fabulous place names around these parts, mostly puddle-centric: Piddlehinton, Puddletown, Tolpuddle – *the* Tolpuddle, of martyr fame – Affpuddle, Briantspuddle, Turners Puddle, Throop…

Throop. Genius.

It's 3.45 as we arrive, so I'm guessing we're alright for time after all. The drive was lengthy, at least blessed with a lack of hold-ups, and as we pull into the car park, all tall, ancient trees and green, I'm quite stunned by the number of vehicles here.

It's a Thursday mid-afternoon, late June. No import. Yet I reckon there are well over 100 cars parked, plus a coach – in the middle of cocking nowhere.

The sunshine holds firm as we walk through the double iron gates into the grounds of the house, and there it is, straight ahead, at the conclusion of the gravel driveway: the place where they filmed *The Seeds of Doom*. Result.

It hasn't changed at all. As you'd expect of an historic house, I guess. Imagine throwing on a uPVC conservatory, double glazed with fake stained glass, to impress the neighbours.

The very first establishing shot in the *Who* story is practically what confronts me now (*pic 7.1*). And that's ideal, because I can readily picture the fully grown Krynoid towering over the building – in CSO, shot from ground level, not the shots where it destroys the place, as that would hopefully have involved a model – this great green lummox the size of, well, a still bigger country pile, all tentacles and vertiginous bulk.

Athelhampton House itself... The only architectural styles I can recognise are gothic and art deco, and it isn't either of those, so I'll resort to describing the scene.

I reckon that's sandstone that has blackened with age, or that's how it looks. An L-shaped building, noticeably angular roof, brick-tiled, plenty of windows... The way they appear barred, this could almost be a romantic prison, the sort of place they'd keep royalty hostage. Perhaps they did? Though the interior shots were all studio-based, Sinead's keen to see the house itself – enjoys that sort of thing – so we're due a visit.

There's been a residence on this site since 1086, when it was inhabited by the Bishop of Sailsbury and his tenant, Odbold (I'm not making this up), though the building we see – give or take a few sections – was constructed in 1485 by Sir Robert Martyn.

Bishop of Salisbury: Odbold?

Odbold [scuttling into lounge, holding dead spider]: Hnn?

Bishop of Sailsbury: Odbold, shall we take elevenses in the garden today?

Odbold [inspecting spider very close-up]: Hnn?

Bishop of Sailisbury: I said, shall we take elevenses in the garden today?

Odbold [eating spider]: Hnn?

Bishop of Salisbury: I wonder, when your parents christened you, whether they were aware of names such as John, James and Peter?

Odbold [looking for more spiders, pauses quizzically]: Hnn?

Bishop of Salisbury: Odbold is such a, well, odd kind of a name, don't you think?

Odbold: Have you eaten all the spiders?

After Robert Martyn, it's all posh types marrying other posh types, buying the place, selling the place, inheriting it. Typical classist England.

The lineage of ownership goes something like this: Henry Brune (ancestor of the Prideaux-Brunes), Sir Ralph Bankes, Sir Robert Long, the fourth Earl of Mornington (nephew of the Duke of Wellington, divn't you know!), the fifth Earl of Mornington, George Wood (good old Georgie, bringing the poshness down a notch, until – uh-oh, who's this?), Alfred Cart de Lafontaine (one does beg one's pardon!), George Cockrane, the Hon Mrs Esmond Harmsworth, Rodney Phillips (Rodders!), Robert Victor Cooke (MP for Bristol West), who passed Athelhampton House on to his son, Patrick Cooke, with wife Andrea, which brings us to the present day.

Judging by the car park, Patch and And are doing alright for themselves. Let's go in, shall we? To the Coach House Visitor Centre!

First, there's the ticket desk to negotiate, via the Topiary Restaurant. Simple, you'd think. You haven't reckoned on the pensioners.

The place is crawling with them. Lordy, but pensioners (and Sinead) don't half love a country house and garden. I bet someone in here mentions their age unprompted once every 17 seconds.

In here, the Grey Pound is King.

Ordinarily, I would think: aw, bless. But there's something about this lot. Well, two of them.

I'm waiting at the ticket desk for the person in front of me to be served, when this old lady sidles up. Stands next to me, but kind of in front. I can see her looking at me in my peripheral vision. I know what she's angling for.

"Would you like to go before me?" I ask, all manners and deference.

Indeed she would. Funny, that.

Sinead nudges me. "Why did you let her in?" she half-whispers.

"She's old *and* a lady," I half-whisper back.

Of course, it isn't a simple ticket-based transaction she's after. Oh no. The old lady has several questions she'd like to put to the cashier.

I wait patiently. Well, not that patiently. Actually I'm thinking she knew *exactly* what she was doing. Spotted the mark. Knew I wouldn't be able to resist letting her push in, her having lived through the war and all that.

Suddenly there's another old git beside me – not behind me (forming a queue, as the British tend to do). Beside me, if you please. And I Know Precisely What Her Game Is. It's as if I'm not even here! As if anyone under the age of 72 is a mere frippery, to be ignored and negated.

Old Git One's *still* asking some tiresome bloody question.

Old Git Two's readying her purse. I feel like telling her, "Excuse me, there is a queue, you know!" But I can't possibly talk sharply to a pensioner. This one probably shook the Queen Mum's hand. And cracked the Enigma Code. While baking scones. Using powdered egg.

Sinead's now digging me in the ribs, as if I haven't already spotted the danger. "Don't let her push in!" she snarls.

I don't reply, keep my strategy hush-hush, but I'm ready. Oh yes.

I'd put two hands on the counter, stake out my territory, but I'd end up hugging Old Git One, who might get ideas. The best I can do is edge forward, merely in danger of a little tweed-wrapped frottage.

Still she's asking questions!

The tension in my head is becoming unbearable. I feel like I'm on the starting blocks at the Olympic 100 metres final, not waiting to buy a ticket to Athelhampton House & Gardens.

Old Git Two knows it. She's edging forward, too.

Then: silence. Old Git One's desire for flora-based knowledge has finally been sated.

Old Git Two's mouth is already opening, a millisecond from vocal-chord launch. But I'm half her age, twice as fast.

Ker-pow! "Two tickets to the house and gardens, please!"

Gotcha!

Old Git Two shoots me a 'I think I was here first!' look.

I shoot her back a 'I don't think you bloody were! Cheeky sod!' look. (It's OK to swear at old people in your head.)

Yes – we're in! Stick that in your colostomy bag and smoke it, Old Git Two! Spoke up before you could! Stood up for my rights in the face of shameless attempted queue-jumping! We're into Athelhampton House & Gardens and you won't be for another good minute – or two if you're paying by card! Several more, if you're planning to ask as many questions as Old Git One! We get to look at the old chairs and stuff first! We get to…

Hang on a sec.

Rearrange these: Victory. Pyhrric.

I hate old houses. Could not give a monkey's. I remember being dragged around Hampton Court at least twice as a youth.

"King So-and-so once slept in this bed," you're told.

So what? He ain't there now!

I did HMS Victory, Lord Nelson's flagship, Battle of Trafalgar, several times, and that was alright for a while because there were cannons and stuff, and a man died and then a man kissed him. But the thrill wore thin.

I don't even need to mooch around Athelhampton House for this book's purposes, but Sinead wants to and she's put herself out for me, so I feel obliged to look at some chairs in support.

Chair, table, painting, painting, chair, lamp, chest of drawers, painting, books, painting, billiard table... roped off. Chair, painting, table, etc, etc.

I pause briefly only in the King's Bedroom, which I suspect might be wishfully named, as I've seen no mention of a kingly visit in the literature. Plus he'd have had to have been a very short king: this bed's about four-feet long! Someone has laid a dead fox along the foot of the bed, touch of 'class', except it has really naff fake eyes, which are too big, like you'd see in a teddy bear.

I'm itching to get outside, check out the *Doctor Who* stuff, find Queen Victoria. But Sinead's lingering and I feel that heading into the gardens without her would constitute treason. Then, hanging around downstairs, tantalisingly close to the exit, I spot someone who works here.

Perhaps I could ask her for some *Who* factoids?

Ordinarily, not a chance. She's a stranger, after all. But my boldness at Chislehurst Caves has buoyed my confidence and without a second thought I march up to her and explain my mission.

Can she help? She can!

I'm all tenterhooks.

"Tom Baker and Elisabeth Sladen filmed *Doctor Who* here in 1975," she says.

I wait for the punchline.

There isn't one.

That's it.

Turns out she's new here and "Tom Baker and Elisabeth Sladen filmed *Doctor Who* here in 1975" is the extent of her knowledge.

Right. There is someone else who knows a lot more, I'm

told, but she's only here on Mondays, Tuesdays and Wednesdays – and I'm certainly not coming back. However, my *Who*-fact-lite new friend is eager to help, so she fetches Athelhampton House's own Fact Pack and flips through to the Film, TV & Media section while I revisit my tenterhooks. Now we're getting somewhere!

My new advisor fingers a point on the page. I squint...

'1975 *Doctor Who – The Seeds of Doom*
Tom Baker & Elisabeth Sladen'

We may have been here before.

Not wanting to appear ungrateful, or even disappointed, I dutifully scrawl down in my notebook some of the other productions that have been here, though sneakily picking out only the silly ones:

'1978 Egg Marketing Board advertisement
1985 *Treasure Hunt* (Anneka Rice & Kenneth Kendall)
1996 Visited by cast of 'Allo 'Allo'

Sinead appears. I make a break for it.

Now the genuine fun starts. 'Find the *Who* landmark!' It's like Treasure Hunt, but without Rice's bottom or Kendall's specs.

We wander through a hedge and immediately get lucky. This, according to the guidebook, is the Great Court. It's also where the trees shaped like stretched pyramids are, which the Doctor and Sarah ran past, though the trees seem slightly fatter and more rounded now.

I drop my notepad and bumf in my excitement, and pretend to run past them for Sinead to take a photograph (*pic 7.2*).

My heart's actually quickening. Where's Victoria?

There! At the end of that grass pathway (*pic 7.3*)! (This is easier than I had imagined.) I fast-walk towards the life-size statue – suitably grey – robed, scowling, more pleased to have found her than to appreciate the statuary. I form a pistol with my fingers and pretend I'm Scobey (*pic 7.4*). Shame I don't have two meathead mates with me, who could play the paramilitaries.

Walking further away from the house, we find a long, rectangular water feature with lily pads (Canal Pond) and a stone arch at the far end, which I'm sure must have featured somewhere in *Seeds of Doom*, though I can't picture the scene. I snap it anyway, in case (*pic 7.4*). And beside us… Can it be? Is it? These trees look more mature – but then *The Seeds of Doom* was filmed a third of a century ago. Yes, this is the place! My 'Small-tree-lined avenue – Body discovered here'. Officially, Lime Avenue, the boughs interlaced to form a pleasing archway overhead, dappling the sunlight. Snap! (Pic 7.7). Check!

Next we head towards the bottom of the garden. A sign. Pfffffftttt! 'RIVER PIDDLE'! Brilliant!

A treasure hut *and* a river named after wee! This is fantastic!

And of course that's the river in which Scobey must have been gobbled up by weed. Double whammy! Come on!

I take a picture of the achingly picturesque wooden bridge, bubbling weir and weeping willows (*pic 7.8*), having no intention of jumping in and pretending to be the character this time.

And I realise I need to calm down.

I can't say that I've taken in any detail because of the pure compulsion to recognise locations, one after another. Bang, bang, bang. I haven't stopped to inspect a single flower or a square inch of pristine English summer lawn. (Phew.) But the place does *feel* different to how it appeared in *The Seeds of Doom*, despite *looking* practically identical.

Perhaps it's the bright sunshine – the weather in '75 was more overcast – perhaps it's the omnipresent old folk, perhaps I just haven't taken enough time to imagine myself into the *Who* situations, in my childish desire to complete my collection. But I have felt no ghosts here – the atmosphere's too touristy sterile.

Though that's a disappointment, I'm still having a quite wonderful time spotting familiarity.

Sinead and I cross the bridge and promenade along the far bank of the narrow River Piddle. Actually more brook-sized, it's perfectly clear, light-coloured stones for a bed, the travelling water catching reeds and bending them towards its own conclusion at Poole Harbour, as if pointing the way.

Stinging nettles and other vegetation (I can only recognise the nettles) line its bank, tree boughs shade us overhead and it is very, very quiet here.

I seek out fish-life. That's a perfect little trout run, down there, and I'm always on the look-out for trout.

I merely alluded to my love of fishing in *Dalek I Loved You*; having over-alluded to my love of *Doctor Who* in the same, I worried that readers might think I had glued myself into corduroy and spoke in nasal tones.

But I am a fishing addict, if lapsed, London's rod-based opportunities being scarce.

I remember as a youngster, hauling in small perch by the dozen at Wellington Country Park in Berkshire; the conger battle in Cornwall; tossing lugworm into the sea whenever we went on holiday, never catching a thing.

Then Dad took me on my first trout-fishing trip, to Ladywell Lakes in Hampshire, I guess when I was 13. Gentle Ken Riley taught me how to cast, and we'd watch a big white fly drop ever so slowly in the water, see these dark shapes dart towards it, turning away at the last possible moment. But every once in a while, one of those shapes would swallow that big white fly. Strike and it's on! The sheer adrenalin trip as I played that trout, as it rolled and darted, leaping out of the water, furiously pumping its tail, then Splash!

After that I was, well, hooked. As a teenager, when other boys my age were trying to touch girls' bits, I'd be painting the garden fence, earning money for just one more trip to Ladywell.

Why? The solitude, the scenery, are so beguiling. Escape into Mother Earth's womb.

Often I leave empty-handed, and that's fine. Fish are exquisite creatures, and wily despite their tiny brains. I have oodles of respect for them...

Sorry, I'm getting carried away here.

Suffice to say that I did spot some brook trout and pointed them out to Sinead. "There, see the weed sticking out? To the right of that and back a foot? Yes, there."

She failed to turn cartwheels.

Just one location remains undiscovered from my hit-list of six. The Cottage, where the human/Krynoid mutant lay in bed and was comforted (vainly) by Sarah. It has to be close. These gardens are perfectly compact. Just need to spot a thatched roof.

We're around the back of Athelhampton House now (pic 7.10), which looks to me slightly less pristine than the front, as if visitors' first impressions are paramount. There's a gorgeous circular dovecote back here, full of pure-white birds and their less-white doings. And there's a building over to our right, behind trees...

Heading for a closer look, we leave the grounds by the entrance gates and hang a right past the Topiary Restaurant and ticket office, as oldsters natter about vegetables. Follow the pathway, trying to gaze through trees... it's definitely a thatched roof.

Stop at the wooden gate before the building's driveway, compare view with memory. Yes, this is the place – we're in. Collection complete!

I take a photograph (*pic 7.11*) and compare past with present. The driveway's different. In '75 that was unruly grass and flagstones, now covered in gravel, but the cottage feels remarkably similar, just a new lick of paint, some careful renovation here and there. The Krynoid was once holed up in one of those bedrooms!

This, I now discover, is Athelhampton House's River Cottage, available to rent: sleeps six (cot also available). So it's necessarily private – as the 'PRIVATE' sign on the gate proclaims – and there's a car in the driveway, suggesting inhabitants.

But my money-shot: putting myself as closely into the scene as I can manage… Staring at the place over a gate really will not do.

Dare I trespass?

It'd only be for a few seconds. Yes I do dare! No harm done.

Next thing I know, I'm unhooking the gate, striding through.

Writing this book has done something to me. It's turned me into a stranger-questioning, minor-law-breaking, scene-seeking motherfucker!

Of course, I don't walk in too far, in case someone spots me and tells me off.

"Quick, Sinead!"

Snap. Mission accomplished. (Pic 7.12.)

And just think about it: the committed *Who* fan – admittedly able to afford a weekly rate of £605-£1372, at the time of writing – could hire and actually live in a genuine location from *The Seeds of Doom*! Sleep where the Krynoid slumbered uneasily. Tread the very same boards as Sarah!

(Thank you for buying this book – every little helps.)

As we're leaving, we consider taking tea in the Topiary, then decide against it because it's hardly our bag. Anyway, our day is not yet complete and the afternoon is no longer on our side.

But there's just enough time to check out the spurious tat in the inevitable souvenir shop. Let's see… Dorset Knob Biscuits, anyone? Jams, chutneys and leather bookmarks? Lavender-scented drawer liners? Or how about a *Bluffer's Guide to Paris*? How exquisitely relevant.

I sneak a quick glance into the Visitor Book on the way out, an opened double-page of spidery writing and comment, in multiple hands.

'Very enjoyable.'

'Very beautiful.'

'Loved the food.'

'FILTHY DISGUSTING MILK JUG.'

You really can't take old people anywhere.

TRIP 8

(Leg 3 of the Mega-Trip)

Thursday, 26 June 2008

Destiny of the Daleks

Binnegar Heath Sand Pit, Dorset

It's now five o'clock, we haven't eaten since breakfast, I'm tired from the driving and excitement, and Sinead's probably tired because she's four months pregnant and isn't used to this level of obsession. We have a room booked in a lovely pub in Swanage, not so far away – and with one more location still tapping a finger in the Fact Pack.

I'm tempted to forego it, but not tempted enough. This book was nearly called *Binnegar Heath Sand Pit or Bust*, if you recall, and I'm buggered if I'm taking the Bust option now. The name has a ring to it – Binnegar Heath Sand Pit somehow parades around the mouth – plus it played Skaro. The planet of the Daleks.

I'm only going to set foot on the planet of the Daleks.

No, there ain't no stoppin' us now.

Happily, the pub nearest to Athelhampton House, The Prince

of Wales, where we might have sought sustenance, has become 'Apartments 1-4', so no diversion available there. But of course, Sinead now wants to drop in on Tolpuddle on the way to the sand, check out the martyring history. And again, given her sacrifices – oh, and the fact that she's my wife (the certificate's in a drawer somewhere) – I feel compelled to humour her, despite the approaching eventide.

I won't trouble you with the details of that little detour. Suffice to say that Tolpuddle was terribly thatched and, besides a short museum that I declined to accompany Sinead into, there wasn't much to see.

"There might be a memorial or something," she had suggested as we entered the village.

"Let's hope so," I'd replied, witheringly.

(We didn't find one.)

So we regain the A35 towards Lytchett Minster, drop down the B3075 Morden Road, hang a right onto the A351, skirt Wareham and join the A352. Sinead, a fan of local radio as well as any old history, has now tuned into Wave 105 FM, which is doing my head in.

[Assume unnecessarily jovial radio voice] "And now the Weather! With Bournemouth Airport!"

How can a place for planes sponsor the weather forecast?

So while Bonnie Tyler or some other ludicrously permed bint clogs up the car with her wailing, we try to find our planet. All I know is, it's near Puddletown Road – Skaro, just off Puddletown Road! – but we've driven down that for a while and saw only farmland and a few houses.

Which leaves us driving up and down the A352, through Hethfelton, Wool and back, seeking any sign Binnegar-related, and craning our necks over hedges and fences, trying to spot a very large amount of sand.

At one point, I notice a house with Binnegar in its name, stop the car and wander into their driveway, look for an expanse of orange in their garden, fail to find one, consider ringing the doorbell to enquire, think better of it, and get back in the car.

The operation, if one could call it that, isn't going very well. As the sun descends, our stomachs rumble.

Only one option: back to Puddletown Road.

We drive further along it this time. And suddenly a bank appears to our right, ten feet high or so, grass and gorse. I wonder what's on the other side.

Then a sign: 'DANGER: DEEP EXCAVATION'.

Fifty yards later: 'DANGER: DEEP EXCAVATION'.

A further 50 yards: 'DANGER: DEEP EXCAVATION'.

'DANGER: DEEP EXCAVATION'.

'DANGER: DEEP EXCAVATION'.

'DANGER: DEEP EXCAVATION'.

'DANGER: DEEP EXCAVATION'.

'DANGER: DEEP EXCAVATION'.

'DANGER: DEEP EXCAVATION'.

'DANGER: DEEP EXCAVATION'.

Woah! There's something over there. Something seriously fucking long. And deep. And I bet I know what it is.

I didn't imagine I desperately needed to re-watch *Destiny of the Daleks* before my location trip, because certain of its Skaro scenes are set in my mind. Three Daleks in a row – being all they could afford to build – rolling through endless sand. Had to be Binnegar Heath Sand Pit, and sand is sand is sand.

I did so because it was an excuse to watch Tom Baker take on the demented pepperpots again, and because Sinead and Dylan were trapped in the flat with me at the time, so I could record the impressions of the unconverted.

Baker's Time Lady companion, Romana, has inexplicably regenerated from Mary Tamm into Lalla Ward, the Earthbound reason being Tamm quitting, while K-9, who has made it too easy for scriptwriters to extricate our heroes from holes (and who was too wobbly out on location), is written out of this story as having laryngitis.

So it's just Baker and Ward.

What immediately strikes me is that we have two distinct quarries being used, my Location Head now being attuned to that sort of deception. Where the Tardis lands, there is not a grain of sand in sight. It's a solidly geological space plastered with age, all fissures and blocks, caves and stacks, in shades of grey, scattered about with man-made brick structures, presumably old mine-workings, half-demolished and dilapidated. Creepy.

"Tom Baker got to go to all the cool locations. Nowadays it's all just computerised," says Dylan, in a surprising turnaround for one of the stomp-footed high-tech generation.

And he's right: the place is indecently cool. It looks like a dangerous playground for the sure-footed, ripe for climbing and exploration. It makes me think twice about my choice of location, though briefly, because…

Here it comes. As the players move stage right they miraculously appear in a vast sand pit, having patently shifted quarries. Binnegar Heath Sand Pit. And it's equally awesome: burnt-orange cliffs, pooled water silted to buggery, patches of grasses and scrub, and deep crevices running down slopes where rainwater has sought a path of least resistance. It might be a more fertile Mars.

A spaceship appears in the sky, the Movellan craft.

"Hahahaha!" goes Dylan. "That's rubbish!"

And normal service is resumed.

I had completely forgotten the central storyline of *Destiny of the Daleks*, though the VHS cover provides a major clue.

The Daleks are drilling down into their own messed-up

planet; the Movellans – incredibly Eighties creations, though this was filmed in '79, looking like refugees from Imagination, the glittery pop group starring Leee with three e's – have no idea why and the Doctor has merely an inkling.

Then I remember. Of course! Davros is down there!

I'd met the chap myself, not a month previously. It's marked in my diary:

May 2008
Tuesday 20   Davros

(How weird was it writing that?)

I had spent much of March, April and May interviewing cast and crew of the new *Doctor Who* series four. Off the top of my head: Tennant and Tate, Freema Agyeman, Christopher Ryan (a Sontaran and formerly of *The Young Ones* – twin delight), Felicity Kendall, Tim McInnerny (who invented 'purest Green' in *Black Adder*), Steven Moffat (*Who* supremo-in-waiting), Peter Capaldi (*The Thick of It* and *The Crow Road*), Georgia Moffett (Peter Davison's daughter)… My anticipation is always further propelled by guest actors' previous associations.

I've interviewed Daleks and Cybermen, Sontarans and Sycorax. But I'd never interviewed Davros. And it felt like The Big One. The Master may have had more appearances in the show, at near-equal billing with the Doctor, but he's humanoid, and if the Daleks represent *Who*'s alien zenith, then Davros, as their wizened creator, is surely the zenith plus one. I couldn't wait. But I had to.

So Davros, played now by Julian Bleach, will be at a photographic studio in West London on the morning of the 20th, and while I can usually cover any fannish glee with some form of professional sheen, I'll admit I was excited. I would get to witness, in latex and flesh, this new incarnation, unseen on small-screens since *Remembrance of the Daleks* in 1988, before most of the rest of the country... *before the rest of the world*! (Sorry, I'm starting to sound like Davros.)

When I arrive, *RT*'s photographer, Mark Harrison, and Art Editor, Paul Smith, are already there, plotting angles and lighting. Not only is Davros coming, so too are a couple of Daleks, the new red-with-wings Supreme Dalek, and Dalek Caan himself. Quite a bonus. (I have no idea at this stage that Dalek Caan is the half-destroyed, creature-exposed bonkers-gonk whose appearances will add a fabulous touch of soothsaying madness to the finale.)

And, as is The Way with these things, I wait.

In fact, I get a bit bored of waiting and nip out for a sandwich. When I return, I'm told that Bleach has arrived and is in the back room, lounging prior to his make-up job.

He's in there. Behind that door. Davros.

I think I'll give him a minute.

As I linger outside, all the Daleks bar Caan arrive – in a rented Luton van. I suppose I should have expected as much, it's just that you do imagine them beaming down from a spaceship with spoilers.

The Luton's gate is lowered and I peek inside. Daleks, unceremoniously strapped to the sides, blankets around them, and at the back, Davros' Dalek base. Looking like that, they'd have a job conquering Argos, but I suppose we all look our worst in the mornings.

(A call shortly comes in that Dalek Caan has broken down on the motorway and won't be able to make it.)

When I finally pluck up the courage to enter the room at the back, Julian Bleach is seated at a table supping coffee. He's an elegant-looking man of distinguished facial features, who has played Frankenstein's Monster and a sinister freakshow type in

Torchwood, has also done Shakespeare and co-created the bizarre dark-comedy musical, aptly named *Shockheaded Peter*. I'm not quite sure what I will make of him.

As it turns out, he's a genial sort, if a man of few words – most of his replies come packaged in just one or two sentences – whose reaction to playing the iconic Davros bats between fascination and bemusement. But he has a way with the words he uses, describing his character as a cross between Hitler and Stephen Hawking.

When the show's prosthetics guru, Neill Gorton, arrives, Bleach takes a different seat, before mirrors, in preparation for his transformation. Alongside the brushes, make-up, glue and latex shapes, Gorton has a life-cast of the actor's head on which he keeps the main mask in pristine shape.

Two Julian Bleaches. One about to become Davros, the other unseeing and slightly macabre-looking. I beat a hasty retreat, so as not to spoil the ultimate reveal…

Which takes a while – during which I discover a quirky touch: a small spirit level at the front of the control panel on Davros' Dalek base – but is worth every thumb-twiddling second. Lower half, striped tracksuit bottoms; upper half, megalomaniacal Dalek creator. Black perv-jacket (modelled on a dentist's) with newly added metal clasps, and that head. That desiccated skin, tautened over its skull, metallic frame glinting, eyeless sockets dripping with darkness, third eye in the forehead yet to glow blue.

Though there is some vision through the mask, via a series of pinpricks that cannot be picked up by the camera, Bleach is guided towards the photographic set. He uses a short stepladder to enter the Dalek base, sits on a wooden bench lined with plain foam, gets comfortable, and the shoulder restraints are lowered in place.

Everyone steps back.

A switch is flicked. The third eye lights up.

Davros is alive!
A seriously iconic moment.

The same happened in *Destiny of the Daleks*, when Davros was played by David Gooderson.

He's been sitting there on the third underground level of Skaro, growing cobwebs, abandoned, lonely in his nightmare, when the Doctor discovers him. He seems devoid of life until a bony hand stretches out its witchy fingernails, wiggles them, and the camera pans up and that blue light comes to life. Cue, inevitably, the end credits. *Whoo-diddly-do-etc.*

Sinead suddenly remembers watching the episode when it first aired, having recognised that very reawakening. How amazing is that, for a scene to be so memorable that it triggers such recognition?

She asks Dylan whether he's enjoying the show, too.

"No," he says, and gets up to make some toast.

Back on Puddletown Road, I at least am on tenterhooks. I can't be certain that that is Binnegar Heath Sand Pit over that ridge, but given those repeated 'DANGER: DEEP EXCAVATION' signs, which went on forever, what else could it be?

I park the Micra just as soon as the signs end, in the entrance to Rogers Garden Stone, its gate padlocked shut. It's 6.30pm now and everyone has left work – good news, since I'm hoping the sand pit won't be crawling with employees, pointing at the 'DANGER: DEEP EXCAVATION' bits and making shooing gestures.

Sinead, tired and very hungry, stays in the car. I, pumping adrenalin, cross the empty road and vault a gate. I suspect this may be trespass, too, so I wouldn't recommend anyone to follow my example. Indeed, please don't. But I have a book to write – and a duty to its readers! (Plus I'm bloody desperate to see what's over there.)

By my reckoning I'm at the far end of what I hope is the pit. So I walk down a dusty, stony path and find a way in through the crappy trees on my right, now heading – if my radar is functioning – towards it. It's barely a path that I'm on, but it suffices. And I'm so pent up with anticipation, I start running. Up the bank, brambles trying to wrap themselves around my bare calves, pulling myself up the steep slope.

Until I reach the top.

What greets me, under the languid blue early-evening sky, takes my breath away. It is incredible. A vista of sand, stretching as far as the eye can see. I'm at one corner, atop a platform before a lengthy decline, which leads down to a flattened base of immense dimensions, over which are spread huge, conical piles of sand in so many shades.

Up here, it's like I'm king of an alien world. Perhaps it's the end of a long day, perhaps it's the anticipation so vividly, extensively realised. Whatever the reason, I feel euphoric.

Skaro!

I snap a couple of photos on my phone (*pics 8.1 and 8.2*), trying and failing to capture the perspective. I can't even fit both ends of Binnegar Heath Sand Pit into the viewfinder, not even from this high vantage point. The place is absolutely massive. I've just consulted the scale on Google Maps, which puts the pit at roughly 2,735 feet in length – that's just over half a mile long!

Now I need myself in the picture. Which means I need Sinead.

Honestly, I feel guilty. Dragging her out here – with another three days of this to go, mind – failing to feed her, clinging to her company and support. This might take a little grovelling.

As I clamber back down the slope, heading for the car, I'm breathing heavily, though through excitement rather than exertion. I make my way back past the crappy trees... And there she is! Already heading this way, packing camera.

God I love her in that moment. My gratitude aches.

"Quick! Come up here!" I call to her. "It's fucking unbelievable!"

(Sorry, I always swear when I run out of hyperbole.)

So I take the hand of this pregnant, ravenous woman, and pull her up through that prickly oomska – in her flip-flops – until she too can witness the sight.

"Wow!" she says.

I run down the sand to stand on the platform, turn and fling open my arms, as if to say, '*Just look at all of this!*' (*pic 8.3*).

Then I try to calm down.

How does the sand pit of June 2008 compare with that of *Destiny of the Daleks*? It feels like it's had a spring-clean. The grasses and shrubs are gone; there are no silted pools of rainwater. Those mounds of sand look pristine.

But the Dalek is in the detail. Down at my feet, heading towards the bottom of that enormo-bowl of sand, the surface is rutted: foot-deep, V-shaped valleys in the sharp white crystals (*pic 8.4*). Deep crevices, formed by rainwater seeking a path of least resistance. Precisely as appeared in *Destiny of the Daleks*.

This is the very same place where Daleks strapped with red-and-yellow bombs once roamed. Three of them (plus some cutouts in silhouette).

Am I going to head down there, get a closer view, seek further recognition? No I am blooming well not. For a start, I doubt I should even be here, and those are the sort of crevices eager young(ish) men losing their balance down slopes break their ankles in. Plus, there's a roadway at the north-west corner, from where a vehicle might suddenly appear.

No, I've done enough here.

Sinead snaps another photo of me, at last becalmed and

contented (*pic 8.5*), for the album, and we depart after one final snap of Binnegar Heath Sand Pit, which we notice afterwards shows the shadows we cast as the button went 'clzzzttt' (*pic 8.6*). And so we add our own dark spectres to that of Davros.

But something was missing. An explanation. In my haste to seek out old *Who*, to boldly go to a bloody enormous sand pit, I had failed to wonder: *what the hell is this doing here?*

No longer. Part of the mission of this book is to not only bring these weird places to life, to seek out the ghosts of recognition, but to put the locations into some real-life perspective.

So I've just Googled 'Binnegar Heath Sand Pit'. And you know what? Besides mention in all the *Who* location websites, I found sod all.

Which couldn't be right.

You don't just dig out – I don't know – enough sand to fill Wembley Stadium ten times over – note to editor: you can check that – which presumably took quite a long time. And never, ever mention it. Anywhere.

Then something clicked. *What if it isn't actually called Binnegar Heath Sand Pit?* Maybe the name was changed? Maybe the *Who* location people plonked that label on it in the 1979 call sheet, for reasons best known to themselves?

After much hunting, I ended up dredging through pdf files concerning planning permission in the Dorset area, which mentioned Binnegar. Yes, *hugely* entertaining. And one name kept cropping up: Binnegar Quarry.

Finally, I found a map: Binnegar Quarry was indeed our sand pit.

(While we're here, I also unearthed an actual 'Quarry Finder' website! The classic *Doctor Who* location bods would have needed to be peeled out of their underwear! It's a learning resource for teachers and students – education being different from in my day, clearly, since we never found great quarries then looked at them; no, we read books until we wished our brains had been pickled in aspic – and is at www.quarryed.co.uk, for those suitably intrigued.)

So, Binnegar Quarry. I'll keep this short because it involves geology.

Look on a map and you'll see the area either side of Puddletown Road is riddled with sand and gravel pits. Amazingly, there's one twice the size of Binnegar, just up the road at Stokeford Heath.

These Dorset aggregates, as they are known, are naturally occurring materials used by the building trade. Soft sand for mortar, sharp sand for concrete. That's what was down there.

They were formed by river erosion in the Wessex Basin during the Quaternary period – from two million years ago until now, which covers a multitude of sins – though some were reworked by more recent river systems.

I can tell you that, in 2003, there were 16 active sand and gravel sites in Dorset, producing 1.6 million tonnes of material. Great. For the building industry. And briefly for *Doctor Who*.

But there's a catch.

I discovered that SITA UK – I don't know what that stands for, and I've managed to quell my disappointment – have been granted permission by Dorset County Council to turn Binnegar Quarry into a 'recycling and recovery park' to recycle up to 122,000 tonnes of waste annually, 'including garden and organic kitchen products and dry recyclables such as paper, cans and plastic bottles'.

Michael Cox, SITA UK's Area Manager, said: "SITA UK's plans for a composting and recycling facility at Binnegar Quarry will play a key role in reducing the amount of material sent to landfill and we're delighted with the council's decision."

Hurrah! Probably.

What it means for the quarry itself, I have no idea. But I'd guess that it will look a lot less like Skaro once the paper, cans and plastic bottles arrive.

Thus does the world keep turning.

And I think we can now safely move on.

TRIP 9

(Leg 4 of the Mega-Trip)

Friday, 27 June 2008

The Seeds of Doom

Buckland Sand & Silica, Surrey

In retrospect, I may have made an error planning a second sand pit trip in 24 hours. It's just that I want to see Antarctica, partner location to Athelhampton House in *The Seeds of Doom*, and the optimum routes worked out this way. It's done now, but Buckland Sand & Silica is going to have to go some to top old Binnegar.

We stayed overnight in Swanage, a staggeringly friendly seaside town on the Dorset coast, which I just so happened to have holidayed in as a youth. Well, if you're going on a nostalgia trip, why go half measures?

The Red Lion (*pic 9.1*) offered a very pleasant double room in an annexe – and 35 different ciders. Hoho. It's my adult version of a sweetshop.

Of course, the wife, not content with sitting on the same chair in the same pub all night working her way through as many of those 35 apple-based frivolities as possible, wants to try other places too.

So after an excellent 'Trio of local fish' and but three different ciders, I'm dragged towards the seafront.

Swanage isn't much as I remember it, from somewhere around '76. Back then we stayed in a hotel overlooking a green, on which I played cricket with some other kids – the sum total of my memories of that week. Now I can see a large white building then grass to my left, some way away – which may just be my former hotel – and a pier to my left, equally distant. I don't recall a pier at all. At my feet, a shallow sea laps gently at the harbour wall.

While we wander around town, which this evening trades quaintness and friendliness for liveliness, I ring my Dad to enquire after our old family holiday. We stayed in The Corrie Hotel, he says, his 91-year-old memory trumping mine. He bets it isn't still there.

I'd naively assumed that it would be, hadn't considered the Brits-abroad exodus once Europe's beaches began prostituting themselves for tuppence. English holidays still rather appeal to me, possibly because I went on so many as a child, was brainwashed towards them. Fish and chips on the beach, sand in children's ice creams, traders smiling and friendly because you're part of their dwindling custom-base (or possibly because they're nice people), monitoring the sun as clouds head its way, soaking up the home-front charm. Add the pubs, of course, when you're old enough.

We try another couple of boozers, argue over a game of pool while Spain thrash Russia in Euro 2008 on a big screen, and end up thankfully back at The Red Lion, where I continue my cider education.

Come midnight, I have attained perhaps degree status.

And come the morning, I've forgotten everything I learned.

Thus works the ebb and flow.

Having asked the breakfast chef for "Everything available to humanity" (he didn't get the *Withnail* reference… or at least he didn't laugh), I run over the day's plans, a bit like Captain Mainwaring. Three locations once again, the first 125 miles away, culminating at a railway bridge in Southall, Greater London, then home, ideally by 19.00 hours. Another packed schedule. And guess what?

Sinead has always wanted to see Corfe Castle, which we passed on the way here, and Durdle Door, a sort of door shape in a rock thing along the coast.

Jesus, I think – it's like going on manoeuvres with Godfrey! "Well come on then!"

Inevitably we visited Corfe Castle during my childhood Swanage holiday, so there is some nostalgia on offer. However, my memories of the site involve it being three very thick walls, unconnected to each other, buried in a hill, and not very much fun.

So I'm surprised to discover that there are many more than three walls. (It's still a ruin, mind, and expensive to get into.) And it's still not very much fun.

Sinead even has the gall to chase after the tour guide, to join his party up ahead, with Muggins in tow. Two Goths, some old people and us, hearing how people used to throw boiling oil over each other. I manage to sneak away when they become entranced by a slit in a wall, and mooch around what's left of the battlements, taking some photos of stone.

Eventually I give up trying to be interested and phone my Dad again, to tell him how we'd stopped by the Corrie Hotel site after breakfast, to find a bunch of old people's apartments. He'd been right.

I try to ring my Dad once a week since Mum went. Though the pair of them talked a right old load of bollocks, I feel deeply for him, suddenly finding himself alone after 70-odd years of companionship.

But he's coped well. Better than I possibly expected. (There was a time when I worried they might go in quick succession, like star-crossed lovers who cannot exist without the other. But he's not that daft. Romeo, noticeably, didn't make it to 91.)

It's funny how my Dad has changed. During our old phone conversations, he'd dutifully always ask me countless questions, trying to eke news from a son who still felt like a teenager.

"Yeah."

"Dunno."

"Yeah."

"Maybe."

Now he talks about himself a fair amount. How he's getting on; what's he's eating; who's been to visit. If I spent a night on the moon, he'd swiftly move on to how he'd just heated up some beans.

Please don't think I'm miffed by that. Quite the opposite: I love it. It's about time he looked out for himself; I can take care of me. (Just.)

Now he wants to survive. And he'd bloody well better do.

I love that old sod, too.

Anyway, I strike lucky this conversation. I've mentioned that we're soon off to Betchworth, see a couple of quarries. Betchworth's near Reigate, which triggers Dad's memory of a time with the legendary 'Nigells' Kemp. (Whom *DILY* readers may recall.)

Nigells and Norman (my dad) are in Reigate, at Nigells' girlfriend's house, and there's a diving board in the back garden, below which is the River Mole. (This must be around 1822, by the way.)

Dad's showing off on the diving board, proclaiming to his

friend that he is the "Olympic champion" – despite the fact that he cannot swim – when he slips and falls off, depositing a layer of chest-skin on the end of the board as he does so.

An eight-foot drop and he's in the river, where our self-proclaimed 'Olympic champion' is unable to muster even a rudimentary doggy paddle. Nigells has to dive in to save him from drowning, and as Dad gratefully stands on dry land, flies already feeding off his bloody chest, Nigells' girlfriend arrives back home to witness the scene. Boys. Tsk.

As I ring off, a steam train passes through trees before me. I feel happy.

Only Durdle Door to go. And I must say, as we head in the opposite direction from the M3 and Surrey, I'm feeling a mite impatient. But compromise is the lifeblood of a marriage, so Durdle Door it must be.

It's £2.50 to stay in the car park for up to two hours, which I pay more begrudgingly than a man forced to pay a ransom to get his severed foot back.

We walk down the stony path, gaze at Durdle Door (*pic 9.3*) from a clifftop, then walk back up the stony path (*pic 9.4*), me wheezing. It says everything that my favourite bit involved finding a stone with two very distinct layers, chalk and something greyer/harder – I was so excited, I took a photo (*pic 9.5*) – and thought about geological strata and the distant ages they represent.

Which doesn't feel quite as scintillating right now.

To Buckland Sand & Silica! (At last.)

We take the A31 back through the New Forest (flat, scrubby), having passed that same way only yesterday. M27, M3, and Sinead has a surprise for me: with her amazing map-reading skills she can guide us to Buckland via Alton, where I grew up. Now there's a diversion I can live with.

DILY readers will hopefully remember the place. Via the magic of cut-and-paste, here's a reminder:

'My parents had picked out a new-build, detached three-bedroom house on a sprawling housing estate that was only just getting going. The address: 6 Princess Drive, perched atop a hill.

Its front garden is a slew of mud awaiting turf and the few houses around are incomplete. It looks a little bit like Noah's Ark, stranded on top of Mount Ararat. The analogy ends there, since we would hardly fill the place with two of every kind of animal. My only Alton pet, after much pleading, was Pebbles the kitten, which Mum took back to the shop after it repeatedly urinated in her shoes.

I haven't kept pets since.

The property has a double garage and front and back gardens, red brick with a grooved, if hardly groovy, white fascia covering its top half.

The gardens slope. In fact, most of Alton slopes. Sit at the landing window after it has snowed and you can watch, chuckling inhumanely, as the drivers slide around while braking when they reach the top of the appropriately named Highridge.

Sit on a wooden sledge in the front garden, having overestimated the descent, and you will slide precisely nowhere, and feel like a right tool.'

Actually, that's more about cat pee and not-sledging, but you get the drift. It was 1973 when we moved there, and Princess Drive was my base until I went to university in London in the autumn of '85.

Many memories, not all of them riveting.

But I haven't been back for eons, so it'll be interesting to see how the old haunt has changed. Take this final small cut-and-paste from the *DILY* paperback, for instance:

'Once, I went to the weekend children's cartoon matinee at the Alton cinema – bet that's not still there, in a town that surely needs all the entertainment it can get...'

Let's see, shall we? It may be just one example, yet certainly my take, lavishly encouraged by the media, is that Britain is a pile of unlovely urban decay that would have gone to the dogs, had the dogs not been stuffed into microwaves by teenagers in hoods. The parks have been built on, or are no-go zones, and the cinemas – nasty, horrible multiplexes in American-style commercial behemoths, notwithstanding – have all shut down. Even the bingo hall that replaced it is now boarded up.

Let's see how realistic that image is. Does Alton still have its cinema?

I sincerely doubt it.

First stop, Princess Drive, where three – count 'em – cars are parked on the drive and the current owners have built an ugly red-brick-cube extension on the front, thus removing the actually-now-I-come-to-think-of-it gorgeous white fascia. Why they didn't just buy a bigger house, I don't know; I hit the accelerator while singing, "I'd rather not go / back to the old house" to myself and thinking that nostalgia isn't always all it's cracked up to be.

Then we drive around town. It may be the sunshine, but Alton looks far more enticing than I remember it. The park has had a facelift, indeed the whole place feels renovated and wanted.

Up the hill, scene of a Silver Jubilee torchlight parade, and my schoolmate Bill Radford's dad's model shop – a haven of Airfix delight – is gone... But there's a huge new model shop on the opposite side of the road! And a bit further on...

Alton Cinema is still open!

I shouldn't feel this joyful!

Put that in your poison pen and smoke it, Tabloid Journo!

Indeed, as we continue our journey, through Farnham – where my unrequited junior-school crush, Georgina Kemp, used to live, and where we'd drive to eat scampi in a basket – along the Hog's Back towards Guildford then find the A25 Reigate Road, we're passing through some of the most delightful countryside I've had the privilege to witness.

Thatched cottages – thatched *pubs* (a killer to motor past) – village greens, duck ponds, lush green vistas, seriously historic dwellings, acres of calm. Storybook England, thriving. And I think again of how, had I not had this seemingly daft idea to track down a bunch of old *Who* locations, I would never have seen these places.

This really is turning out to be a most excellent day.

(And just you wait till the end…)

We drive through Betchworth – where the quarry is next on my list – to Buckland, because it goes in that order in the Fact Pack and I'm not changing it now, no matter what order logic now dictates. From www.doctorwholocations.net I know there's a narrow tree-lined roadway that leads down to the stacked sand. Which we just need to find…

Inevitably I end up driving out of Buckland, having failed to spot it, and am forced into my 572nd about-turn of these trips.

However: there were a couple of signs involving Hanson, the building suppliers, and I bet…

We take a left at the second sign and I instantly recognise the road from a photograph on the location website. Oh yes, we're in.

Now, the website's photographer declined to go any further down this road than its beginning, since the site is private. Proving the point, we park up on a muddy driveway with barred gate, where we see a large notice that states, 'All visitors and drivers must report to the site office. Do not enter site unless authorised to do so.' (Pic 9.6)

Beneath that little deterrent are no fewer than nine different warning signs, including, 'Beware moving plant'. *Perhaps the Krynoid is still here*? (My little *Who* joke.)

Do I have the authority? Of course I do!

"Stand aside! I am writing *a book*!"

(Again I must stress: please do not follow my example. I'm on a roll and easily confused.)

I cross the road, mount a small bank and peer through young trees (*pic 9.7*). Ahead, past wasteland, is a mass of pale sand with woods behind, a bulldozer and assorted other heavy machinery. Shit – and there's someone on the wasteland. A bloke. And he's… Hang on. He's playing golf by himself.

Presumably a slow day for sand, he's putting a ball down and twacking it as far as he can into the natural detritus.

He hasn't spotted me yet, but he will do.

I'm getting nervous.

We shouldn't be here.

The asphalt road widens as we approach the quarry (*pic 9.8*). There's a dinky JCB bulldozer to one side, what appears to be a visitors' reception – an official-looking hut at least – a few outsized piles of sand and a large overhead conveyor belt up ahead. All it has on Binnegar Quarry – because it's a mere fraction of the size from this viewpoint – is the ominous thrum of working machinery.

Sinead and I dare to go still closer (*pic 9.9*). There are towers up ahead, for what purpose I have no idea, and I can see the golfing bloke clearly now, who must surely in turn have seen us, based on Ostrich Law. Why is he not running towards us, shouting, "Hoi! You!" as red-faced men did in the *Just William* series?

And so the tension builds.

It's a stand-off, if barely worthy of a Western.

I reach the reception and walk up the wooden steps, preparing to explain myself, to drop to my knees imploring, "We mean no harm!"

'No unauthorised personnel', it says on the door, meaning me. I knock but there's no one in, so I have a nose through the window. Just some paperwork and a hard hat.

The confrontation has to come.

I've just visited Hanson's website. Check this out:

'Hanson is one of the world's largest suppliers of heavy building materials to the construction industry. We produce aggregates (crushed rock, sand and gravel), ready-mixed and precast concrete, asphalt and cement-related materials and a range of building products including concrete pipes, concrete pavers, tiles and clay bricks.

We are part of the HeidelbergCement Group, which employs 70,000 people across five continents. HeidelbergCement is the global leader in aggregates and has leading positions in cement, concrete and heavy building products. [Blah blah, etc. Whatever.]

Hanson's UK business has an annual turnover in excess of £1.8 billion...'

Heavy building materials are worth *£1.8 billion* in the UK alone? My writing business is worth nearer £1.8 – clearly I am in the wrong game.

There's more worth boggling an eye over: Hanson's sand and gravel output last year weighed in at 32 million tonnes and the company operates 90 quarries such as this one.

They produce sand for building, though my 'expert' eye reckons Buckland's pallid crystals look too fine for that. The options, according to the website, are: 'silica sands for glass making, hydro sands for filtration, top dressing and horticulture, and other sands for golf courses, gardens and play pits.'

Speaking of which…

Golfing bloke's looking my way, calling to me.

"Hello?" he says, a question mark hovering at the end.

"Hello!" I call back. Act friendly. Brazen it out.

Shit. He's going to perform a citizen's arrest, I'll be banged up and our baby will never know its father.

"You having a look?" he asks.

Maybe I was being hasty? Perhaps "having a look" at a great deal of sand is perfectly normal?

"Yeah… Is that alright?"

Golfing bloke nods.

It's alright! We're in!

Except I have no intention of pushing my luck. No doubt he's OK with us hovering at the entrance to the site, thinks we're sand-fetish loonies (unless of course we aren't the first *Who*-location hunters here?). But I bet if we went in any further he'd be on us like 32 million tonnes of sand and gravel – which he has access to, don't forget.

The 'Safety on Site' section of Hanson's website includes this:

'Hard hats, high viz jackets and safety boots should be mandatory on site. Eye and ear protection, along with overalls and gloves may also be necessary.'

I'm wearing an REM t-shirt, my garish Top Shop jacket (flimsy) and some long shorts. Not a hope in hell.

Equally, Buckland Sand & Silica, which I suspect should really be named Hanson Sand or perhaps Buckland Quarry, isn't terribly impressive. After Binnegar, it's frankly a let-down.

Does it look anything like Antarctica, as portrayed in *The*

Seeds of Doom? No, it bloody does not. Nothing like. That Antarctica was covered in fake snow, had ice cliffs, but even if you stripped that fakery away, the terrain looks completely different. In *Doctor Who* they had boulders and rocks. This is flat, flat, flat, then mound, mound, mound.

I wonder whether this really was the site that doubled for Antarctica.

But – there is a but – it does look almost exactly like the 'nice deserted place' Harrison's Chase's dodgy chauffer refers to in episode three, where he plans to bump off Sarah and the Doc. There was a giant hopper in the middle of the quarry back then, which has unsurprisingly disappeared, though the industrial machinery now present offers a passable double.

Although it's consolation of sorts, I'm eager to move on and am actually texting distractedly when Sinead takes the money-shot (*pic 9.12*).

It's 4.15 pm already – curse you, Durdle Door – after a long drive, and Betchworth Quarry beckons.

TRIP 10

(Leg 5 of the Mega-Trip)

Friday, 27 June 2008

Genesis of the Daleks/ The Deadly Assassin

Betchworth Quarry, Surrey

Genesis of the Daleks and *The Deadly Assassin*! One of *the* iconic Dalek tales of the classic era, as well as my personal favourite *Who* story. Both filmed at Betchworth Quarry, which played Skaro (again) and the Matrix (I'll come to that shortly). That's quite some sexy baggage down there in Surrey, except...

Except I've done just enough research to know that they filled the whole darned thing in and landscaped it. All gone. A deceased quarry. These days just green field, as far as the eye can see.

Why do I still want to go there? In collectors' terms, I've done a few quarries already, but not one of them has been landfilled and levelled off, so there's that aspect. But also, these places I've visited – Dungeness in particular – can give off a sense of *Who* all around the site of a specific scene. Like the sugar that becomes scattered around a sloppily plated doughnut.

I'm not suggesting that a stranger to the show would suddenly stop in the environs of, say, Binnegar Quarry and think to themselves: hello, something odd here I can't quite place. But if you know the history, it's often there in the ether, triggered perhaps by familiar scenery nearby, or by some tangible other-worldliness.

There's one other factor. Skaro and the Matrix may have been obliterated from view – but they are still down there. Hundreds of feet down, conclusively interred, but still down there. Betchworth Quarry is effectively the grave-site of a double-slice of *Doctor Who*.

And I could stand there, clutching flowers.

Thanks to the magic of video-recording, I can still see what the site once looked like. The action in *Genesis of the Daleks* opens up on it: khaki-clad soldiers wearing red and yellow gas masks, shrouded in mist, battling through an angular landscape of boulders and barbed wire. And who's this appearing through the swirl? It's Tom Baker's Doctor, soon to be confronted by a fellow in a jester's outfit dyed black.

This is the time of the birth of the Daleks, created by Davros, making his debut in Baker's fourth story, in early 1975. The Time Lords, represented by the dark jester, want the Doctor to halt that process once and for all, so the terrible creatures would never have existed. Wipe out all that future destruction in one fell swoop.

Persuaded to accept the mission, the Doctor asks for the coordinates.

"You're here," says the jester, rather smugly. "This is Skaro."

Betchworth Quarry, by another name.

Much of the first episode finds the Doctor, plus companions Sarah and Harry, wandering about its floor, so there's plenty of reference material that I could have looked out for – now sadly redundant.

Boulders, large and small, in off-whites to light greys. Chalky looking, sheer cliff walls, atop which shapes in rags loom. Behind our heroes at one point can be seen a scree slope that looks almost glacial. The place looks vast.

Ask any child to imagine an alien planet's surface and such Betchworth scenery would not be far from their minds.

So it's no surprise that not only did *Who* film here twice, but its celebrated BBC counterpart, *Blake's 7* – sci-fi renegades! – pitched up there on several occasions. For that show it became the planets Suarian Major, Cephlon, Exbar, Sardos, Xenon and Betafarl. (As well as appearing in *The Professionals* and *Robin of Sherwood*.)

Quite the star, for a hole in the ground. Time for its close-up...

Having already driven past the road, we're at least sure where to go this time: back along the Reigate Road, right at the roundabout into Station Road, then drive until The Coombe on our left. I park at a bend just after the Old Well House, close in to a hedge so as to not annoy the (precious few) locals by blocking their roadway.

We've been very lucky with the weather today, although it's now verging on muggy. I've parked so close to the hedge that I have to exit via the passenger door, negotiating the gear stick on my way, and as I fall out of the car I check to see that no one has spotted such ungainliness. In places as remote as this, the local papers can be pretty short of news. I can imagine the headline: 'Geek Parks Poorly, Tumbles from Vehicle'.

This is the North Downs Way, which continues through trees towards Box Hill, a National Trust site. Before that landmark is our own quarry and I'm aware that it might be tricky to recognise, being now effectively a field.

Past a couple of homesteads, silent and expensive, the path

suddenly opens out and the eye is drawn instantly to a vast chimney-thing that dominates the landscape, square in cross-section, red-brick in construction. There's scaffolding only at the top – why and indeed how it got up there, I have no idea – and there are two short trees somehow growing from it (*pic 10.1*)! It must be more than 100 feet high and at least 20 feet wide. Why is it there? Quite mystifying.

Nearer the base is a dark archway, which from another angle reveals itself to be a tunnel straight through the structure, and clustered in the gravel road at its very bottom, as I gaze down from the top of a grassy bank, are vehicles, parked so that some block others in. Lorries, vans, possibly abandoned, certainly unused, since not a soul is around.

To my left is a large, rusted cylindrical tank, seemingly unconnected to anything.

Could this be part of the old quarry workings? If so, what is that very large chimney-thing – and where is the quarry itself? Not here, where mature trees grow and the contours are too steep.

However, there is a flicker of recognition where I stand, though not from *Genesis of the Daleks*.

Half of the second and the entire third episode of *The Deadly Assassin* take place inside the Matrix – the most surreal sequence of events in all of *Doctor Who*, and utterly wonderful.

The Master has returned, albeit as a mere shell of his former self, all slimy skull with wibble-eyeballs and hooded cape rescued from a spent bonfire, intent upon revenge. Tom Baker's Doctor is without companion for the only time in *Who* history, so the actor is required to talk to himself rather a lot at the beginning of the story.

Someone is about to assassinate the President of the Time Lords on Gallifrey – and they plan to frame the Doctor for it. (Even non-*Who* fans must have guessed who the 'someone' and 'they' are.)

As his Tardis lands on Gallifrey, the Chancellery Guard surround the Doctor's capsule.

"I must get past them and warn the President!" he says to himself.

It all leads to Baker being strapped into the Amplified Panatropic Computer Net – it's OK, I won't test you on this – and entering the Matrix, where he will battle the Master's pawn, Chancellor Goth, for control. The Matrix is a collection of Time Lord thoughts, a dreamscape if you will.

So many scenes set within that cerebral arena boggle the mind of the *Who* fan unused to such gleeful weirdness: the terrifying Samurai warrior who slices through Baker's scarf, to send the Time Lord tumbling down a cliff face; the clown's head reflected in the mirror the Doctor uncovers beneath the Matrix surface, who laughs a clown laugh that could give men with no hearts coronaries; the lunatic behind scarf and dark glasses who drives the train at Baker, his foot trapped in the tracks; the biplane straight out of Hitchcock that buzzes the Doctor and strafes his fleeing form with bullets...

Inspired surrealism, worthy of *The Prisoner*. Except this is *Doctor Who*, ostensibly for kids.

In reality it's all Betchworth Quarry, of course, readily recognisable as the Skaro of *Genesis of the Daleks*, aired 18 months previously. The same chalky slopes and rocky bits. However much of *The Deadly Assassin*'s action occurs in an area that has been allowed to overgrow, where shrubs and saplings subsist, before switching to a flooded area (in reality a few miles away), where the Doctor looks like drowning in the episode-three cliffhanger.

What I will always remember from that near-drowning scene were the flowers. Pretty, if I may use that word, meadowland flowers. The sort of flowers that are here, at my feet (*pic 10.2*).

It just *feels* as if I'm somewhere in *The Deadly Assassin*. Feels *right*.

It's that sugar from the sloppily plated doughnut I mentioned earlier: a sense of *Who* ghosts floating in the environs.

If only I could find the epicentre.

So we set off once again along the North Downs Way. To our right is a very steep bank: the type of thing that quarries lurk behind, as the Binnegar experience taught me. I eye up the chances of negotiating it and decide it's a no-go. Way too steep, and far too overgrown with stinging nettles and all manner of spiky vegetation. No, other people came here before us and found the quarry, *Blake's 7* fans as well as *Who* fans, and I certainly can't see the *B7* lot climbing that.

Betchworth Quarry must be somewhere else.

Soon we're into a lightly wooded area: gnarled short trees cling to a mudded slope to our left (*pic 10.3*), which must be a nightmare to climb when the rains come. Again, there's a sense of *Deadly Assassin* here: Baker was chased through trees like these. Down the bottom, amid the shadowy trunks and branches, there's a field just visible, its grass glowing under the sunshine. Might that be my quarry (*pic 10.4*)? I need to get closer.

I might be 42 but exploring woods is in my DNA. It's practically all I did as a child, in the days before computer games, satellite telly and communicating with your mates using colons, parentheses and wantonly appalling English.

Back in Alton, around the time of *The Deadly Assassin* in fact, I'd wander up the 'back alley' behind our house, maybe call on the Janson brothers or Simon Axtell along the way, hit Whitedown common, slide down the chalk on my bottom, use the Green Cross Code – not SPLINK (see *Dalek I Loved You*) – before crossing the Basingstoke Road to enter Anstey Woods. Boyhood heaven.

The fallen tree that we'd clamber over and make camps beneath; the pit further in, which we ran down into, trying not to fall over (brilliant!); the stile that segregated the muddy section of Anstey Woods from the grassy section; collecting butterflies in the net my parents made between them; taking in nature's sounds. Freedom and adventure.

That's what it feels like now. Sinead has scooted ahead so it's just me, and I have a slope to get down. The boy in me can't wait; the adult is a bit worried about spraining his ankle.

What's odd is that someone has built a crude railing down one route, fashioned from trees, for people to hold on to. There are even steps dug into the soil, shored up with branches to foil erosion. It's still a tricky descent and I find myself clinging to convenient vegetation and easing myself down in places, but the route peters out at the bottom of the slope and I'm standing among a load of old leaves with nowhere to go; the field before me is fenced off with barbed wire.

If this is a dead end, why on earth did someone go to all the trouble of building railings and steps down to it? It's deeply odd.

There's a deflated black cycle-tyre inner-tube hanging from a particularly gnarled tree in front of me. *Why?*

The barbed-wire fence is hardly in good repair but still tricky to clamber over, so I content myself with assessing the quarry-worthiness by peering. A rolling expanse of lush green dips down towards clumped trees ahead and disappears off to the right, further than the eye can see.

It's a very big field. Bigger than I would have imagined a quarry to be. Yet, again, I think of Binnegar and the vastness of that bugger. Yes, I'm *fairly* certain this could be it. Skaro and the Matrix, down there? It's all I've got at the moment.

I need Sinead and her nifty camerawork again, but first I have to get back up the slope. The adult suggests the path, the boy urges me straight upwards and hang the conveniences.

The boy wins.

Tree roots popping out of the ground act as ropes to cling to, and I haul my way back up feeling terribly nostalgic. I used to do this sort of thing as a matter of course. These days I feel I've achieved something if I haul my sorry ass to the local shop for a newspaper, rather than reading it on the internet.

I catch up with the wife around a bend, having passed a cyclist and a squirrel. The left-hand edge of the path here is fenced off with wire-mesh panels, as there's a drop down that side into a bowl of trees spattered with the sort of pretty flowers witnessed earlier (*pic 10.5*). On the other side, the ground just keeps on rising. Surely there's no way these contours signal a quarry?

But: look beyond the trees and there's that field I recently inspected (*pic 10.6*). Surely I've walked far enough along the North Downs Way to spot Betchworth Quarry, and that's the only terrain that could feasibly be my goal. That *has* to be it. So why am I not fully convinced?

Knowing that Sinead is four months pregnant and will need to get down that same awkward slope I just stuttered down to take photographs, guilt compels me to find her a long stick. If it's not the most efficient stabiliser, it at least makes her look a bit like Gandalf.

In the end, she reaches the bottom more gracefully than I managed (*pic 10.7*) and I stagger through the barbed wire out into the giant field. As is becoming traditional, I throw my arms out... half-heartedly (pic *10.8*).

Sense of *Who*? Zero.

Sense of standing in any old field? Ten.

The ground slopes downwards towards a copse and meanders off to my right forever. There are rolling contours on the surface (*pic 10.9*), not what you'd expect if someone were to dump a load of soil on top of rubble and rubbish. Surely they'd just flatten it off?

Instinct tells me this isn't Betchworth Quarry, but I'm all out of ideas. Anyway, we're hungry and the sky is clouding over, a light breeze now cutting through the mugginess.

As we head out of the woods, back towards The Coombe, I spot a sign I had missed earlier (*pic 10.10*): a red line through a pedestrian, plus the warning, 'Access forbidden to all unauthorised persons'. But access to what? That patch of crap vegetation beside it? I just don't get it.

Sinead, meanwhile, has launched into a *Famous Five* fantasy, involving robbers, those old vehicles parked down by the chimney-thing and buried loot, and has scrawled 'TREASURE' with an arrow pointing back the way we came in chalk on the back of an adjacent sign (*pic 10.11*). If you see it, please don't be taken in.

I'm not happy; I don't feel I've solved the Mystery of the Somehow Elusive Quarry. All I can say is that we have done our best... Hang on, how did it go? 'As long as we have done our best / Then no one can do more / And life and love and happiness / Are well worth fighting for.'

The theme tune to *The Flashing Blade*, a show I adored as a child! Hopefully it won't come down to fisticuffs for the life, love and happiness bit.

Interlude: I couldn't help it. I've just listened to *the Flashing Blade* theme tune via www.thechestnut.com and have entered a dreamlike state of pure wistfulness.

Interlude 2: Now I've become completely sidetracked in that same site, which archives the 'Golden Age' of children's television. *The Changes*, anyone? *Murun Buchstansangur*? *Marine Boy*? *Michael Bentine's Potty Time*? *White Horses*? *The Singing Ringing Tree*? (But no *Gold on Crow Mountain*, sadly.) I've just listened to the doleful theme tune to *Belle and*

Sebastien for the first time in 30-odd years and it sent shivers up and down my spine.

Oh my word, I've just done the same for *The Adventures of Robinson Crusoe* – and it brought tears to my eyes. What is it about nostalgia, coaxing bittersweet sensations of misted pasts from the very depths of our souls? Is that why we watch *Doctor Who*, and why I'm batting about the country on this bonkers quest? I imagine that it is.

So: what is the answer to The Mystery of the Somehow Elusive Quarry? Was I standing in the correct spot?

I've been trawling a succession of webpages and have cracked it, finally, at the website of the Surrey Wildlife Trust.

And the answer is: No.

Ah.

The Surrey Wildlife Trust provide a downloadable *Visitor Guide and Self-guided Trail* to the Brockham Lime Works, which are next door to Betchworth Quarry. It has a map and key.

What the wife and I actually walked along was believed to be Pilgrims' Way, which pilgrims used to visit Saint Thomas Becket's shrine at Canterbury Cathedral. Such unexpected history feels rather cool: that we might have followed in the footsteps of pious folk in sandals some 600 years previously. (Ignoring any picky bugger who suggests the pilgrims would more likely have taken the old main road to the south.)

At the point where we stopped and turned back (*pic 10.5*), we were in danger of stumbling upon Brockham's Lime Works.

The men used to dig out chalk by hand, to be burnt in kilns at intense temperatures to produce lime, which was used by the construction industry (for mortar) and in agriculture (as fertiliser). A small network of narrow-gauge railways – one section appeared in *The Deadly Assassin* – was once used to transport materials around the sites.

Such is the toil that occurred here from the first half of the 19th century, until 1936 in the case of the Lime Works, and until the early 1970s in Betchworth Quarry's. So I bet that chimney-thing (*pic 10.1*) is a surviving lime kiln. Makes sense.

The SWT's *Visitor Guide* also includes this: 'Ahead is Betchworth Quarry, once part of the thriving chalk industry here and until recently a landfill site. Some fine old lime kilns can be seen from the path but access to them is prohibited and dangerous. Betchworth Quarry is privately owned, although the surrounding area is managed as a nature reserve and it is possible to cross the site by following the North Downs Way.'

So how the hell did I miss it?

A glance at the Google satellite map that I link to on my site may solve this quandary. Being out of date, it actually shows the quarry prior to landfill – and it seems that I missed a glaring right turn, at the very beginning of the walk. Easily done. Honestly.

What I was standing upon was neither Skaro nor the Matrix, but a Big Field. Which at least justifies my instinct that my *Who* sense was registering zero. Still it's rather embarrassing.

Can't win 'em all.

TRIP 11

(Leg 6 of the Mega-Trip)

Friday, 27 June 2008

Day of the Daleks

Bulls Bridge, Southall, Greater London

But, boy, did I win this one.

It's late afternoon by the time we've revived our spirits and tummies with an excellent meal plus elderflower squash in The Jolly Farmers (*pic 10.12*) in Buckland. (Apologies for that sentence sounding like something out of Enid Blyton; clearly Sinead's *Famous Five* fantasies were contagious.)

This is our second day, it's practically chilly now, we have two 'A' roads, a brace of motorways and a final few squiggles to navigate, before the final destination of the first half of this Mega-Trip. Are we knackered? Yes. Was Bulls Bridge at the very top of my list of desired locations? Yes also.

I do feel obliged to suggest to Sinead that we call it quits, she being with-child, and this adventure being more my pet project than hers, but the lady-with-child's not for turning, she assures me.

We have a convert!

From the A24 we hit the M25, and thank higher beings we're going clockwise – the opposite lanes are chocker; you'd be lucky to pass a wafer-thin mint between the bumpers. Radio traffic reports suggest that the jam in that direction covers half of the entire motorway.

Imagine doing that journey daily, wasting all those hours, sitting in a car watching a family of beetles undertake you on the hard shoulder, getting home for a dinner that resembles interesting archaeological finds at ten, watching *My Family* re-runs on UK Gold for an hour, retiring to bed with all the sexual urges of a flat-packed wardrobe, then getting up at six to repeat the entire fiasco. The mind numbs.

Thus feeling smug, we complete the M25 leg at a reasonable speed, join the M4 and turn off onto the A312. It's almost 7pm and headlights are required.

The Fact Pack suggests we park in the Tesco car park, which we find readily enough, it being a commercial behemoth amid lots of roads. I park, climb over a wall, cross the crossing and there it is: Bulls Bridge (*pic 11.1*), a pleasing pair of curves in white-painted brick, one for pedestrians to walk over, the other for barges to pass beneath. Clearly designed by romantics rather than computers. That it's Grade II listed is no surprise.

After the palaver of Betchworth, this all seems too easy.

However, it's not Bulls Bridge itself that I'm after. It's the railway bridge further up through its arch, which is just about visible if I squint. It's hardly within touching distance – it's not even within pole-vaulting distance – but it's there.

Erm, on the other side of the canal.

Anyone for a swim?

Bulls Bridge was built in 1801. The canal branch our railway bridge spans was opened four years later, linking to the Paddington basin. Known as the Paddington Arm, it's 13 miles long, has no locks and joins the Regents Canal at Little Venice. Canal-workers used horse-drawn barges to transport heavy traffic – building materials, essentially – up it to north-west London.

Back then, when the Industrial Revolution was at its peak, they could cover the 20 miles from Uxbridge to Paddington in around six hours, which was considered speedy. Compare that with the M25 of today, and it still is.

Of course, the trains took over in the mid-19th century and Britain's canal network began to fall into disrepair. Those that still survive – a few thousand miles-worth, mind – are now used purely for leisure. You could boat all the way from London to Birmingham on the Grand Union Canal, assuming you weren't in a hurry.

I have a couple of London friends who live in narrowboats. It's an existence a million miles from the average flat-in-town. Leisurely doesn't cover it. Their top speed is 2mph, with a prevailing wind and parping for Britain. I've joined them on cruises, puttering up the still waters, sipping G&T, taking it easy. The only effort required is to crank open the occasional lock gate, then wait patiently as the boat rises or falls while the diesel fumes take minutes off one's life. Sitting there, not quite able to understand how the system works, but marvelling at the engineering ingenuity.

The boat people are a community unto themselves, who have opted out of the rat race and who understand engines. Forgive me for sounding sexist, but even the women have toolkits. Everyone talks to everyone else and they party at weekends in boathouses up and down the canals. The booze is cheap and the chatter easy. It feels idyllic, until you remember they have to throw their own poo away.

You can catch a sense of the solitude down here at Bulls Bridge. Southall has a population of 90,000, majoring on South

Asians – more than half that number are Indian alone – yet here, even beside a 24-hour Tesco, it's damned quiet. Step beside the water and all around is blotted out. Even the continual traffic thrum disappears, somehow muffled by the peacefulness.

A few narrowboats are moored along our side of the bank, dark-hulled, colourfully-topped, female-named, some with potted flowers decorating their roofs, curtains drawn. Which reminds me that time is getting on, and we have a canal to cross.

Looking up and down, I can't see any footbridges. To my left, a knot of tarmac fit only for cars; to my right, view blocked by a boathouse. I try left and discover, well, it's hard to say, but there's a sign: 'This area has been refurbished by TESCO STORES LTD as a non-working example of a canalside dry dock'. So it's a dry dock! And in case anyone isn't sure what 'non-working' means, the notice concludes: 'This is not operational'. No shit, Sherlock!

But it's full of crap! Not actual crap but proverbial crap. Boxes, cartons, cans, bags, packaging, dirty, overgrowing and clogged with pondweed (*pic 11.2*). Unloved and ugly.

If you're going to refurbish something then gloat about it, at least maintain the poor thing. Perhaps Tesco spent all their money on Jane Horrocks?

Further along the towpath the route is blocked by a wire-mesh fence with a hole in it and, beyond that, in a boat, there's a bloke reading a paper.

"Ask him!" hisses Sinead.

"You ask him!" I hiss back.

"Come on, you're good at talking to strangers now," she says.

No I'm not, I think, Chislehurst and Athelhampton feeling a long time ago.

We bicker for a while until Sinead loses her patience.

"Excuse me," she calls out. "Is there anywhere we can cross the canal?"

"Arrr," says the watery bloke.

Actually, he didn't say "Arrr". He told us to go back the other way, where he said we could find a footbridge.

So we try that, end up walking through an industrial estate, wander around some floating shacks and after many fruitless minutes reach an impasse. Bastard must have lied.

Now I'm stuffed.

That 20 feet of water between us and the far bank might as well be 2,000.

It is at this point that we make a near-fatal error.

We buy a map, and Sinead reads it while I drive.

It's Sinead's excellent Plan B: if we can't cross the canal by foot, we can surely do so by car. It's just that our *Mini A-Z* doesn't cover Greater London. So we buy a lovely red *London Maxi Scale Street Atlas* in the Tesco petrol station, which Sinead instantly fawns over, get back in the car and head for Bulls Bridge Road, which sense should have dictated we head for in the first place. Bless my little Fact Pack.

Then we get lost. Tempers fray. Well, not so much fray as burn in hellfire. Madness gets the better of me and I suggest to my wife that her map-reading prowess is matched only by that of her driving. (Yeah, I know.) Signalling her disagreement, she attempts to exit the car while it's moving.

Though we call each other rude names and dismiss each other's skill sets, the situation fails to improve.

As I come to a halt in traffic, Sinead surges out of the car dispensing red mist, slams the door and disappears into Southwell's belly. I sit in the driving seat wondering how Plan B could have gone so horribly wrong.

I'm not sure how she intends to get home, because her bag and purse (or wallet, as she prefers) are in the car. I ring her.

Her phone, in the passenger footwell, rings back at me. Hmm.

As the unnecessary ire subsides, it's replaced by mere annoyance mixed with guilt. You may recognise that combination, dear reader. Gradually, as I sit there wondering what to do next, the annoyance disappears, leaving just the guilt.

In a flash of inspiration, Plan B becomes a Rescue Mission. I shall rescue the wife from Southwell!

Except that when I spot her on the other side of the road, walking quickly, clearly upset (I know, don't rub it in), and suggest she gets back in the car and – spot the error – stops being so childish, she keeps on walking.

That goes on for a while. Sinead is eventually cajoled to return to the Micra's bosom, however remains put out. So when I park in Bulls Bridge Road, she demands the car keys. She wants to go home, leaving me to my own devices. She has had enough of the Mega-Trip.

Untaken with this new version of Plan B, I exit the car and head towards the canal with Sinead in hot pursuit. While punters smoking outside the Grand Junction Arms look on, we wrestle each other for the keys, shouting.

I bet Bill Bryson never had to contend with this sort of thing.

Let's step back from this for a second.

Sinead has been a goddess, cooped up in a car while we drive around south-east England, getting out only to look at lots of sand or a field that isn't a quarry. She has the supportive gene, always there when I need her. Where am I? Let's not go into that. Suffice to say that I mean no harm.

Sadly it's that same old heat-of-the-moment thing.

One thing's for certain: it's up to me to sort this out.

So I apologise, put an arm around my wife and with the other point out some wildlife. Yes, that should do the trick.

"Look!" I say, "Some ducklings with their mother!

159

Aw!" (*Pic 11.3*)

I feel a bit like Alan Partridge.

Further up there's a coot – or possibly a moorhen, or possibly something else entirely – on its nest, a stack of grasses poking from the water. On our side, a lone coot/moorhen/something-else baby, all fluffy-feathered, paddles furiously away from the humans (*pic 11.4*).

Such wildlife, amid such peaceful scenery, in the middle of a people-packed, car-clogged conurbation. It's amazing, really. These pockets of tranquillity exist in the unlikeliest of places. You just have to stumble across them.

And, of course, some council idiot with a signage fixation has to ruin the effect by stamping nanny-state bureaucracy in your path. On this private stretch of the Bulls Bridge Road there is a sign, which I felt compelled to photograph (*pic 11.5*). Red triangle; inside, a depiction of a car falling into water. Now tell me: which is the driver liable to spot first, the sign or the canal? Or perhaps everyone is pig-stupid?

Sigh.

Now, I confess: I omitted to take any notes from Bulls Bridge onwards. I was just too wrapped up in the project, too lost to the adrenalin.

I knew that many *Doctor Who* fans had previously visited the site and had photographed the tunnel the Daleks and Ogrons had emerged from, back in '72, from the opposite bank of the canal. Such images are readily found on the internet.

The far bank, where the tunnel is, is inaccessible for some reason. I couldn't remember why. But I knew it would be a coup if I could stand in front of that tunnel, the first person to do so in a significant number of years. A *Who Goes There* exclusive!

I tell you, I was buzzing.

So: what follows is all from memory.

All the while I'm walking along the east bank, where the towpath is, I'm sizing up the potential access along the west bank, where the tunnel is. At Bulls Bridge there's an old house, boarded up, its garden full of Triffids. Then, a narrow pathway in front of another abandoned property and a section where the hedging has gone wild, perhaps blocking the route.

In front of that is a blue and yellow dredger, its cabin high up, a curious outsized-lawnmower construction attached to the front (*pic 11.6*). If they made a model of it, a small boy would be stupidly excited to receive one at Christmas – it's that kind of a machine.

Unfortunately it's listing badly, all messed up, and I notice a sign on its side, proudly stating that pupils from a local school helped to come up with its name. TARANCHEWER. No idea what they meant, but a great name. The Taranchewer has since become the Taranchewed and I wonder with sadness whether the children have seen it recently.

Further along, narrowboats are moored: blue, blue, red, green (*pic 11.7*), like painted crocodiles, waiting. A man and a woman appear on the opposite bank, walk through a gate and head for their boat. If they can do it, so can I! And their boat is just 100 yards from the railway bridge. My hopes are high.

Should I carry along this towpath, wasting time, when I could be on the goal side of the canal? I think: better not be hasty, ought to see what's up ahead.

The sun is low on the horizon now, the sky a carpet of undulating cloud in colours the mildly depressed might relish. The railway bridge is getting nearer, a dark length spanning the water.

Still eyeing the opposite bank, I register the terrain: path, path, path, path... And beside the bridge, on the Dalek-tunnel side, a tangle of nasty-looking vegetation, spilling towards the water. An unkempt beard of thorns. It looks bad, but perhaps not mission-concluding.

And I'm there. Where that tangled vegetation is, guerrillas on the Doctor's side, wearing khaki and toting futuristic guns, once spilled down the bank, hunting Daleks.

And the tunnel itself...

Momentarily, I'm stunned. I've seen *Day of the Daleks* so many times that I don't even need to watch it again to know what to look out for – guerrilla forces from the future travel through time (via Bulls Bridge railway bridge) to assassinate idiot whose actions led to the Dalek takeover of Earth – and I was convinced that the tunnel entrance was set into the wall of the bridge itself; in other words, that the tunnel was at right angles to the towpath. It's not.

I briefly wonder whether I've got the right tunnel, but no, this is it. I can picture the alien foe emerging from it in line: Dalek, Dalek, Ogron, Ogron, Dalek. Off to the big house to fight with UNIT soldiers.

So the tunnel actually *follows* the towpath. Makes far more sense. It might seem like nothing, but to me it's a revelation. For all those years, I'd seen it wrong. An optical illusion. Weird.

And after all those same years, I'm here. Bulls Bridge railway bridge. That dark opening and the memories of Daleks. The same scene, now distorted by decay.

Sinead takes a picture on her decent camera (*pic 11.8*) and I take one on my phone (*pic 11.9*). Impressions? Nature – and man – have been unkind. The brick is stained and blackened, the path before it shabby and tat-speckled. Someone has graffitied... is that '220' or a duck then '20' in bold black numerals outlined in white? (Which suggests that I wouldn't be the first person to stand beside that tunnel in a significant number of years, though I didn't suss that at the time.)

But I'm excited. I reckon it might just be feasible to do the same walk on the opposite side of the canal. To stand where the

Daleks trundled. I'm determined to give it a shot.

I ask Sinead to wait here with the camera and, relations still being understandably cool, start running back up the towpath so as not to make that wait too long.

I cross Bulls Bridge and immediately encounter my first obstacle. I'd expected steps down to a towpath. Instead, it's fenced off.

Balls to that!

I pull the fence to one side and squeeze through, then drop down into the garden of the boarded-up house (Lock House/Cottage, I later spotted). It's like a greenhouse left unattended down there. Access to the front garden is blocked by a sheet of corrugated iron, so I wander around the back, but that's conclusively boarded off. Try the front again. Oh, just go for it. Pull on one side of the corrugated iron (which is already bent outwards, so I'm not the first), breathe in again.

Yes! I'm in the front garden. Through the gate and onto a proper path, if long disused. Moving quickly. Past the dredger, plunge through the overhanging bush, past another garden, now I'm at the bit where that couple appeared. Follow in their footsteps.

A gate. Ah. 'Private'.

Ordinarily, I'm Britain's most law-abiding citizen. Petrified of authority, opposed to revolution. Not tonight, baby! Not now!

Through the gate, which creaks. But I'm thinking: there are half a dozen boats here; how would one boat person know I'm not planning to visit another boat person? Mind you, they could easily challenge me...

It's a risk I'll take.

The pathway here is at least well-kept, so easily navigated. I'm walking fast, light on my feet trying not to disturb, and as I pass each narrowboat in turn I avoid looking in through windows in case someone looks back. As I continue, I'm rehearsing a pitiful "I'm writing this book, see…" speech in my head. I pray I don't have to use it.

Hoses across the path. I tiptoe through them. But it's quiet; I can't hear anyone moving about.

The last boat before the tunnel is twice the size of the others and the path narrows, so I have to put a palm on its prow to balance as I step past. Still no "Er, excuse me…?"

I'm now maybe 15 yards from the tunnel and… Fuck.

Fuck, fuck, fuck.

Someone has erected a ten-foot-high wire-mesh fence slap-bang in front of me, which extends a foot or so beyond the edge of the path, out into the water, just in case anyone planned shimmying around it. And it's lined with barbed wire.

Game Over.

I look across the canal towards Sinead, despairingly. She's still gamely waiting there, despite our previous to-do. God love her.

I call quietly towards her, through clenched teeth, "I can't get past," hoping she might have a suggestion but knowing that's hardly practical.

I stand there, adrenalin depleting, gutted.

I look through the fence. All that tangled vegetation I'd spotted before is ahead: brambles and stinging nettles I can see clearly now, armed and ready. A further nightmare.

I study the extent of the fence. I could try to swing around it, but I'd be hanging out over the canal and what if I fell in the water? Drowning might be preferable to the embarrassment.

Then something surges inside of me and I think: sod it, I've come this far!

Before I know it, I'm clinging to the wire mesh with my left hand and leaning backwards at 30 degrees, my entire body over the still, dull water. The barbed wire on the outside of the fence is all over the place, so I have to edge my right hand carefully into a safe spot on the mesh. Grab hold. This is it. Please-please-please. Let go with left hand... and swing...

Fence, don't you dare give way! Shuffle, shuffle.

And I'm only bloody over! (And not looking forward to repeating that in reverse.)

Now the nettles and brambles. I'm wearing long shorts, calves and ankles exposed – this is going to be No Fun.

But really, I'm almost there.

As I tread carefully on each evil bramble branch, pushing it down to the ground so it doesn't rip across my flesh, massed stinging nettles feed on my exposed legs. Each ginger step is the same; I just have to blot out the pain. (Is it really worth it? Obviously not, though I wasn't to be told at the time.)

Then I'm through! I'm at the bloody tunnel! First person here, perhaps since Pertwee and co, 36 years ago! (Not counting the graffiti youths.) YES!

I know it's pathetic. What have I achieved? I'm standing next to an old tunnel beneath a railway, somewhere on a canal in Southall. And I'm elated.

It's not the building; it's the significance. Plus all I went through to get here. I have my exclusive. I made it, by stealth, guile and determination (and relentless stupidity).

And the *Who* ghosts scatter, wondering who's disturbed them after all that time alone.

Before I go any further, I have to stress: this one really was daft; I just got carried away. Definitely, please, without a shadow of a doubt, do not try to repeat my madness. It was foolhardy, dangerous and mildly illegal. And the view from the far bank's more than adequate.

Please let my description of the site suffice:

Well, it's very dark inside the tunnel because, as Sinead

could have told me, having taken a photograph from beneath the railway bridge (*pic 11.10*) of its far end – all of ten yards from its front end – it's been bricked off. So there's no way you could approach this from the other direction.

Why anyone even bothered building it, I have no idea. What possible purpose could a ten-yard long brick tunnel beneath a bridge on a towpath serve? Other than being ideal as a portal for Daleks in *Doctor Who*?

I really couldn't begin to guess.

The light's seriously fading now – today has taken far longer than expected. Sinead snaps me from the other side (*pic 11.11, enhanced from gloom using Photoshop*) as I take stock. In reality, it's a grotty fraction of England. A large, unruly bush is growing in the entrance to the tunnel (*pics 11.12 and 11.13, both enhanced*). The walls are covered in a whitish growth and more graffiti. 'BLAPZ'? 'ONA'? Why would you even bother?

A train roars by overhead, thunder in my ears, oppressive. I don't plan to hang around.

My abiding memory of the tunnel interior? Stalactites. The ground inside was just a stony mess, but there were short stalactites all over the roof. Silvery and smooth, hanging down from the brick in a random pattern. Not formed by any fossilisation, of course, but by glop and slime seeping through over the years, then solidifying.

No self-respecting Dalek would set castor in the place these days. Yet they did once, back in 1972. Actors in Dalek casings and others dressed as Ogrons hung about in there, waiting for a director to call, "Action!" Perhaps discussing last night's pub or the price of peas. A little bit of history.

Time for one last picture (*pic 11.14, also enhanced*) from the far bank – me, fingers as a gun, pretending to be an Ogron – and it's time to go.

Job well and truly (over)done. Actually, I seem to have cut my arm on some barbed wire (*pic 11.15*).

I catch up with Sinead heading back along Bulls Bridge Road and throw an arm around her. What a fucking star. If she'd driven home and left me dangling over a canal, I could hardly have blamed her. But she didn't.

Though I'm still buzzing on adrenalin, I get the feeling she doesn't quite comprehend my excitement. Sees it more as I outlined above: '...standing next to an old tunnel beneath a railway, somewhere on a canal in Southall'.

Still she stayed.

Back at the car, we were tempted by a swift jar in the Grand Junction Arms, but it looked solidly like a 'locals pub', and when Sinead nipped in for a wee she heard people arguing – and we'd had quite enough of that for one day.

We didn't get home until gone ten, ordered a delivery curry with relief, ate it while slumped before the telly, and hit the sack around midnight.

By 2am my stinging calves, which felt like they were under attack by swarming fire-ants, were still keeping me awake.

TRIP 12

(Leg 7 of the Mega-Trip)

Saturday, 28 June 2008

The Android Invasion

Worsham Quarry & Tubney Wood, Oxfordshire

While I'm on the go, occupying my mind, it's fine. It's only when I stop that I think of Mum.

In honesty I've been lucky, not having to cope with the death of one so close until the age of 42 and with parents teetering either side of 90. On the other hand, I've had to live with the fear of expecting the worst. As it turns out, I'd have happily continued with that.

But there's a strange twist in the tale, which is providing some comfort.

On 31 March, at around 10pm, Sinead came into the lounge while I was watching telly, and announced that she was pregnant. The following day, a little before noon, my brother Gordon phoned and said that Mum had passed away.

That was a Tuesday morning. I'd expected to visit Mum at the weekend, had planned some things to say, stave off that ridiculous silence. But it wasn't going to happen. I'd already had my last chance and I hadn't even known it.

I called Sinead at work, blurted it out and, bless her, she said she'd come home straight away. I really needed her company that day. Her cycle ride should have taken half an hour, but it felt quicker than that, surprised me. I remember the relief when I heard the key in the door. I hadn't moved since receiving Gordon's call.

I needed to do something, couldn't just sit there inactive. So we decided to drive to Kent: I imagined my Dad could do with some support. During the journey, Sinead and I discussed whether our tiny new life would turn out to be a girl. What a strange and rather beautiful coincidence that would be. That day, I was pretty convinced.

Dad was in the lounge with Gordon. Mum's armchair was empty. The armchair where Mum always sat. Read her books or fell asleep with her chin on her chest. My wonderful Mum. Never there again. I knew it was true though it felt neither real nor right.

Sinead sat next to my brother on the sofa. Only one chair left: hers. Should I? I just did. Couldn't think it through.

Beside her chair was the bag she'd taken into hospital, now filled with the neatly folded bedclothes she'd been wearing. No longer inhabited. The nightgown she'd been wearing. My Mum. No longer wearing it.

Dad and Gordon talked of her last moments, how she'd given them both such a smile, the moment before she went. And I thought: she gave me a smile too! An amazing, gorgeous smile, and she glowed.

They talked about their smile and I didn't want to interrupt. We all wanted to lay a claim to her, all wanted our own personal moment. Something to treasure just for ourselves.

I really wanted to tell them about my smile. But Dad, his hurt must have been the greatest, poor soul, and Gordon, well, he's my older brother for a start. Everyone in my family is significantly older than me, so I always feel like the child, even now.

So I really wanted to tell them, but I kept it to myself. And I comforted myself that I knew.

All those thoughts and memories were there, just behind the eyes, during these trips that I've made for this book. I was lucky to have landed the project when I did. It got me out of the house, focusing on other things, and it drew family around me.

So this was the second half of the Mega-Trip, and the time of Fact Pack 2. Another wad of paltry notes and insufficient directions, which would take us into places so very English, so very traditional, that time itself seemed to have stood still. No wonder the Doctor had been drawn to them.

We were going to have fun, the boy, the wife and I. But first, the traffic. I imagine it was my M25 smugness coming back to bite me.

Heading out on the A40 towards Oxfordshire, nothing was moving. In two hours, we travelled the sort of distance a pea might travel through tar, if swatted by a squirrel on crutches.

I'm worried about Dylan in the back seat. Aged merely 13, near the bottom of the familial food chain, he doesn't really have any choice but to join my roadshow of geekdom. Still, I desperately hope he enjoys the process, witnesses sights new to him, catches a flavour of the passion, hopefully gleans something for himself from the weekend. At the very least, that he isn't bored.

I remember as a small boy, being dragged by my mother to meet her lady-friends, and when I think of those occasions now all I hear is a drone of nattering voices, like the teacher's in *Peanuts*. "Wha-waow-wha-wha-wha, wha-wha-waow-wha-wha-waow…" While I was obliged to find a pencil fascinating, or somesuch.

Dylan plays his cards fairly close to his chest, so I sometimes need to look for signs of covert enjoyment, but he's a lovely, bright child with a heart as wide as Africa. So I don't want to let him down.

Neither do I plan to let him out of the car.

And we are stuffed. Driving nowhere, driven crazy. It's so bad, I'm genuinely relieved when Sinead pulls out the new *London Maxi Scale Street Atlas* and starts plotting alternative routes off the A40.

Not one of them works. Every new road we turn down has a multi-coloured steel snake of tedium up ahead, unmoving and simmering. It's also hot, which would be fine if we were on a beach.

Come 2pm, we haven't done much more than 2mph. I'm beginning to wonder whether someone bought just one car too many, the final vehicle to join the queues, producing a perfect and inescapable gridlock. And there we die, in our cars, stationary with the engine running.

It's so exceedingly frustrating, I suggest we give up and go home. I'm half-serious. As the idea is batted around with reluctance, a miracle happens. The speedometer registers 5mph, then 10, then 15… Watch Out! Suddenly we're back on the A40 and the traffic's running smoothly. We're free!

Thank fuck for that.

Interlude. I've corresponded with some lovely, kind people, who have emailed me having enjoyed one or other of my books. One, Ifan, a Brit now living Down Under in Tasmania, just sent me a photograph of his four-year-old daughter, Morgaine, cuddling a Dalek. And informs me that she's convinced they're saying, 'Excuse-me-mate! Excuse-me-mate!'

What does Fact Pack 2 – The Return to Fact Pack – have in store? Only the second- and third-placed locations on my wish-list, that's what. East Hagbourne in Oxfordshire today, Aldbourne in Wiltshire tomorrow. A pair of English villages, each one of which gave off a perceptible aura during their moments in the *Who* limelight. Given that English villages don't tend to change very much, I'm highly hopeful of basking in some of that aura.

First up, East Hagbourne, which provided the backdrop for Tom Baker's *The Android Invasion*, of 1975. Though Jon Pertwee's *The Daemons*, in which Aldbourne appeared, is by far the more seminal tale, it's Hagbourne I have always longed to visit the most.

I can't really explain why. *The Android Invasion* won't figure too highly among many fans' favourites, yet it captivated me. Partly the aliens, partly the location.

Once again, I watched this with Sinead and Dylan...

"Just let me get my magazines ready," quips the wife, as the tape kicks in.

In a galaxy far, far away, aliens have replicated the entire village of Devesham, right down to the last thatched roof, where they can practise for Earth takeover (starting with Devesham, for some reason). At a wood on its outskirts, the Doctor and Sarah arrive in the Tardis. As they explore, they're watched by an oddly twitchy soldier in combats, hiding among the trees.

"I bet after doing *Doctor Who*, Tom Baker got no girlfriends," says Dylan, apropos of nothing. (How wrong can one person be?)

Next thing, our heroes are being chased by four beings in seriously cool spacesuits: white jumpsuits with helmets, the visor blackened and bulging, firing bullets from their index fingers. They're like something from a more fanciful episode of *The Avengers*.

The fleeing Sarah inevitably falls into a quarry, where she is soon followed by our twitching soldier, whom Baker pronounces dead.

Cut to Devesham, which *Metropolitan* magazine journalist Sarah recognises from a previous assignment. It's unnervingly quiet, no one around, and there's a tall stone monument – and I think that's what drew me to East Hagbourne: that something so instantly recognisable would be there at the end of my journey. Baker is tied to it later in the story, and I could stand *exactly* in the same spot.

So that's the village itself, the woods and a quarry so far, added to my checklist. But there are two more locations to come from *The Android Invasion*.

The village pub, the Fleur de Lys, which Baker and Sladen go inside seeking signs of life, to be met by empty chairs and tables – until shortly before 8pm, in a tantalisingly spooky scene, when zombie locals are driven in on the back of a truck, take up positions in the boozer and, as the wall-clock chimes eight, come to life as if co-starring in *Bagpuss*.

Needless to say, we'll be trying out the Fleur de Lys.

And finally, there's the Space Research Station, where UNIT are based, to whom the Doctor goes for help. According to www.doctorwholocations.net, that building is owned by the Health Protection Agency, which has something to do with radiation, and is located at the nearby Harwell International Business Centre.

Five locations – a lot for one day. Or for what's left of the afternoon, as it will turn out.

As episode one ends, we catch our first glimpse of one of the controlling aliens, a Kraal named Styggron – cross a bulldog with a rhino and melt – as he spies on the Doctor and Sarah through a grille at the research station. And though Dylan is trying to maintain a teenage aloofness to the dated proceedings,

I definitely saw him start.

Hehehe.

We work out a sequence of attack and end up driving to Worsham Quarry first by mistake. Look, let's not focus any longer on map-reading altercations. The three of us will pull together as the day wears on. It's been frustrating thus far, and we all seem tired.

Here, beside the Burford Road in Witney, conveniently off the A40, should be our quarry, which both Sarah and the soldier fell into. I'm not exactly desperate to visit another big gouge in the earth's crust, but Dylan seems fairly keen and, well, we're here now.

We're looking for Moor Avenue and a pathway off to the north, which are easily found. It feels like an inauspicious start, at a merely minor location, but the sun's still out and rural England awaits.

The pathway, houses one side, greenery the other, begins with the latest sign, which has a 15mph limit warning and a home-made-looking thing that says, frankly, 'HUM' (*pic 12.1*). We decline to do so, being from London, and continue up the path with the boy as eager staff photographer (*pic 12.2*). Do you know, I could swear there's a spring in his step.

Twice, on this latest pathway with sun dapples, a ferocious dog tries to claw its way over a fence at us, barking furiously; I flick Vs at the pair of them, confident that their owners have got the dog-height:fence-height ratios right.

I'm not entirely sure where the quarry is going to be, but it's a quarry and you can't easily hide one of those (Betchworth, notwithstanding). Actually, the Betchworth experience is already tugging at my ear lobe.

We reach a T-junction. Housing estate to our right, fenced off large yard with back gardens to our left. Neither looks remotely correct: a suspicion confirmed by rudimentary investigation.

This leaves only forward, down a pathway diminishing in size, through increasingly rampant vegetation. And who's this going past, heading that same way? It's a family, with buckets, nets and small children. Er... nets?

I could swear I hear running water.

Yet at the start of the path, we had also spotted another of those 'Private property' signs *(pic 12.3)*, so well worn as to be redundant, but as if there were something here once that members of the public were supposed to avoid. A quarry, for instance. And I've come across no mention of this one being filled in.

"Remember Betchworth," goes the voice in my head, sniggering.

Sinead, aware that I have reverted to being petrified of talking to strangers, asks the family if they know of any quarries in the area.

They don't, the female leader of the group says, and they've lived here for years. Which just doesn't add up.

With nothing else for it, we follow them down the diminishing path, and end up at a stretch of water *(pic 12.4)*. Quite a picturesque stretch of water, with a man-made bank on our side and a green panorama on the other, but hardly what we're after.

"Hang on a sec," says Dylan. "So instead of finding a quarry, we've found a river?"

That does appear to be the case.

Stumped, we try further along the overgrown track to our left, where I get stung yet again. It's amazing: I doubt I've been stung by a nettle in 30 years, yet suddenly I'm the prime target of every formic-acid-toting weed for miles around.

Can I find a dock leaf? Can I heck. When I were a lad, I tell Dylan, everywhere there were nettles, you could find dock leaves. No longer. (If he takes nothing else from the weekend, at least he has that flora-based tale of woe.)

Eventually beyond confusion, having tried every possible angle, we end up back at the T-junction and I start rubbing my chin, detective-style, in front of that housing estate (*pics 12.5 and 12.6*). Those sandstone bricks surely do look pristine. On these lawns before me, that grass seed is only just taking hold. And those trees planted amid them – mere saplings…

So Sinead, Dylan and I stand there debating how long ago we think the houses were built, and at what stage of germination we reckon the grass seeds are. Thankfully no one can hear us.

Despite my failure at Betchworth – and despite what that woman who claimed to have lived in these parts for years said – I stand firm on this one.

"That housing estate has been built slap-bang over Worsham Quarry!" I declare. "And now it's time to move on."

Was I right?

Yes! (For a change.)

Take a look if you can at the Google satellite map on my site, which, being out-of-date, still shows the quarry, and you'll see how a network of roads, shaped like a hooded man dancing uncoordinatedly, has been slapped over the top of it. Stenter Square, Meadow Lane, et al. Those are the names I wrote in my Notebook of Suspicion.

And those houses must have flown up, because a Google search for Worsham Quarry returns the website of Smiths Bletchington, suppliers to the construction industry, founded by Arthur Smith, great-grandfather of the current directors. It notes:

'The former limestone quarry at Worsham was acquired by Smiths in 2004 as a major development in their recycling business.

Construction and demolition waste is reprocessed on site using crushing and screening equipment to produce hardcore, sub base and fill materials which complement and supplement our primary quarried materials. The inert residue left from processing is infilled on site as part of the quarry's restoration works.'

All that was going on just four years ago! Britain's dock leaves might no longer be relied upon, but its home-builders certainly seem to have pulled their socks up.

It's with a small sense of deflation that I leave Witney. Though the detective aspect of the chase is always fun, it's seeking the sense of *Who* that drives me, and you couldn't more conclusively crush the ghosts of *The Android Invasion* than by dumping a load of rubble, soil and new buildings over the top of them, then planting saplings.

It feels an ignominious end to the site of one of my favourite stories. But then the quarry did play only a small part of the action. One should hardly become despondent.

To Tubney Wood. Or rather: to East Hagbourne but spot a sign for Tubney on the way so go there first.

On route, waiting at a quaint humpback bridge for some traffic lights to change, I spot a pub name and urge Dylan to snatch a photograph (*pic 12.7*). The Rose Revived! Geddit? (For non-*Who* fans: Billie Piper played Rose, the Doctor's first companion, who left but then was *revived* to appear again at the end of season four. No, I'm not proud.)

I've stuck a link to the pub's website on my own because, had we not been running late, we would definitely have stopped. Although the bar looks a bit stiff, the exterior seems enticing – and the River Thames only flows past the beer garden. (To join, nearby, the lovely-named River Windrush, which we had stumbled across in Witney.)

It amazes me that *my* river, the Thames, in London, the same one from The Town of Ramsgate, reaches all this way into the interior. I know it shouldn't, rivers generally tending towards ostentatious length, but it does.

And it must be said that the Thames, in these parts, is far more picturesque than our London portion ever manages. Indeed, the countryside I've passed through so far on this Mega-Trip has rarely dipped below eye-popping.

Why do we choose to live in the city, and why is my son being raised the same? (Just wait until Dylan's quote at Four Barrows.) We sacrifice such tranquillity and such visions for the cosmopolitan lifestyle.

It has been positively heartbreaking to keep zipping past public houses hundreds of years old, oozing history and cider fumes, with thatched roofs and roses trailing, where old blokes in beer gardens talk through pipe stems, supping ale the colour of yesterday's canal.

Actually, you can keep the ale part.

It just makes me keenly aware that these trips are barely pinpricking the surface of what is out there, like performing languid acupuncture on a Sumo wrestler.

I expected Tubney Wood to be a modest copse. It's not. It's huge – feels like it ought to feature in history books, the sort of leafy acreage where outlaws hung out and kings hunted. It's also bisected by the A420, along which the traffic is doing mad speeds and I have a Mercedes up my backside.

When we leave the car and try to cross the road, we're taking our lives in our hands. Despite such greenery all around, the air is rent with Doppler Effected vrooms. It feels threatening and hardly conducive to the environment. I suspect all three of us have a case of the nerves.

We were also forced to drive around the woods twice, just trying to find somewhere convenient to park, having failed to come across anything resembling a car park. In the end, a lay-by had to suffice. As to spotting the precise sites where the *Who* crew filmed, we would have more chance of spotting Lord

Lucan, befriending him, getting him to confess all to the filth and claiming a rich reward.

Despite the history I suspect Tubney oozes, there's a paucity of information on the internet. Plenty on Tubney House, mind, which I believe we spotted through trees, but which fails to concern us. I did find this brief gem, from the *Topographical Dictionary of England* (1848, edited by Samuel Lewis):

'TUBNEY, a parish, in the union of Abingdon, hundred of Ock, county of Berks, 4 1/4 miles (W. by N.) from Abingdon; containing 190 inhabitants, and comprising 1124a. 2r. 36p. The living is a sinecure rectory, valued in the king's books at £3. 1. 10 1/2., and in the gift of Magdalen College, Oxford: the tithes have been commuted for £147. 10., and the glebe contains 10 acres. The church has been demolished, and on the induction of a rector, the ceremony takes place in the open air. The parishioners attend Fyfield church.'

I thought topography was the study of contours? Still I find the olde language and preoccupations fascinating: sinecures, rectories, glebes and all that. The 'hundred of Ock'.

There's also a little info available from the Oxfordshire Wildlife and Landscape Study group, who note that Tubney Wood is ancient (more than 400 years old) broadleaved woodland, involving oak, ash, birch, cherry, filed maple and beech, with carpets of bluebells. And the soils are acidic-sandy, which fails to excite me.

My favourite mention of Tubney Wood comes from a blogger called Tim, who took copious amounts of drugs and attended an illegal rave there back in '92. His tales are fabulous; however this is his best sentence: 'The night is great for accentuating the drug/music induced mayhem, but it gets a bit annoying when you keep tripping over tree stumps.'

I'm finding Tubney Wood as disappointing as Worsham

Quarry (or the lack of it). I feel lost in its anonymity and pestered by cars that seem more like hornets.

Still, there must be a money-shot and I might as well take it anywhere, since everywhere looks the same (trees). First, I take a photo of a 'TUBNEY' sign (*pic 12.8*), in the absence of anything more authentic, then Dylan and I climb over a farmer's gate, where I can stand in woodland and he can snap away (*pic 12.9*).

After Dylan has shown me the best way to climb back over a gate – I love it when the educational roles are reversed – we gratefully reacquaint ourselves with the Nissan's interior, having managed to avoid becoming roadkill, and the boy takes one final fleeting picture of the clumped-green woodland (*pic 12.10*) under a bruising sky.

East Hagbourne had better be good.

TRIP 13

(Leg 8 of the Mega-Trip)

Saturday, 28 June 2008

The Android Invasion

East Hagbourne & Harwell Campus, Oxfordshire

We come off the A34 on the A417 – noting signs for Harwell and another location, but avoiding the diversion as time is short and I must to be consoled with something fleshy – then take the first left on country lanes towards West Hagbourne and, inevitably, its eastwards cousin.

The first sight that confronts us as we enter the village is that curious monument the Androids tied Baker to (*pic 13.1*). The very thing that I suspect drew me here in the first place. And the second sight, as we round the corner past Church Close? Up ahead, in a row of buildings on the left: The Fleur de Lys (*pic 13.2*)! Finally, things are looking up.

It's almost too easy after the travails of earlier, seems to take away some of the fun – but, wow, is this some place: ludicrously quaint, unfalteringly English, all cottage, beams, thatch and blooms. A church that looks far larger than its potential congregation dominates one corner, pigeon calls mock the silence, and the overwhelming sensation is one of age. Serious age. Nothing 'mock-' about this place. This, without a doubt, is the genuine article.

A sign advertises the 4th Annual Scarecrow Trail in East Hagbourne, 'Scarecrows up for 28th June 2008' – today, by chance. 'Theme: As Church Fete – Heroes, Heroines and Villains. Join in the fun and make a Scarecrow of your favourite character.' And beneath a drawing of a happy scarecrow: 'Cup for the Winning Scarecrow. Teas in the Church.'

Teas in the Church. I told you it was unfalteringly English. Already it feels a delight and a privilege to be here.

A quick wander. The Old Bakehouse... Apple Tree Cottage.... Lime Tree Farm.... Sundial Cottage... You get the idea. And indeed there are scarecrows in most gardens, presumably because you don't turn down the chance of a good Scarecrow Trail in a place this low on strip-lit entertainment. There's one creation across the road, resting on beanpoles, in stripy tights and woolly hat (*pic 13.3*), an indeterminate hero/heroine/villain; along the way, a shark atop a hedge; up there, beneath the eaves of a roof, something sinister in black; and before me now, hanging from the front door of a typical property – all white plaster crisscrossed by ancient beams, tiled not thatched roof though still full of character (despite being just a roof), colour rioting in the garden – is a rather incongruous green Hulk (*pic 13.4*). The children of the village, and no doubt their parents, have been getting imaginative with masks and straw.

I shall discover my own choice of winner shortly.

We're hungry. It seems we're always doomed to be hungry on this Mega-Trip. Fact Pack and Fack Pack 2 – The Return to Fact Pack – are simply too factual to allow such frivolities as meal-breaks.

Though where better to seek succour than the Fleur de Lys (*pic 13.5*)? Unless of course it happens to be closed. Closed! I thought every pub in Britain remained open all day – but not here, not in a village of population... According to itraveluk.co.uk: 1881. That's the same number as drug suspects arrested in the Guangdong province of China between 1 January and 27 May 2005. Or, put less sordidly, every villager could have travelled to Scotland to watch East Stirlingshire play at their old Firs Park ground – provided one was happy to sit outside.

A sign at the pub notes that it will open again at 6pm. The time now? 5.20pm. Time enough to explore.

The starting point is obvious. The monument. It stands defiantly in the junction of Main Road and Church Close, on a base of stone steps that look hewn directly from a mountain. Immovably solid, yet the tapering shaft rooted centrally in the steps exudes a kind of grace.

Atop the shaft sits a cuboid construction housing what appear to be gnomons, then further tapering until an orb. What it represents I have no idea, but I'm thinking: weird sundial. It is probably significant that it sits within easy view of the church.

Can I sense the old ghosts of *Who*? Not enormously, no. Though the recognition factor has gone through the roof, since this multi-ton orb holder looks unchanged since 1975, its surroundings have such an intense personality that *Doctor Who* feels just a bit-part in the teeming history.

Not that passing Alsations will stop me mounting those same steps that Baker once bestrode.

The lowest step is quite a hike, after which summiting is a doddle. I'd like to stand up and pretend to have been attached there by Androids, but there are a few people around – one man and his dog, some blokes working on a house – and I'd be in danger of looking silly. Though I doubt I would have been the first.

(Interlude: yesterday I spoke to Gary Russell, former fan turned *Doctor Who* script editor, and mentioned this book and East Hagbourne. He told me he'd done the attached-there-by-Androids thing. It was I who felt silly.)

Instead, I sit at the top of the steps, trying to look the casual tourist, and Dylan takes the first money-shot (*pic 13.6*). Behind me, grey-tinged clouds the size of football fields do their best to blot out the blue sky.

Where next? As we wait for the Fleur de Lys to open, a simple stroll the length of the village seems in order. East Hagbourne, this living museum, should be savoured. Craftsmen of yore built this place and only a fool would see fit to change it.

A local woman, who has been scattering seed for chickens ranging free in an orchard, says "Hello" to us as we stop and stare. (You don't often see live poultry where we come from.) After she has gone, the birds mass and head towards us (*pic 13.7*), walking like Egyptians, imagining that we too have snacks for them. I feel bad disappointing them, though they are only chickens.

A notice in the orchard boasts that East Hagbourne has won Best Kept Village in 1996, 1999, 2003 and 2004. What on earth could have beaten it in the intervening years boggles the mind.

The wind gets up, rustling leaves as if in a ghost story, as we reach the end of Main Road and the extent of the village. There's another monument here, like the one I just climbed, though smaller. Because it didn't appear in *The Android Invasion*, I don't find it terribly interesting. How poor is that?

With Sinead on a personal mooch, Dylan and I retrace our steps back through the village, with plans to glance inside the church, and in Church Close I espy my Scarecrow Trail winner.

Outside the cottage nearest to the monument, someone has built a Dalek (*pic 13.8*). That family knows their *Doctor Who* history, I think proudly.

Its construction is both mad and brilliant. Upturned dustbin decorated with silver balls, stood upon a small table covered in a black throw, sink plunger (natch), plastic basket as collar and foil-covered bowl as head, with – *piece de résistance* – tufted straw in place of lights. If anything else wins, there must be witchcraft in the air.

Behind the Dalek, the cottage wall features ornamental brickwork inlaid between black-coated beams; to its left – I'm guessing – trailing clematis. Just so very East Hagbourne.

Further up the close, a slate sign introduces The Old Vicarage and, beside it, lounging on two white metal garden chairs, is another scarecrow (*pic 13.9*). It's just some straw in a wetsuit, really, which makes me think of a stereotypical vicar, eager-eyed and jovial, keen to demonstrate to parishioners that he too can be a little crazy at times.

So Dylan and I decide to photograph St Andrews Church rather than going inside (*pic 13.10*), in case the vicar appears, goes all Tigger on our asses and forces tea into our mitts. And then we shall never be set free.

Edging back towards the pub, craving six o'clock, I have an unexpected flash of recognition (*pic 13.11*). I could swear this corner is where the van loaded with zombie villagers stopped, before they trooped into the boozer. Had I been too focused on the one landmark when it was the bigger picture – this entire end of East Hagbourne – that offered the greater sense of *Who*?

Now I can feel something: that same sense of rural queerness that pervaded the television story. It feels right, contents me.

I check my watch. 17.57. Bugger it, we can walk slowly.

Time to enter the hallowed portal of the Fleur de Lys (*pic 13.12*)...

Though it's six on the dot as we go in, there's already a local sitting on a stool at the corner of the bar, chatting to the barman.

First impressions (*pic 13.13*)? Frankly it's nothing like the ancient wooden, spartan alehouse that Baker and Sladen entered in *The Android Invasion*. This feels warmer, smacks of layers of renovation. Not that I had expected any different, having always imagined that *Who* interior to be a studio set, though I can't help a twinge of disappointment.

While we order dinner and drinks, I debate internally whether to quiz the barman. It's touch and go. Were we the only people here, I'd definitely come clean. But we aren't, and I guarantee that sole local will be earwigging. There's always the *Withnail* Approach: that I am "doing a feature for *Country Life*. Survey of rural types: farmers, travelling tinkers, milkmen; that sort of thing…" but I don't have the chutzpah to pull that off.

The truth, it transpires, proves easy.

The barman – also the landlord – is indeed aware of the televisual history of his boozer; he produces a VHS of *The Android Invasion* from behind the bar, which a regular has presented to him. So I press further: has he had many *Doctor Who* fans in?

Just the one or two, he says, though he and the wife have not been *in situ* for so very long. He's a friendly chap, soon offering information unprompted – he has some *Android Invasion* illustrations upstairs that he sells for the local artist, Linda Benton – and revealing that the pub interiors actually *were* filmed inside the Fleur de Lys.

I'm quite stunned. So we are actually there, *in the scene*.

The far wall, the landlord says, where the chalkboard is now, is where the old bar used to be (*pic 13.14*). To the left of us, currently another seating area, they once offered off-sales. As I turn to look, I'm confronted by a notice pinned to a pillar concerning Didcot Pubwatch – 'Barred from one, barred from all' – which lists a series of names. Several of them are female. I think: that would never have happened in '75.

Our host ushers me into the corridor outside the loos – through the same doorway which, memory suggests, the Doctor and Sarah once hid behind – where there are framed souvenirs of *Doctor Who*'s time here.

One is a collage of photographs taken by Willie Pereira, dated July 1975, generally featuring awed local children crowding around Baker, in costume, as if he were some kind of visiting Santa. Baker used to love that sort of thing, meeting his junior public, and indeed still does.

Another of my *DILY* e-pals, Nicky, told me how she attended a *Doctor Who* convention earlier this year with her daughter, and met our Tom. Often the star expects some kind of remuneration for their mark on a photograph; Baker, well, he gave the kids a quid each. His pocket, she recalled, was bulging with the thick coins.

The centrepiece of the Pereira collage (*pic 13.15*) is captioned: 'Doctor Who (Tom Baker) and Sarah-Jane (Elisabeth Sladen) flanked by Harry and Phyllis Bartlett', being the landlord and lady of the time. He, wearing spectacles, looks like he once served in the forces; his wife, the smallest of the quartet, smiles proudly.

Thirty-three years ago, that photograph was taken. Thirty-three years. To put that into perspective: Margaret Thatcher became leader of the Conservative Party that same year, the Birmingham Six were (wrongfully) sentenced to life in prison, Ali beat Frasier in the Thrilla in Manilla and, on the island of Morota, lone Japanese soldier Teruo Nakamura finally surrendered and accepted that World War II had ended.

The past is perfectly captured in these monochrome photographs, fading over time. To their left is a fan certificate, framed, noting that 'The Lords of Time Meet Here, Time

Stream Permitting'. I'd imagined I wasn't the first.

And to their right is one of Linda Benton's illustrations (*pic 13.16*), a black-and-white line-drawing of the Doctor being tied to that monument by two black-visored Androids. It makes me realise: I really should find out what that monument is.

"Is it some kind of sundial?" I ask the landlord.

No, it isn't, he says, and I feel slightly foolish. It's the Upper Cross. And that smaller version at the opposite end of the village is – anyone? – the Lower Cross.

East Hagbourne simply *is* history. Check out, if you can, www.easthagbourne.net, the East Hagbourne Village Website. For a population of 1881, they are terribly organised.

An erstwhile visitor is quoted: 'The beauty of this sequestered village as you come down into it is almost bewildering... Out of the houses clustering round, you might almost expect to see folk in ancient costume issue forth, move up and down the little street, and form themselves into picturesque groups, because it is more like a village on the stage than anything else...'

Git put it better than me.

It turns out that several of these properties are yeoman houses, dating from the 15th, 16th and 17th centuries – so there are buildings still standing here that were constructed in 14-something! Woah.

The name 'Hagbourne' derives from the Saxon chief Hacca, who settled there beside a stream (Bourne being Saxon for stream) that now runs past the Manor House. By the time of the *Domesday Book* of 1086, Reinbald of Cirencester was in charge and the entry runs: '[Reinbald] held it himself from King Edward. 15 hides; but then and now it answered for 12 hides less 1 virgate. Land for 12 ploughs. In lordship 2 ploughs; 18 villages and 16 cottagers with 10 ploughs. 6 slaves; a mill at 12s 6d; meadow, 30 acres. The value was £15 now £18.'

If you want to know what all those Olde English terms mean, check out the website; personally, I prefer to wonder.

The tales of the crosses alone are fascinating. The Upper and Lower Crosses and the door knocker on the north door of St Andrews Church form a triangle within which a criminal on the run from the law could, in days of yore, seek sanctuary. Safely inside the invisible force-field, he could confess his crime to an official, forfeit his goods and agree to depart England's shores sharpish. Any deviation or return meant certain death.

A devastating fire here in 1659 took out all the dwellings between what are now East and West Hagbourne – physically separating into two villages what was once simply Hagbourne. Who'd have thought?

The original Upper Cross, it is suggested, was destroyed by Oliver Cromwell, but its replacement's square capital (my 'cuboid construction', correctly termed)... hang on... 'has three sundials (the fourth side has an inscription, now much faded)...'! So I am not entirely foolish, after all.

Equally fascinating, and which I had failed to spot earlier: there is a small alcove within the shaft of the cross that 'is reputed to have contained vinegar to disinfect coins during times of plague.'

No wonder the *Doctor Who* page of the same website comprises just two sentences. Perspective.

The thrills continue inside the Fleur de Lys, where our host kindly presents me with one of Linda Benton's A4 illustrations, which has become too worn to be saleable, and reserves us a table at the corner of the seating area – right where the old bar of 1975 would have ended.

I suspect Sinead and Dylan are also enjoying the ghost of the association, and I readily convince myself that everyone is Having A Good Time.

I did wonder about the need to reserve a table. Though a few people have begun to patronise the Fleur de Lys, it's hardly buzzing. Then something uncanny happens. Nearer seven than the 8pm of *The Android Invasion*, admittedly, but all the customers arrive at once (*pic 13.17*). It's just like the scene in *Doctor Who* when the villagers suddenly come to life! Like they played it out, especially for us! Sinead notices it too.

It's a tickling end to our East Hagbourne experience. (And the food and service were excellent.)

We're booked for the night in the Swindon Marriott – all the pubs were full – and are eager to get settled. It has been another long day.

However, having already been tantalised by signs to Harwell, which also happens to be on the way to Swindon, we decide to complete the job we signed up for: to visit the final location in the Saturday section of Fact Pack 2: *Doctor Who*'s Space Research Centre.

As we pootle down Main Road (Only Road might be nearer the mark), Dylan drops the shutter on the Lower Cross (*pic 13.18*) for our files and we swing towards Didcot.

The Harwell Science and Innovation Campus is hard to miss off the A4185, being vast and dominated by something ostentatious resembling a football stadium cum UFO. Its website notes that: 'The Harwell Science and Innovation Campus in Oxfordshire is a vibrant and growing community of science and technology based innovation and enterprise including major national and international science projects and facilities. Over 4,500 people work on the campus in some 100 organisations.'

Covering 640 acres, it's set within an Area of Outstanding Natural Beauty, if hardly contributing to it.

This same area used to be RAF Harwell, then the UK's centre for government-funded nuclear power research, feeding off the grey matter of the local Oxford-educated boffins. When *Doctor Who* visited, the buildings they used were owned by the National Radiological Protection Board.

Its funny how Cold-War-era that sounds, despite such research being ongoing and with a potential increasing global reliance on nuclear fuels.

I wonder what they did in there? Blokes in lab-coats handling things through rubber gloves in vacuum chambers? Ladies in cropped lab-coats making suggestive moves with Geiger counters? Sorry, that's the plot to *Carry On Up the Mushroom Cloud*.

It wasn't a thrilling looking building back then. And it still isn't. In fact, it's barely changed.

Fortunately, since I have no idea where exactly on this 640-acre site to look, we recognise it immediately. It's on the right off the main road into the Campus, Fermi Avenue, past that football stadium cum UFO. I notice now the roads to the right are named Road 1 – can't see a 2 or 3 – Road 4, Road 5, Road 6, etc, up to Road 15. How perfectly scientifically minded.

And, brilliantly, the single road in the area with an actual name is... well, picture the road-naming meeting:

Boffin 1: Any advance on Road 15?

Boffin 2: How about Road 16?

Everyone bar Boffin 22: Brilliant!

Boffin 1: Right, so we're all agreed...

Boffin 22 is waving his arm frantically.

Boffin 1: Yes, Boffin 22?

Boffin 22: I'm rather a fan of Dido...

Boffin 5: Me too! I admire her mellow lounge vibe and inoffensive way with lyrical construction.

Boffin 11: Oooh! And the way the arpeggio structure in her work is overshadowed by the counterpoint!

Boffin 3: I find her legato to be too often accompanied by

the ritardando, when a little mezzeforte might be more usefully employed.

Boffin 9: Isn't Stan brilliant!

Everyone: Oh yes, Stan etc. etc. etc.

Boffin 17: Actually, I quite like Simply Red.

Boffin 1: Shut up, Boffin 17. Dido Road it is!

Bet it went like that.

It's a very grey place under a diminishing sunlight, the Harwell Science and Innovation Campus. More like a low-rise industrial estate. Yet you can imagine the sheer collective force of brain-power at work here during opening hours: a perceptible neon glow hovering above the rooftops.

When we arrive (somewhere after 7.30pm), the place feels completely abandoned. And there's me thinking that people so intent upon innovating would be working all hours.

It's interesting how often, on these trips, we are either the only people around or are not exactly claustrophobic. A result of the obscurity of the locations, our visiting times and the distance from clustered humanity, I would guess. But it's another reason why I am enjoying myself so much: we have these places to ourselves. Beats Alton Towers.

Our Space Research Centre has a sort of Reception cabin outside, unoccupied I am relieved to note, then a car park, which I stop in. In April 2005, the National Radiological Protection Board was swallowed up by the Health Protection Agency so this site now houses the Centre for Radiation, Chemical and Environmental Hazards, which sounds dangerous.

What I am increasingly aware of – as, I suspect are Sinead and Dylan – is that we are sitting in a vehicle on a Saturday evening, for reasons unknown and likely to be bewildering to anyone else, with cameras, in front of a government installation where they research radioactivity. During an era when our security forces are hypersensitive to terrorism.

What's the betting there aren't CCTV cameras trained on us at this very moment, as people in front of monitors start pushing buttons on telephones wearing frowns on their faces? I'm not joking.

After taking just one photo (*pic 13.19*), I get the creeps, slide the gearstick into first and drive out of the Centre for Radiation, Chemical and Environmental Hazards car park as fast as I can, without going so speedily as to heighten suspicions. (At least easy when you're in a Micra.)

"Dylan – take some more pictures through the window!" I cry, and we're outta there. His fleeting images are *pic 13.20* and *pic 13.21* on my site. Skid-marks not pictured.

Let me now describe the three photographs we managed between us, since I really didn't take much in at the time.

As I said, the building's exteriors haven't altered noticeably in 33 years. It's all windows and people-boxes stacked side-by-side, with some sort of vent poking out of the top, in shades of drab. The single glaring difference between reality and television is that the *Who* people slapped a large radio dish on the roof in CSO, no doubt to add credence to the idea of that being a Space Research Centre. One can hardly research space if one cannot see into it.

The instant recognition certainly enhances the sense of *Who* – Tom Baker definitely once ran about on *that* roof, avoiding UNIT buffoons with guns – but the notion that we had no place being there hardly soothed the nostalgic thought processes. I wouldn't go again. People take national security very seriously, and you really don't want to have to explain to some humour-free droid in uniform about androids invading Earth. They might not hear the "In *Doctor Who…*" bit and you'll end up starting World War III by mistake.

That talk of seeing into space has reminded me of a story I came across while researching East Hagbourne. It's on the BBC News website, dated November 2004.

Deborah Hambly, who lives in the village, is a keen astronomer and averse to street lighting. The story begins: 'She says [the street lighting] is so bad, she is fighting plans for a school crossing near her house because of up to 10 streetlights that must go with it – taking the total in the village to nearly 100.'

John Napper, who runs a mobile planetarium and observatory from his home, also in the village, adds that growing light pollution is affecting his livelihood: '"It's hopeless. I was out here in my garden at night the other day and I could literally read a newspaper," he said.'

What stuck me first was that Hambly was trying to stop a school crossing being built so she could see some stars – she wasn't, it was explained later; she was merely after regulated lighting around the crossing that wasn't on 24 hours a day – but also that in a village as small as East Hagbourne there were at least two people out in their gardens at night, eye glued to a lens attached to a chunky telescope, gazing among the constellations.

Hambly was introduced as county representative for the Campaign for Dark Skies, which sounds like something out of *The X-Files*, but is real. Makes me want to join, although I'd need a telescope first.

The night sky and the Race into Space fascinated me as a child. *Who* fans become understandably enthused by all their exciting Doctor-based science-fiction – but there are real people out there with their hearts and minds actually out among the galaxies. People who train their sights on nebulae, quarks and black holes. Who track the stars – pinpoints of light that took millions of years to reach these shores – as they pass through the heavens.

When you close the covers of this book and tuck yourself into bed tonight, spare a moment for all those romantics around the globe with imaginations full of heavenly bodies, sat in sheds in back gardens or in silver-domed observatories on the tops of lonely mountains, gazing upwards through the darkness, blissful in their solitude, wondering what next they might witness among the far reaches of time and space. Because that, my friends, is where *Doctor Who* started.

TRIP 14

(Leg 9 of the Mega-Trip)

Sunday, 29 June 2008

The Daemons

Aldbourne, Wiltshire

Another day, another village.

We forego the offer of breakfast (not included in the room price) in the Marriott and head towards Marlborough, where we find a pleasant little café with outside tables and I spill orange juice down myself.

I love these little trips away as a family. Dylan's the right age for banter now, and – for example – as we head for Aldbourne, we urge Sinead to find rude place names in the *Road Atlas of Great Britain.*

"Is there a Shitting in there?" he asks eagerly, and I wonder whether I should reprimand him, or whether geographical innuendo is acceptable.

It's hardly a testing drive to our destination, on the back roads through Poulton, Mildenhall – where everyone is either washing their car or mowing their lawn, this being a Sunday – Axford and Ramsbury, before heading north on the B4192.

Contrary to my previous good fortune, the clouds are winning the battle of the skies and there's pressure in the air. Gloom inhabits the horizon.

Ask any ageing *Who* fan which is the most iconic location and I reckon the majority would say Aldbourne, aka Devil's End, as it was known in the story. Why? Partly because *The Daemons* itself was so iconic, featuring Roger Delgado's Master, UNIT, paganism, devil worship, witchcraft, one of classic *Who*'s most sinister and brilliantly realised monsters in the gargoyle Bok, and – the bell-legged, stick-wielding icing on the cake – Morris dancers. But also because the village was truly a co-star.

Usually the action bats about over four or six episodes (unusually, *The Daemons* had five), often tarrying in the studio; in contrast, filming during April '71, the *Who* cast and crew stayed resolutely in Aldbourne, sucking out every last drop of English-village weirdness. Where East Hagbourne's similar vibe felt alien in origin, there it felt largely human, centred on the villagers themselves so it was more readily related to.

How can I best describe the sensation of watching *The Daemons*? Imagine turning a corner on a country lane to find those above-mentioned Morris dancers bearing down upon you astride hobby horses, wearing unsmiling faces, and all you hear are the bells and the rhythm of their boots on tarmac. Cue God-fearing scream.

It is, as they say, a cracker; still I had to watch it alone, two *Who* stories in a row being too much for my alleged loved ones.

The very first shot is of the church, St Michael's in real life, in a storm of epic proportions. Stock footage of rats the size of cats, a frog, a crow and a normal-sized cat add to the eeriness. A hunched figure leaves The Cloven Hoof pub (actually The

Blue Boar), follows his dog into the church graveyard, and there dies of fright. I can only imagine five-year-old me watching this when it first aired, saucer-eyed and leaking.

The following day: cut to a BBC crew at a barrow (one of the Four Barrows – we'll be off there later), where a blundering archaeological buffoon plans to dig open the ancient burial tomb.

Cut to: Jo banging on about the dawning of the Age of Aquarius, being such a bloody hippie, and the occult and witchcraft, which the Doctor (Jon Pertwee) dismisses with a flick of his velveteen wrist.

"How do you know there's nothing in it?" asks Jo.

"I just know, that's all," he replies. "Everything that happens in life must have a scientific explanation."

And I think: hang on, that's exactly the sort of thing I've been coming out with – to my wife's consternation, since she has 'an open mind' – for years! And I heard that very exchange at the age of five… How it all adds up.

Then we're back at the barrow with a pompous BBC reporter, harking on about Matthew Hopkins, Witchfinder General, pagan man, unspeakable rites and witchcraft, noting that the workers on an earlier dig at the barrow abandoned their employer and ran all the way back to Cornwall. *From Wiltshire?*

"What's in the barrow?" he asks the archaeologist.

It's a question that both Sinead and the boy will put to me later.

Treasure, reckons the *Who* digger. This, he says, is the tomb of a Bronze Age warrior chieftan, dating from 800BC.

Next, we're back in the village, in reality at Crooked Corner, where a copper plans to drop a small boulder on the head of white witch Miss Hawthorne, during a strange and unnatural wind.

My word, it's great stuff.

The action thereafter centres heavily inside and outside the church – whether that crypt is genuine and actually beneath St Michael's, I have been unable to confirm, but it surely looks real – with gun battles in the graveyard and a devil abroad.

The Cloven Hoof/Blue Boar also plays host to the majority of the players, including upstairs in its bedroom. There's a scrap on the green, which leads to the Doctor being tied to a maypole, and Bok gets the bazooka treatment before freezing in the graveyard.

It really is all there. We just have to find it.

I park by the pond before midday. Dylan goes to inspect (*pic 14.1*) and returns with news of a small dead fish floating at its edge. It's only a mini-pond and he wonders how it got there, so, in return for his gate-negotiating tuition of yesterday, I explain how birds eat fish eggs and poop them out as they fly or paddle – in this pond, for instance – which is how fish get everywhere.

I imagine he's suitably impressed, and I only hope it's true. (My Scottish friend Gordon told me that as we were perusing a loch, without explaining the provenance of such an excellent fact.)

With the father-son bonding in fine fettle, we shimmy right of The Crown and continue past the sort of property we have become used to of late (*pic 14.2*): red brick, old-roofed, achingly pretty and suffused with blooms, though this village doesn't feel quite as ancient as East Hagbourne – seems larger and more spread out. Where yesterday's location was so resolutely tranquil, this one has a potential for *Camberwick Green* bustle.

And there it is before us (*pic 14.3*): the green, church behind, and among the buildings on the right, well, you can't miss a boar that's *that* blue. It's a scene straight out of *Doctor Who*, as if the years since 1971 never happened. It's almost uncanny. A snapshot out of time.

As we head for the pub, a middle-aged woman walks past wearing a silly woollen hat, socks and carrying a ski pole. A rambler. I avoid her eye in case she stops and starts reciting the Country Code at me, while I poke her repeatedly above the chest and demand to know whether she thinks she's Franz fucking Klammer. (That ski-pole thing really bugs me and I don't know why.)

So we halt for a breather at a table outside the Blue Boar, which gives me a chance to take everything in.

The immediate difference between The Blue Boar and The Cloven Hoof is that the former is absolutely covered in flowers (*pic 14.4*). It's as if the boozer, single-handedly, is trying to win Britain in Bloom. Hanging baskets, ivy, climbers, creepers, trailers, red and pink and blue and mauve and purple and orange and green… Woooah, felt a little faint just then – hideous flashback to being forced into the chorus of the *Joseph and his Amazing Technicolour Dreamcoat* school musical.

And that pub sign! It depicts a boar, so vividly blue that orbiting astronauts might become blinded, about to trample on the flag of St George. Which can't be right.

Gorgeous pub, though.

Already there's a bunch of well-heeled folk here, late-twenties, all dressed up and boozing early, clearly waiting to attend some sort of function. Across on the green, curiously, two men appear to be dismantling some sort of recording equipment propped on a monument – not dissimilar to East Hagbourne's – while a colleague parked outside the church waits for them.

What can that be about? I imagine this place is a honeypot for the *Who* bees, so they might well be here on similar business to myself.

It makes me feel slightly jealous – they've got recording equipment! Why haven't I got recording equipment? Maybe they're been interviewing people? Perhaps I should interview someone? I look around hopefully.

Beside us, two old chaps on motorised wheelchairs trundle past each other in opposite directions. They exchange a cheery "Morning!", though when I check my watch it's 12.07.

"Everyone here gets around in those!" says Dylan, exaggerating wildly.

Perhaps that's what village life feels like to him: pottering along in life's slow lane, bag of veg on the handlebars?

It is time to seek him the truth.

Aldbourne also has a website of its own, at www.aldbourne.co.uk, but where East Hagbourne's is the 'East Hagbourne Village Website', this one is the 'Aldbourne Community Website'. It's a subtle difference that I may be overplaying, but the two do seem to have different focuses.

Aldbourne's is less devoted to history and more to contemporary village life. Perhaps because it's a third more populous – 2,500 live here – so there's more to natter about?

The Discussion Board makes great reading. There's a lengthy, heated thread concerning the dismissal of the local postman (Paul, I hope you win your tribunal, old son), 'Aldbourne wins Calor Village of the Year', and among the Chit-Chat section: 'Gardeners please be careful when using slug pellets', 'When did rubbish collection start?', 'Humphrey Lyttleton dies' and 'Anyone fancy being bodypainted today?'. The sort of stuff you might find on any community messageboard. Roughly.

And what of *Doctor Who*? I found a link to a BBC story of the filming of *The Daemons*, which proved to be broken. But hold on... A search for '*Doctor Who*' within the Discussion Board has unearthed a few gems (and plenty of iron pyrites). The shiniest by far is a YouTube link to some home-movie footage from the days of filming – Delgado signing an autograph in shades and robes; Pertwee chatting over a wall;

Bok having his feet put on (!); the Master in Bessie (!!) – overlaid with Pertwee's odd I Am the Doctor 'song'. A reply posted by Daleksrule runs: 'I met Roger Delgado when I was 8 in 1973. He was a lovely guy. My Dad used to service his car! and I met both John [sic] and Roger at a school fete in 1971.'

It's such genius I've linked to it on my site.

On the general-history side of Aldbourne, we are better off elsewhere.

The village, I discover, was best known for its bells (its bells). The Cor family opened a bell foundry here in the 1600s and three of the eight bells in St Michael's Church were cast locally. But the Aldbourne folk – known as Dabchicks, after a mythical bird said to have landed in the pond – have been bell-obsessed for centuries, and held a legendary piss-up on the green in 1460 when drinking from the new church bell.

The village's name? We already know what Bourne means (stream, for those at the back), and the 'Ald' bit derives once again from the name of a Saxon chief: Alder, who settled here in olden times.

What else? Melinda Messenger and Johnny Ball hailed from these parts.

That's enough general history – Ed.

After a quick snapshot outside The Blue Boar (*pic 14.5*), suitably self-conscious, we head across the green towards St Michael's (*pic 14.6*), scene of such *Who* activity, pausing first at that strange monument.

It doesn't look as old as East Hagbourne's and feels to me slightly sinister. At its top is a cross (*pic 14.7*), which is facing the church but leaning dramatically away from it. An act of supplication, I suspect. (I've just zipped again through *The Daemons*, and you can spot it behind Pertwee in episode five, when he's waiting for the Brigadier to come and blow everything up.)

That's a teeny role compared to that of this building in front of us. The steps up towards St Michael's main door alone played such a part in the story. The Master, the Doctor, Jo, UNIT soldiers, Bok... They all paced that way. Turn around and you're looking back towards the Blue Boar/Cloven Hoof over the green (*pic 14.8*). This area is simply alive with memories.

The path is cobbled, with weathered, aged gravestones to either side (*pic 14.9*). It's no crowded graveyard, mind. There's room to breathe, if that's the right phrase. The crew filmed front, back and sides, and I swear I can picture some of the grave formations that appeared in *The Daemons* (*pic 14.10*).

There's one particular money-shot I'm after that should be easily spotted: the Master, hands on a gravestone, thinking the Doctor has been killed by a helicopter crashing into Bessie. He went straight back into the church afterwards, so that must be next to the entrance.

And indeed, here they are, just to the right of the door: four in a row, descending in height. The ones Delgado was seen behind. It's rather thrilling to think that that man, who died tragically two years after *The Daemons* was filmed in a road accident, stood in this very spot. In his honour, I pull a Masterly scowl (*pic 14.11*) – and turn out looking more like Victor Meldrew. And boy, do I look knackered.

It's been a hell of a four days. I must have driven more than 500 miles, as the bag of memories fills up on the back seat. But I don't *feel* tired. Not a bit. Way too much excitement and anticipation for that.

There's been a church on this site since before the *Domesday Book*, and this current incarnation – it was dedicated to St Mary Magdalene until 1460 – really is magnificent. Gothic architecture, with Norman features dating back to an 11th or

12th century church incorporated into the evolving design. Even the pews are 150 years old, set in place during a Victorian restoration.

The tower, from the 1400s, dominates. This great, high block with its clock and crenellations, topped with the flag of St George. I mean no blasphemy, but put it in a thunderstorm at night, back-lit by lightning strikes, and it wouldn't look out of place in the *Hammer House of Horror*. In fact, it's just clicked: that's practically what they did to set the scene at the start of *The Daemons*. So I'm not the first to think it.

Inside is a different matter: pure worship.

You know that church smell? Must mixed with religion? It's here, inside this cavernous venture. The sense of space, as light streams in through the windows. And of course the sense of *Who* – I'm pretty sure the Master and various characters mingled in this south aisle.

To my left is the base of the tower; to my right, up ahead in the sanctuary wall, a stunning triptych of stained-glass windows (*pic 14.12*). I've no idea what they are depicting – pious types being bloody decent, at a guess – but the colours are so vivid they look like some sort of piercing laser projection.

Though I'm an atheist, I can't help thinking: aren't churches brilliant? The sheer scale of them, the man-hours required to build them, the architecture and morality – and all, essentially, at the time of construction, to overwhelm and subjugate the people. Brilliant.

I check first for any signs of a crypt, though admittedly the only way I can think of doing this is by looking for a sign that says 'CRYPT' with an arrow pointing downwards and to look for a big hole in the floor with steps. I find neither, which is a shame since those scenes with villagers in dark robes led by an arms-aloft Master, and the appearance of the Daemon himself, horned and huge – not actually the Devil, but an alien named

Azal who looked very much like him, to placate religious viewers – were among the most memorable. I consider asking someone; there are a few people in the church, but sadly none look like a vicar, who would know about such things.

I'd be after, according to the Vicars of the Parish list (*pic 14.13*) posted in the northern aisle, one Mary Crameri, who has been vicar at St Michael's since 2000. The list dates back, incredibly, to 1301, when Richard de Whityngdigh was in place. Some exquisite names – Thomas Shortbrygge (1475), John Parker Cleather (1872), Selwyn Swift (1981) – among, I note, a disproportionate number of Johns.

I walk quietly – it's a given inside churches both to tread lightly and to whisper – to the chancel end (if you're wondering how I know all these church terms, I have the St Michael's leaflet in front of me) and discover in the lady chapel a memorial to two brothers, William and Edward Walrond, who died in 1615 and 1614, respectively, and I wonder who they were.

Now I discover they were related to the Goddard family, whose own monument (*pic 14.14*) is in the Goddard Chapel in the south transept. None of the family members appear to have hands, which is mysterious. Richard Goddard, it is believed, was a 15th century benefactor of St Michael's; hence, I imagine, his kin's place among its stone-workings.

Earthly cash always did do one favours in God's good books.

As we leave the church, a friendly, well-presented old couple turn and accost me. The gentleman of the two tells me – I'm not entirely sure why, but Christians do this sort of thing – how the lady who did the floral arrangements in the church died suddenly, so the flowers in there are for her funeral next week.

I don't really know what to say, but make some sympathetic noises.

"We had a fete here yesterday," he says.

Again stumped for a response, I ask whether they remember *Doctor Who* filming in Aldbourne.

"We only moved here in 1977," he explains. "But there are many villagers who do remember it."

Great, I think, maybe they could help me with an introduction?

"I'm writing this *Doctor Who* book…" I tell them. But before I can explain properly, they seem suddenly desperate to get home. She's already halfway down the street and he's looking from her to me, her to me, panic swimming in his eyes, as if he's just remembered he left the bath water running.

"Yes, well, that'll be an interesting book," the chap blusters, and I'm convinced he doesn't mean it.

Yes, well, please do tell me more about the church fete.

I suppose Aldbourne must be pestered by geeks passing through. I'm wearing my (Spurs player) Aaron Lennon 'Give pace a chance' (geddit?) t-shirt, which depicts a dove carrying an olive branch, and wonder whether they misread the pun, taking me for some sort of pious refusenik.

I consider following them home, offering tales of Binnegar Heath Sand Pit and picturing we tickled trio guffawing delightedly, but decide against it. They were very friendly to this complete stranger, after all, even if they did run away shortly afterwards.

After a tour of the graveyard, where I am pestered by a blurry *déjà vu* of scenes half-remembered, the wife, the boy and I debate our next move. Since none of us are hungry, we postpone a trip to The Blue Boar and decide to head instead for *The Daemons*' Devil's Hump – aka one of the Four Barrows. As a huge *Time Team* fan, I bloody love that kind of thing.

The route takes us along Crooked Corner – the road's real

name, not one invented for *The Daemons*, though it seems ideally suited – where the white witch, Miss Hawthorne, played by the fabulously named Damaris Hayman, narrowly averted having the local, possessed copper clocking her on bonce with a boulder.

Were it not for the general need to renew window frames, so all those at number 3, outside which the action took place, look pristine, and the presence of a gleaming Audi by the property, it all looks pretty much the same. This is definitely the place.

I've been unlucky with the weather. In Dungeness, when I needed snow, it was gloriously hot; and here, where I could have done with a disconcerting squall, it is merely overcast and lightly breezy.

Not to worry. This remains a moment that deserves capturing, so I suggest Dylan plays Miss Hawthorne and demonstrate the character's spell-casting pose as she called upon pagan gods (or somesuch) to calm Satan's winds. I'm not sure I got it right, because he looks more like he's auditioning for *The Sound of Music* (*pic 14.15*). At least the essence of the moment is there.

There simply is nowhere in this village that you can walk without being followed by a sense of *Who*. Hanging baskets may have been added, and windows replaced, but, of all the locations I've visited so far, this one retains the most authenticity. It's inescapable.

So it's no surprise that even the cast and certain crew members have returned here, numerous times, since the filming, for conventions and most notably to film the 1992 indie-produced *The Return to Devil's End*. Naturally, I bought a copy some while back.

Actor and Dalek voice Nicholas Briggs, well known to fans, did the interviewing, and Pertwee, Nicholas Courtney (the Brigadier), John Franklin (Captain Yates), John Levene (Sgt

Benton) and director Chris Barry all took part. A nostalgic bout of joshing and reminiscing followed, as Briggs led them around the same locations described here.

The only problem with asking actors to remember scenes from several decades ago – I have encountered the same myself, many times, while working for the *Radio Times* – is that their memories can be hazy.

There's a very funny moment, right at the start, where Briggs asks Pertwee, "What do you remember about the shooting down here?"

Pertwee [brightly]: "Nothing at all!"

Which didn't stop him returning once again, to discuss the production, in 1996 for a *Doctor Who* convention – three weeks before his untimely death – accompanied by the usual suspects plus Damaris Hayman.

DS Carlin documents the day in his e-zine, *Sparrows Fall* (www.sparrowsfall.co.uk), with photographs – Pertwee grinning, magnificently white-haired; panel discussion in a marquee on the green; Mr Carlin himself beside the former Doctor.

The fate of Bok is revealed there by Pertwee, who took the gargoyle statue (the moving Bok was a bloke called Stanley, wearing a costume) home and put it in his garden, where it gradually disintegrated, being not really made of stone – though not before his Irish gardener had chanced upon it in a hedge and refused to go anywhere near it.

TRIP 15

(Leg 10 of the Mega-Trip)

Sunday, 29 June 2008

The Daemons

Four Barrows, Aldbourne, Wiltshire

Around the Crooked Corner there's a bridle path on the left, so
Fact Pack 2 notes, which leads to Four Barrows. It's a walk of
about a mile, which I fail to mention to Dylan, since he is a
teenager.

The sun is trying to assert itself, in testing conditions, so
once again I find myself off up a light-dappled right of way,
branches overhanging and distant calls of nature in my ears.
Sinead and Dylan have zipped ahead (*pic 15.1*) and I am
lagging. I'm thinking about the Dark Arts.

Not long after the bridleway entrance, someone has dug a
ditch into which someone else has lobbed a haphazard pile of
branches. Just one pile, all higgledy-piggledy (*pic 15.2*). What
the hell for? It's the sort of thing they'd have found in *The Blair
Witch Project.*

I imagine it's the influence of all this Daemon-ic nostalgia,
but I definitely have a sense of something in the ether. It's all

in the mind of course, since the occult is basically tosh. Oh, I've met witches, or women convinced they are witches, but never quite managed to pin down what it was they did. Seemed to me more to do with a healthy connection to Mother Earth.

Still, there's something slightly amiss in my psyche, which is aided none when a passing helicopter – I've heard a lot of helicopters on this Mega-Trip – rattles its blades and sends a murder of crows squawking into the sky.

The symbolism is not lost on me.

I'm not about to turn tail squealing like a joyrider's tyres; I've just let *The Daemons* get under my skin, that's all. It will pass.

The path continues to narrow. Through the trees on either side, there is farmland. Indeed, everywhere around is farmland. I imagine people have worked these undulations for centuries. Look back towards the village and you can just make out the flag of St George flying over St Michael's (*pic 15.3*). We are on our own out here, in this peaceful corner of England.

The field to the left contains wheat, which I have to identify for Dylan. City living does preclude a certain basic knowledge, so I'm glad he's here with us; and he hasn't started asking whether we're there yet, so I assume he's enjoying this country stroll.

Way up ahead, one field on the left is a gorgeous shade of lavender – and *I* don't know what that is. Sinead reckons it's cornflower. I'd imagined it might be actual lavender, but I suppose there's only so much call for pot pourri. We're all learning something here, away from our habitual environs.

It starts to rain. The wind has got up, too, blowing the chill drops into our faces. Dylan refuses to put his hood up, in case it ruins his hair. (I can't complain – I refuse to use an umbrella because they look so square.)

We really have been walking for quite a while – surely for more than a mile – and still no sign of anything barrow-like. Dissention is creeping in among the ranks.

"What does a barrow look like?" the boy asks, beginning to doubt that I know myself, imagining that we are walking aimlessly through fields while passing a succession of barrows unawares.

"They look like a big mound," I say, beginning to doubt myself too.

We all scan the area for big mounds. Then for big mounds that might have become disguised among crops. Nothing.

"What's in the barrow?" Dylan asks.

"Yes, what's in the barrow?" asks Sinead.

And for once, I have the answer. Though my pre-trip research here has been habitually minimal, my love of all things long-buried compelled me to check this one out in advance.

Aldbourne's Four Barrows, on Sugar Hill, are – as the buffoon archaeologist in *The Daemons* correctly stated – from the Bronze Age. They form a cemetery, dating from 2500-1500 BC. That's BC. They're up to 4,500 years old. Not wishing to labour the point, but that's seriously old.

Three of the barrows are bell barrows (surrounded by a ditch); the other is a mere bowl (no ditch).

Yes, yes, I'm getting to what's inside them.

The barrows were excavated by W Greenwell, who wrote up his work in 1890's *Archaeologia*, Volume 52. And here, according to Wiltshire and Swindon Sites and Monument Record Information, is what he found: 'Primary adult cremation, a small vessel (pygmy cup?), 7 amber beads, a bone pin, a flint flake & secondary cremations. Part of beaker base and ox and pig bones found in the mound material.'

Three bodies in total, plus trinkets and possible food for the afterlife. Whose bodies, one cannot say, but it's safe to assume they were high-ranking (I know that from watching *Time Team*). All Greenwell's finds were packed off to the British Museum.

(In *Doctor Who*, the same barrow contained a miniaturised alien spaceship that had once brought the Daemon to Earth. But that's television for you.)

That's a mind-blowing amount of ancient history and English heritage, right there. You don't mess about with that kind of stuff. So I explain to Sinead and Dylan that I imagine the mounds would be fairly overgrown – you wouldn't have farmers bowling combine harvesters or ploughs over them, for instance. What I'm suggesting is that these Four Barrows are going to look like mounds with shaggy hair.

To them, I suspect I am sounding increasingly desperate. (You know when you take someone somewhere – talk it up – and it's not working out, and you feel responsible for their lack of entertainment?)

What feels like far more than a mile into our stroll, in danger of becoming a hike, we are all beginning to wonder aloud whether we took the correct bridleway off Crooked Corner, when we come upon a strange scene (*pic 15.4*). It looks a bit like a UFO landing site (at least it does if you've watched too much *X-Files*).

"I bet you I find a dead body here!" announces Dylan, and I almost hope he does, just to raise his spirits.

The crops have receded here, the ground is largely bare, and there's an area of charring. In it are some bits of metal machinery. Farm machinery, no doubt.

"Do you think that's part of an old plane from World War II?" asks Dylan.

No, but I think they should get him to write *Doctor Who* with that imagination.

It's a diversion of sorts, but the fact remains: we have come seeking Four Barrows and we have found Nought Barrows.

By committee, we decide to give it until the next bend then quit the search. And then it happens. I espy something up ahead. Two hillock-y shapes up there (*pic 15.5*). Raggedy. Could that be half of the Four Barrows?

It's a couple of hundred yards away, and not wishing to drag my loved ones any further, I tell them to wait here while I jog ahead to investigate.

I'm only halfway there when I spot the iron gate. The same iron gate (or newer but similar enough) that *The Daemons*' BBC3 – see what they did there, back in '71? – crew covering the opening of the Devil's Hump rolled equipment through.

"That's it!" I call back, delighted, vindicated, downright relieved.

And I was right: where all around is carefully sewn, shaved and ordered, these ancient burial mounds are indeed rife with stinging nettles and lengthy grasses; left to their own devices. Undisturbed.

It feels great to be here. There's a double-whammy of knowing that Pertwee and Katy Manning once possibly stood on this same spot as myself, 'entered' the barrow and were pursued by Bok – obviously the barrow interior was a studio set, but they showed the gargoyle's entrance from the outside – and that these four barrows were constructed perhaps 4,500 years ago by people wearing animal skins, laying dead leaders here, burning their bodies, placing jewels and food around them, before piling earth upon earth on top of them. Such a ceremony.

I climb the first barrow nearest the gate as the others catch up, and take a photograph looking along the line of mounds (*pic 15.6*). The nettles sting my exposed ankles yet again – will I never learn? – even the knee-high grasses, which whip past my legs, are beginning to irritate. The ground is pitted and uneven. But the toil has been justified.

The barrow is only ten feet high; however, there is a sense of being king of all you survey up here. It's wide, too. A serious structure when you consider the crude tools used to make it.

Atop this mound atop Sugar Hill, Dorset stretches out before me in all directions. Hamlets, villages, and fields, fields, fields. Birds call, a dog barks and the ghosts of Saxons sleep beneath my feet. This green and pleasant land.

"Look, Dad!" says Dylan, who has a long blade of grass between his teeth. "I'm going to be a countryer!"

Aw. I love him to bits.

"It's countryman," I say, though even that doesn't feel right.

He could have moaned bitterly as we trudged onward through the needling elements, but he didn't. Like Sinead previously, he's put up with being driven around the country, visiting odd places on his Dad's behalf, and he's making the most of it. Will he remember this weekend with fondness in ten years' time? I would love to think so.

For Aldbourne's latest money-shots, I'm photographed, arms akimbo, on top of the first barrow (*pic 15.7*) and draped awkwardly over the iron gate (*pic 15.8*); and I can't resist taking one for the miscellaneous files of that lovely trapezium of maybe-cornflower (*pic 15.9*), which is now but a field away.

We have walked a blinking long way – surely that was more than a mile? – and we have it all to do again, to return to Devil's End.

I close the gate behind me with some reluctance. I feel like we're leaving Mother Earth back there at Four Barrows, to return to modernity, away from such earthly beauty.

The adrenaline passed, my ankles are now driving me nuts. I look down and discover a mass of red blotches and swollen veins, more grass rash than nettle stings, which does nothing to placate me.

I ask Dylan to take a photograph, and plan to caption it: 'The things we do for love'. (*Pic 15.10*)

As we walk back, I have a brainwave. There's a classic *Daemons* re-enactment that I had unforgivably omitted to consider: 'Jenkins, chap with wings! Five rounds rapid!'

The line, one of the Brigadier's, has gone down in *Who*-lore as a classic. He barks it to a UNIT soldier on spotting Bok – and it's just his phrasing. Not 'that gargoyle' but 'chap with wings'.

I tell Dylan of my plan. I'll be Jenkins, he can be Bok. And I show him how Bok moved: a sort of bow-legged stalk with tongue sticking out, leering. Most sinister.

"I can make my tongue really wide," says the boy, demonstrating.

"Bok's was much pointier," I say, though impressed.

He tries again.

"That's it!" I cry.

So we find ourselves once again in the graveyard of St Michael's, Aldbourne, out front. This is roughly, I'm hoping, where Bok sat down and reverted to stone once the Daemon had been defeated, after which the entire church was destroyed in a huge explosion.

Sinead takes the photograph over my shoulder, looking towards a quite magnificently played Bok, as I shoulder an imaginary rifle and fire off the first of my five rounds rapid (*pic 14.16*). I dearly hope that no one is watching.

And we're there. A job well enough done, I believe, that we deserve a trip to the Cloven Hoof... Sorry, the Blue Boar.

As we return, that well-heeled drinking party we'd sat beside previously are just heading off across the green, to a christening in the church, we overhear. I leave Sinead and Dylan sitting at a table outside and enter the pub to order. It's packed with punters.

Inside is a gorgeous oak-beamed space with fireplace. Strange beers in bottles have been lined up above the bar, as ornaments. One named Kripple Dick.

What do I recognise from 1971? Well... the interior was far simpler then, sparse frankly. The walls looked unpainted and adorned only by a few plates and some horse brasses. I could also have sworn that the bar itself was on the opposite side of the room. I'm disorientated. It's been a long four days.

A local lady comes in and tells those gathered at the bar that someone has parked an Astra right across her driveway. The subtle implication being, I suspect, that the 'someone' is from out of town.

I'm just glad it's not me.

Though the staff seem friendly, I'm definitely not going to ask, in front of this lot, whether I can nip up to the bedroom, check out where a recovering Jo Grant once lay. Neither will I pluck up the courage to take any photos.

I feel I've already filled my boots with memories of *Doctor Who* here in Aldbourne. I'm sated. And my eyes are starting to itch. Though it's hard to rub them vigorously with contact lenses in, I do my best. Bastard grasses. I can feel my eyelids reddening and my eyes becoming bloodshot as I order our drinks – we've decided against eating – and imagine I look a right state.

Leaving the drinks outside with Sinead and Dylan, I manage one last mission: I nip out back to the loo, to see what's there. And I find just one link to April 1971: a framed certificate on the wall, beside some countryside scenes.

'The Lords of Time Meet Here, Time Stream Permitting'.

Beaten to it again.

There's a fabulous story doing the internet rounds, courtesy of Aldbourne resident Marion Deuchars, who well remembered the filming. Fancied Pertwee in his dashing cloak.

A local girl, she recalled, had planned to get hitched in St Michael's and told this to her fiancé's father.

The father replied, said Dechaurs: "'You can't. It was blown up in *Doctor Who!*" He was convinced it had been destroyed.'

If there must be a suspicion of chinny-reckon in there, it's still far too excellent a tale not to pass on.

TRIP 16

(Final leg of the Mega-Trip)

Sunday, 29 June 2008

Pyramids of Mars

Stargrove Manor, Hampshire

We make our way back to the pond and I climb into the Micra while my suffering eyes weep uncontrollably.

"Are you sure you're OK to drive?" asks Sinead.

"Yes, I'm fine," I reply. I'm not quitting the driving seat now, not on the final leg of the Mega-Trip.

Our destination is fewer than ten miles away, as the crow flies – a car will have to negotiate windy country lanes – and relates to the story that came third in my *DILY* Top Ten *Who* Stories Ever. *Pyramids of Mars*. (No 'The…', and I like that.)

Boy, do I adore *Pyramids of Mars*.

Of course, Stargrove Manor did also appear in Tom Baker's later story, *Image of the Fendahl*, which I enjoyed but for me is totally overshadowed by its predecessor – so that's the one I shall focus on.

To cut a long story short: archaeologist Professor Marcus

Scarman disturbs the Osiran alien Sutekh (think Egyptian God with a head a bit like Skippy's) beneath an Egyptian pyramid. Sutekh, naturally, plans to bring his 'gift of death' to Earthlings. Scarman's home is The Old Priory or, as we know it, Stargrove Manor.

Why is the story so deeply alluring? It has the hand of Robert Holmes all over it, who heavily rewrote the original scripts, and that of producer Philip Hinchliffe, who understood his gothic horror.

But on-screen it's the monster: the Mummies. Towering, musty-bandaged creations with twin deep, sunken eye sockets that fill the face, a bizarre chest extrusion – a cheeky reference to 'Mummy' sounding feminine? – and a lumbering, sideways gait as they walked. Genuinely unsettling.

As with Athelhampton House in *The Seeds of Doom*, the action occurs inside and out – and I'm fairly sure those interiors actually are Stargrove's – with Mummies waddling dangerously after a succession of characters, including the Doctor, Sarah, Mr Bronson from *Grange Hill* playing Prof. Scarman's brother Laurence and, most memorably, a poacher.

Said pheasant-plucker gets offed in one of *Doctor Who*'s most original and startling death scenes: squashed between two Mummies, suffocated between those scary chests. That happens outside the Lodge, where Laurence lives and which is in the Stargrove grounds.

In *Pyramids of Mars*, those grounds are far less kempt that Athelhampton's were, and more wooded. There's a fallen tree where our heroes shelter from sight, in the hole gouged by the ripped-out roots, and what looks to be a sunken garden, where the Doctor and Sarah tend to a shot Dr Warlock. (Don't worry about him – he dies in episode two.)

But the scene I'm most eager to capture is the one where the Mummies stand guard before a pyramid erected in front of the manor house, a pyramid that happens to be an Osiran War

Missile. It looked so cool. A tableau of ancient Egyptian evil. Yes, that's the one that I want.

However, I am reminded of an early scene in the story. Prof. Scarman's Egyptian servant, Ibrahim Namin, complete with fez (in case we weren't convinced of his provenance), has been disturbed while playing ominous chords on the organ. It's the butler, Collins, announcing the arrival of an uninvited guest...

Collins: I'm sorry, sir, but the gentleman insisted.

Namin: *Gentleman? What gentleman?*

Collins: He's an old friend of Professor Scarman's, sir.

Namin: I ordered that no one was to be admitted, Collins! I told you: *no callers*!

And guess what?

Stargrove Manor isn't open to the public.

But I'd love to get in. For the book. I've been aware of this since I drew up the Fact Packs and I knew that it was going to be a severe test of my nerve.

I'd pictured the scene in my mind and I pictured it again repeatedly as I drove down those country lanes towards Hampshire. Me, standing at a pair of ostentatious gates, wringing my hands, announcing myself on an intercom, dribbling with fear. *How dare I disturb the aristocracy?* (No, really – how dare I disturb the aristocracy?)

As I drove, I rehearsed a little speech over and over in my head, which changed a little with each new attempt, while never sounding convincing.

It reminded me of a news story I read about one of Madonna's stalkers, who buzzed the intercom at the end of Madge's enormo-driveway and, when asked to identify himself, went, "Hi, honey – I'm home!"

That won't work here.

Didn't work for him, either, funnily enough.

Happily we get completely lost, delaying the Dreaded Moment.

According to Fact Pack 2, which even for Fact Pack 2 is woefully short of information, Stargrove Manor is in East End. But we can't find East End. We can find East Woodhay and West Woodhay and North End, then East Woodhay and West Woodhay again, then return to East Woodhay... and what's this sign up ahead? Oh, it's 'North End'. And there are roadsigns that point to East End but we keep going round in circles.

Frankly, I don't mind. I'd drive around here until we run out of petrol then scrape a living catching bugs in some woods while my hygiene becomes undesirable – anything to avoid having to announce myself on that inevitable intercom – but I have my family with me and they might not be so sold on urine-stained fashion.

It's terribly green and posh around here. We're distracted by at least two other vast country piles set back from the road – or possibly it's the same country pile twice – and eventually I spot a lady in her front garden, screech to a halt and reverse back towards her.

My window's nearest her, so I have to do the talking; but also, I realise, it will be good practise for the Dreaded Moment.

"Hello!" I call to her.

"Hello!" she calls back, perfectly jovial.

"I'm looking for Stargrove Manor?"

She knows of it. Well, even we can't be so lost that we're outside the antenna-range of a pile once owned by Mick Jagger. (Oh yes, Jagger once lived there – was the owner at the time of *Pyramids of Mars* filming. Stargrove Manor is where, some say, the alleged, infamous Marianne Faithfull Mars Bar incident occurred, though I'm pretty sure they're mistaken. That was another of his various country mansions.)

The gardening lady's directions involve half a dozen twists and turns, so I ask her to repeat them, just to be on the safe side.

As I thank her and wind the window back up, all but the first slip my mind. Well, not so much slip as career away in a convoy of juggernauts, leering out of their windows while eating chocolate. Porky gits.

"Can you remember any of that?" I ask Sinead desperately.

"I couldn't hear what she was saying," says Sinead.

So we drive round and round in circles again and eventually stumble upon East End.

Please, no.

There's a Y-shaped junction and a pair of wooden gates ahead of us. The gates look nowhere near as ostentatious as I had imagined, but the gravel driveway behind them, lined with huge, mature trees, does. There's a building behind them and to the right, set back a bit, which looks suspiciously like the Lodge where Mr Bronson lived.

However, there is no plaque, which I had expected. Nothing to say for certain that that is Stargrove Manor. I'm dearly hoping it isn't.

Just to check I take the right junction off the Y, where there are a series of buildings... And a sign... 'Stargrove Cottages'. My stomach turns over.

"Yes, that was it," I say. "That's Stargrove Manor."

So I park and walk with Dylan to the wooden gates. Sinead says she'll wait in the car, reticent for once, and I bet I bloody know why. What's in front of those gates, on a wooden stand?

An intercom.

I can't remember any of the rubbish speeches I have only recently concocted in my mind, but I do remember my single tactic: mention the *Radio Times* early on.

In all my journalistic dealings, noting that I'm from the *Radio Times* not only opens doors denied to more salacious publications, it also puts people at their ease. The *Radio Times* is a part of the BBC, sweetie. No upstanding hack from the *RT* ever stitched anyone up.

So it's going right at the top of my speech. "Hello, I normally write for the *Radio Times*, but…"

"Let's have a look at the Lodge," I suggest to Dylan.

Stalling tactic. Brilliant.

I peer over the wall, already feeling like an intruder, and take the first money-shot (*pic 16.1*) in these parts, realising that it may also be my last. The building's surroundings feel leafier than they looked in '75; there's ivy making its way up the front wall, but the white pillars of the porch are instantly recognisable.

The poacher ran out that way, and the Doctor and Sarah ran in, pursued by a Mummy.

So, yes, that's the Lodge, definitely.

Right.

The Dreaded Moment has arrived.

I wasn't sure whether Dylan would cotton on to how downright terrifying and daring this was going to be, but he has. I can see it in his eyes. I'd tried not to give my fear away, lest it travel and return to me ten-fold, then breed. But he has.

He's itching.

I eye the intercom. Lots of buttons in silver. One labelled 'Call'.

I could turn around now, get back into the Micra and speed back to London and no one need ever know. I could delete this chapter heading, pretend a trip to Stargrove Manor had never once crossed my mind.

But I can't.

This is the culmination of all the balls I've mustered so far on this Mega-Trip – Chrissy in Chislehurst Caves; the guide at Athelhampton House; the madness at Bulls Bridge; even the recent gardening lady – right here and now. I have to do it.

I press the buzzer. Dylan makes a snuffled giggling sound. I want to dig a big hole in the ground and live in it.

And there's this ringing, like a phone's. Which goes on and on and I pray it never stops.

And then it does.

"Hello?"

A male voice on the other end. Saying, "Hello?" With a question mark on the end. Requiring an answer.

"Hello," I say. "I normally write for the *Radio Times*, but..."

Google 'Stargrove Manor' and all you'll get back is a bunch of *Doctor Who* location mentions. It's another case of perpetuated misinformation. Try 'Stargroves' instead – as it should be known – and the story begins to unfold. (I've used all the common *Who*-locations monikers, correct or not, on my website, since those are the place-names I sought.)

The trouble with Stargroves, history-wise, is that it is so steeped in rock stars that the people who originally built it, when and why, fail to get a look in, as far as I have been able to make out. Celebrity trumps nobility these days.

Hilariously, I can find claim that the building was once the headquarters of Oliver Cromwell, presumably sometime around the the English Civil War (1642-1651), then nothing until it was bought by Mick Jagger in 1970, for around £30,000. Evidently, Mick, Keef, Christopher Gibbs, Anita Pallenberg, Robert Fraser and Terry Southern drove down to view the property, stopped off at a few pubs on the way and were pretty half-cut by the time they got there.

Who inhabited the place after Cromwell – those intervening 320-odd years – fuck knows. Mick, right? And Keef, yeah? When they got there – they was pissed! Off their tits, yeah! Legend!

"Oliver who? Wasn't 'e in The Grateful Dead?"

"Nah, mate. New Model Army."

The Stones recorded at Stargroves, as they would – songs destined for *Exile on Main Street, Sticky Fingers* and *It's Only Rock 'n' Roll* – as did visiting pals The Who and Led Zeppelin.

The mind boggles at the prospect of what went on behind those doors – although I do wonder how many rock star myths begin as tittersome exaggerations to journalists eager to believe.

I found a discussion board concerning Stargroves that contains this comment from one 'dodgy': 'i ACTUALLY VISITED sTARGROVES WHEN THE sTONES WERE THERE AND CAME ACROSS KEITH RICHARDS SAT ON A FENCE HAVING A VERY DEEP CONVERSATION WITH A HORSE.'

Hardly the likeliest of stories, is it?

Is it?

One dreads to imagine what Led Zep got up to, since their apocryphal story involves not a Mars Bar – how tame! – but a dead fish.

I can tell you at least who owned the pad after Mick.

Formula One's Williams boss, Frank Williams, who purchased the pile off Jagger when it was said to be on offer for £2 million – a tidy profit, as one would expect of the shrewd fellow – in 1993.

Williams moved on in 1998, selling Stargroves for a reported £2.5 million. To Rod Stewart. *The* Rod Stewart.

And there the trail goes cold.

(I tell you, I'm glad I did this research after the event, because if I'd thought I might be buzzing Rod Stewart's intercom, I'd have had to wear a nappy.)

"Hello," I say. "I normally write for the *Radio Times*, but now I'm writing a book about *Doctor Who* locations and

Stargrove Manor was used in *Pyramids of Mars* in 1975 and I wondered whether you'd be kind enough to let me have a look around at the places where they filmed for my book if you wouldn't mind." I stop just short of calling him 'Sir'.

"Where did you say you were from?"

So I repeat the whole thing again – *Radio Times* at the top – barely perceptibly slower.

There's a long, agonising pause.

Finally, the voice again: "I'll open the gates for you."

Fucking YES! We're in!

Dylan and I jump around while I go, "Yes, I did it!" until I wonder whether the intercom channel is still open and the gentleman at the end of the voice can hear us.

Then we wait. And nothing happens. No 'Bzzzzt!'. No opening gates.

Nothing.

And I wonder: have I blown it?

Sinead finally musters the courage to join us.

"What's happening?" she asks. Only blooming everything!

After what feels like eons, the gates still haven't opened. There's only one thing for it: I have to press 'Call' again. I've only been here a few minutes and already I feel like I'm pestering the bloke.

"Hello, erm, I just spoke to you and the gates haven't opened."

Pause.

Further pause.

"Hold on."

Silence. 'Bzzzzzzzzzt!'

And the wooden gates slowly being to part (*pic 16.2*).

Get in!

Now, I have to describe us, walking up this driveway that

stretches as far as the average Yellow Brick Road, multi-million-pound manor house way out of sight, lined by trees the height of giants.

I'm wearing my aforementioned 'Give pace a chance' t-shirt, an old green jacket that I've been sitting on in the car, some ancient three-quarter length shorts and skate shoes, though I fail to skate. My ankles have cleared up but my eyes are leaking pus. My head looks like an outsized canary died and fell on it.

Sinead is matching the latest line in three-quarter length tracksuit bottoms with a dark blue cardigan and black top. She is a bit pregnant.

And Dylan: knee-length shorts, t-shirt with some sort of writing and combat-style top in shades of grey. His hairdo, which he straightens every morning despite it already looking straight to me, is, he stresses, terribly fashionable. I wouldn't understand.

It's motley invasion force led by Worzel Gummidge.

You must forgive me if I recount this from memory because I'm hardly making notes as I go along. I am both on tenterhooks and crapping it. All three of us are inhabiting a carrier bag of tension.

I'm long past the spot where the poacher got sandwiched between Mummies, without having given it a second thought, instead simply taking in the magnificence of this estate and the length of its entrance. The verge to our right has been mown precisely parallel to the driveway, where signs dictate a 10mph speed limit. I'm taking this in while wondering whether I really should have brought the car.

It takes a good few minutes before we reach a bend in the drive and see a gentleman ahead of us, dwarfed by a lawn so lush it should appear in a novel about arrogant men in breeches and their simpering womenfolk.

"Why didn't you bring your car?" he asks, as I head across

the grass towards him.

"I didn't realise your driveway would be so long," I reply, pleased that it sounds both like the truth and a quip.

His accent is South African. He's wearing a salmon-pink shirt and jeans, and there's a pen in his chest pocket. He has white-ish hair, a beard and is of neat stature. He could easily dress up as Santa, given pillows.

Hardly surprisingly, he seems wary.

I'm wearing my sunglasses, however remember that old Army recruitment advert in which the British soldier's being hassled by the other guy – until he takes his sunglasses off, when the other guy calms down. Eye contact: it encourages people to trust you. At least the Army reckon it does.

So, as I reach the chap, I remove my sunglasses with one hand and extend the other in greeting.

He shakes. Warily.

In my peripheral vision, far right, I can see a bloody big house.

I don't remember what I said next, but I imagine I explained my mission yet again. I doubt he was thinking afterwards: oh, I get it now! Your barging in here with your ragamuffin family suddenly seems perfectly reasonable.

But I do remember then turning to look at Stargroves and going, "Nice place you have here."

Nice place you have here.

Actually it's incredible (*pic 16.4*). Watch *Pyramids of Mars* and there's a sense of it teetering towards dereliction. The walls were grey and greening, out of sorts. The windows looked tired. The whole thing felt unloved.

Yet this place – this place is immaculate. Fit for a king.

Crenellations and fairytale towers, pure-white window frames, bays and ivy. The colour: something lighter than latte with perhaps a hint of green. Picked, I imagine, from Dulux's

English Heritage range. Jigsaw-box material.

And guess what, I discovered just now, won 'Best repair/restoration of an historic building/structure' in the Basingstoke and Deane Design and Conversation Awards 2005?

The citation reads: 'For large scale repairs and restoration to a very high standard. Repairs to the external render were extensive and required a high level of craftsmanship and attention to detail to achieve the quality of finish that was accomplished.'

Yup. Stargroves.

"Would you mind showing me some of the places they filmed?" I ask.

I get the distinct impression that he might mind, and I can't say I blame him. I mean, who the fuck am I? And why have I bought a family with me? Do I actually even own a car? Maybe I'm just a chancing tramp and the woman and boy are there to put him off his guard, so I can clonk him over the head with a tin of Tennents Super wrapped in a wet sock, then nick stuff?

I feel incredibly uncomfortable. As, I imagine, does he.

However, fair play to him, he leads us to the right of the manor house, along the side, and points at a small gravel courtyard (*pic 16.5*), hedging on one side, red-brick buildings on the other two. Car, not posh. And, I've only just spotted in the photograph – a red telephone box!

This, he explains, is where they filmed the pyramid scene.

My Holy Grail scene! Yet, well, it doesn't feel remotely right. I'd imagined they filmed that slap-bang in front of the manor house. This is no bigger than a private swimming pool.

I'm not convinced.

Is our reluctant host just trying to get rid of us? Seems reasonable.

I'm trying to make conversation as I go, to put him at ease, but it doesn't seem to be working.

He tells me more than once during the course of our visit – about half a dozen times, actually – of how a BBC crew visited some years ago – eight, I think he said – to make a film about the locations used in, what he calls, "Planets of Mars". I don't correct him.

What he's trying to say, I deduce between the lines, is: "Please go away, watch the DVD and leave me alone."

I've started to feel bad for intruding on him, but I'm here now and I have to see it through. We're back on the front lawn.

"I wonder," I say, "whether you wouldn't mind showing me some of the other places they filmed, if that's alright?"

By now, yes, it seems that he would mind. I've basically asked for a tour of his estate, which has swerved past Cheeky and has entered the red-shaded Impudent zone.

They did film down by the old sunken garden, he says, but the previous owner built tennis courts over it, so there's no point going down there. And then he stops talking. There's no, "But I could take you to the fallen tree – that's still there!"

Well, we really must be going.

I ask Dylan to snap one final shot, of me standing before that gorgeous building (*pic 16.6*). You only have to look at my body language, arms wrapped tightly around me, hands clenched, rictus grin on face, to see how uncomfortable I felt. I'm aching for that shutter to close.

The bearded gentleman makes a point of escorting us back up the driveway, perhaps in case I double back and sleep in his pond, during which time I resort to asking how old the trees are.

Sinead helps out, wondering aloud whether he's had many *Doctor Who* fans here before us.

"No," he says, pointedly, and once again mentions that BBC

visit, which means absolutely nothing to me.

"Is the house open to the public?" I enquire.

"No, it isn't," he says.

Desperate to fill the painful silences, I promise to send him a copy of this book once it's finished. I won't, of course, not because I'm a bloody big liar but because he hardly wept tears of joy when I suggested it.

And finally we're back at the gate. No one is finding the parting sorrowful.

As I turn to shake his hand and thank him effusively, he cracks a smile for the first time. Mainly, he's pleased to see us go, I'd imagine, but also I think he'd finally started to believe my story.

It was quite a coup. And hugely nerve-wracking.

I'm just very grateful to the bloke and implore others, please, not to do the same. You really don't want to put him, or yourself, through that. Trust me.

Two mysteries remain.

Was he the owner? I'm writing this more than a month after that trip and my memory is hazy. Both Sinead and I recall getting the impression that he was. Something he said, presumably. Having now discovered that Rod Stewart bought Stargroves in '98, and finding no internet mention of him selling it, I'm no longer 100 per cent certain.

It doesn't really matter.

The more relevant mystery is: what's that bloody DVD he kept banging on about?

I found the answer to that a week or so ago.

I only own the thing, and didn't realise it.

Oh, Fact Pack 2.

Remember how my *Claws of Axos* DVD had a 'Now and Then' special feature, which provided a map of the precise filming locations? My *Pyramids of Mars* DVD has a 'Now and

Then' special feature, too. Subtitled: 'The Locations of *Pyramids of Mars*'.

Can't say I'd ever noticed it before.

I'm glad I hadn't, though, because watching that extensive tour of Stargroves' grounds, comparing current scenery with snapshots from the 1975 story, would have done my work for me. Made me redundant. It certainly would have removed any sense of adventure.

However, I can watch it now and find out exactly why our reluctant host pointed me towards that silly little courtyard and assured me that's where they filmed the pyramid scene...

First, some handy historical fact in voiceover, by the sadly departed Mr Bronson/Laurence Scarman, namely Michael Sheard, who died in 2005.

Stargroves was built in the 15th century, he tells us, and was probably named after the landowner, John Stargrove.

It was destroyed by a fire in 1840 and the rebuilt manor house was bought by one Frederick Carden, who commissioned the towers...

Hang on, let's try Googling Carden... Aha! Bingo!

From *A History of the County of Hampshire*, Volume 4 (1911):

'The property at STARGROVES, designated a manor in the 16th century, was probably represented by the land held by John Stargrove in 1428. John Edwardes is the first known holder of the manor as such, and he sold it in 1565 to Vincent Goddard, from whom, in 1570-1, it was acquired by Edward Goddard, who appears to have been a nephew. The latter died in 1615 seised of 'a manor or capital messuage in Eastwoodhaie,' leaving a son of the same name, who in 1616 obtained a lease of East Woodhay manor-house from the bishop.

Edward, son and heir of the last-named Edward, died in 1669, and was succeeded by his son William, who died in

1690; William's heir was his son Edward, who dealt with the manor by fine in 1692 and died in 1724. In 1755 Edward Goddard, possibly a son of the latter, was holding, and in 1782 William was the owner; another Edward Goddard held in 1814.

Mr. Richard Hull ultimately acquired the manor which he was holding in 1848. He sold the old manor-house and about 35 acres of land to Capt. George Graham Ramsay, who was living at Stargroves House in 1875, and who sold his portion to Lieut.Col. Sir Frederick Walter Carden, bart., in 1879, the latter acquiring the rest of the property in or about the year 1896 from the representative of Mr. Richard Hull. Sir F. W. Carden died in 1909, and was succeeded by his son Capt. Sir F. H. W. Carden, bart., the present lord of the manor.'

All that missing history! Involving all those military types and knights of the realm. Wonder what they'd have made of Mick 'n' Keef?

No mention of Cromwell there, which calls that previous claim into doubt – and I must say I was dubious, old wart-face himself appearing from nowhere.

Filling in that chunk of the puzzle has made me very happy. But what of our mysterious shrinking pyramid scene? It's here, on the DVD, 4.44 in. Take it away, Mr Bronson (all the italics are mine)…

'In between the stable block and the main house stands the *surprisingly small* courtyard in which the [Osiran] War Missile prop was situated. The use of *wide-angle lenses* made this location *appear much larger than it is in real life.*'

Gotcha.

So that's it. The Mega-Trip completed. It feels like weeks, not days, since Sinead and I stopped outside Chislehurst Caves. So much *Doctor Who* history. So many counties.

Kent, Dorset, Surrey, Greater London (is that a county?),

Oxfordshire, Wiltshire, Hampshire. And that's not including those we passed through. In four days!

How do I feel? Amazed that it actually happened. Grateful to have witnessed so much of this beautiful land. Awash with memories of the ghosts of *Who*. And utterly sodding knackered.

But my work isn't quite over. No book of *Who* locations would be complete without a trip into new *Doctor Who*. So, a trip to Wales, where so much of that triumphant revival is based.

I've already been in touch with my old flatmate from university days, Karl, who lives there and whom I haven't seen in – ooh – 20 years? (*DILY* readers may recall me being his best man and no one laughing at my speech.)

Karl's happy to chaperone me as we take in a few juicy locations, so the train's booked for Friday. The Cardiff department store overrun by the new Autons? The cemetery in *Blink*, anyone?

Just, please, let me grab some shut-eye first…

TRIP 17

Friday, 15 August 2008

Rose

Howells department store & Queens Arcade, Cardiff

Plenty happened on the home front between the end of the Mega-Trip and now. I've been writing this book solidly, for a start, and am grateful for the diversion of thoughts from the events of the spring.

Dylan's up in Scotland on his summer holidays, staying with his mother's relatives. He adores it up there with the beaches, his cousins and the dogs, untroubled by me driving him to nuclear research facilities.

Sinead's now in Cornwall with her folks, on the traditional week's visit. I'm so snowed under it's just me back here in London, alone, beavering away. A martyr to the cause.

I turned 43 last week and couldn't quite believe it. I used to be seven!

Sinead arranged a surprise party, my first ever, and indeed it was a complete shock. I remember walking into the pub, seeing my mate Mark first and thinking: what the hell are you doing here?

A fine rabble attended, karaoke had been arranged, and

Sinead and I finished off the night with our habitually magnificent – given beer-ears – rendition of The Pogues and Kirsty MacColl's *Fairytale of New York*. Yes, a Christmas song in August.

It's been a time when I needed all the friends I could get and, bless them, they're there. Always trust your friends. You can wallow in a DVD collection, but it won't buy you a drink and offer words of wisdom.

The wife, lest we forget, is now five months pregnant and visibly so. The major news is that she had her second scan a couple of weeks ago and we both saw for ourselves, on the monitor, what gender the baby is. That tiny person, kicking and wriggling, then staring intently at its toes. The 'Toomp-toomp-toomp' of its fragile heartbeat.

Remember how Sinead discovered she was expecting the night before my mother died and, on the drive to Kent on that horrible day, I was as good as convinced that it would be a girl?

Well, it is.

Amazing.

It is a girl.

I left the hospital, stood outside and phoned my Dad with the news.

"It's like Mum's carrying on," I said to him.

"It is," he said. "I'm over the world." (I assumed that, at the age of 91, the moon was a leap too far.)

It proved too much for both of us.

I said goodbye and put the phone down.

But happy.

By mid-December I'll have a daughter, a second child after a gap of 14 years. I never expected that. Then again, what can you expect? Ups and downs and Christmas on the 25th – that's about it.

And before Sinead births our little girl, I have to birth this book. I definitely wouldn't swap. No siree.

Just 14 days until my deadline, and I haven't finished *The Daredevil Book for Cats* either. Zoiks.

Anyone got some skates?

I've become used to the London-Cardiff trip since *Doctor Who* returned under Russell T Davies. Annual trips to the *Who* studios in Upper Boat, where the Tardis and *Torchwood* Hub sets permanently reside, to meet cast and crew, or to the BBC Wales studios for *Radio Times* photoshoots with interviews. I was in the city only last week, for a readthrough of *Torchwood* series three scripts, which is all terribly top-secret.

But I haven't properly explored the place, not since Spurs lost to Blackburn in the Carling Cup final of 2002 at the Millennium Stadium, after which we wandered the streets to find beer to ease our pain, yet succeeding only in prolonging it. We should have just given up and gone home.

Karl Thompson was one of my housemates during the university days in London. We were one-third of a group of six who met at an intercollegiate hall of residence in '85, when we shared its fifth floor, who then moved into a house together in Tottenham for the second year. Dart-holes in my Duran Duran poster and Bucket Man in the garden. (Bucket Man was a life-size creation, constructed from Kentucky Fried Chicken boxes and buckets, of which we were unnecessarily proud – *see button on page 17 of website.*)

Karl, me, Quinch, Funk, Bruce and Ralf. You had to be there. Consider yourself fortunate that you weren't. It's all in *Dalek I Loved You.*

And now we're meeting up again, Karl and I, for the first time since… I can't really remember when but it's a significant period. As I said, I was his best man, not that long after we graduated, so it seems reasonable that we would have stayed in touch. But you know how it is: one in Wales, the other in London, kids, diverging lives…

If you actually ponder on it, it can make you feel guilty, how you let a friendship slide. Until you think: hang on, they were hardly battering my door down! It just happens.

Luckily, Karl got in touch out of the blue, having chanced upon the *DILY* website, and most provident his timing turned out to be. Three months later, I could email him and write: 'By the way, I'm planning a trip to Wales for the new book. Any chance you could, erm, drive me around and put me up?'

'Of course,' he replied. 'No problem.'

And that's the thing with friendships that drift apart. Some of them never die, they just fade away, and can be revived at any time with a few simple words in the right place. I'm looking forward to our reunion.

Although I do have one memory…

No fault of Karl's, but I visited his family home in Bargoed, 45 minutes north-west of Cardiff, with Andy, who was once known as 'Funk' (see above), and we went to the local pub. Just Andy and I, since Karl is teetotal. We were happily drinking away, chatting between ourselves, when a young Welshman turns to us and wonders aloud why we don't piss off back to England. It's a rhetorical question, fortunately, so we don't have to go over the whole met-Karl-at-college-shared-digs-in-Tottenham tale, but it's hardly conducive to our enjoyment of the evening. We left shortly afterwards.

There are tossers like that the world over, of course, but still it disconcerted me and remained lodged up top. I certainly don't intend to go to that pub when I'm back in Bargoed.

I have already put together Fact Pack 3. Oh yes. Given that I'm spending not much more than 24 hours in Wales, I need to know exactly where I'm going and what to expect. So Fact

Pack 3 offers just slightly more depth than its predecessors.

The first task was to choose my locations. And the immediate quandary was: which ones in so short a space of time? The BBC Wales crew has batted about all over the country, from Llansanor Court (scene of Agatha Christie's garden party in *The Unicorn and the Wasp*) to Fitzalan High School (*School Reunion* interiors) to Nant-Fawr Road (where Donna lived) to Swansea Central Library *(Silence in the Library)* to Vaynor Quarry – indeed, a quarry – where the Doctor fought the Master in *Last of the Time Lords*... There are dozens of locations already, after only four series and three Christmas specials. So where to start?

Initially, I clicked all over www.doctorwholocations.net, thinking: oooh, that looks good! But then so does that! And that! And that!

Eventually I reverted to my previous system: go with my favourite stories. Which led immediately to *Blink*.

The cemetery where the Weeping Angel looks over Sally Sparrow as she visits her friend Kath's grave – St Woolos Cemetery in Newport. And of course the hugely ghostly house where Sally first meets the flatulence-inducing, pointy-toothed statues – Fields House, also in Newport.

Which left enough time to visit two more, I reckoned.

Freshest in my mind was *Journey's End*, the season four finale: that epic battle against Davros and the Daleks, requiring a host of returning companions. Those scenes on the beach where the Doctor bids a second farewell to Rose, bittersweet since she now has a Doctor of her own to molest, the blue-suited one, back in her parallel universe.

Ideal for my purposes, since I'm yet to add a beach to my itinerary – and Southerndown Beach, where they filmed, also played host to the first farewell, in *Doomsday* at the end of series two, as well as having a cameo backdrop in that season's Cyberman story, *The Age of Steel*. Nice.

Journey's End feels apt, too, since Wales is my own final stop.

One more? Well, it has to be. *Rose*, the very first, Christopher Eccleston in leather. The one that brought it all flooding back. Though necessarily flawed, since there was so much to explain to the new viewers of 2005, it also links perfectly with my own first trip from this book. In 1970, the Autons burst out of the window of Marks & Spencer, Ealing; thirty-five years later, updated Autons burst out of the windows of shops in Queens Arcade, Cardiff. I'll just have to work out which ones.

Let's start there, shall we?

The plan was to meet Karl at Cardiff station, after which we'd join his family and head for the Queens Arcade. Since I had to be on the ball, it meant viewing *Rose* on my own, prior to our meeting.

It's interesting, watching that very first episode again, not as a fan thinking: blimey, it actually is *Doctor Who*! Being simply too bowled over to take in the detail. But, with the benefit of hindsight, being more calculating and wondering: right, what were they trying to achieve?

Pace is the trick. The story hits the ground running and never lets up, bar a lengthy Rose/Doctor stroll during which they fill in loads of back-story.

The introduction of the Doctor is genius. You have Rose cornered by Autons, about to strike, when someone grabs her hand and shouts, "Run!" And they're off...

Eccleston's Doctor is so matter-of-factly great.

Doctor: What's your name, by the way?

Rose: Rose.

Doctor: Nice to meet you, Rose. Run for your life!

Since writing this book, I've become acutely aware of the physical scene settings, which is odd. I guess I now view programmes like a locations manager. And you spot things.

For instance: Rose leaves her flat in London, dallies with boyfriend Mickey in Trafalgar Square and goes to work in a department store – in Wales! That's Howells, 9-19 St Mary Street, Cardiff CF10 1TT.

All the Auton scenes, supposedly in London, are also set there. At the Queens Arcade. And the bit where plastic Mickey's head comes off and he marches through the restaurant with hands like chopping boards – also in Cardiff; the La Fosse restaurant to be precise, which is handily close to the arcade if you're carting cameras and lighting around.

I reckon you could drop a bag of flour from a hot-air balloon floating over the centre of Cardiff, and coat a good half-dozen prime new *Doctor Who* locations in white dust.

By the end of the episode, we're all set up. We're acquainted with Rose, her Mum, Jackie, and her fella, we understand the very real alien threat, and we know that the Doctor is the coolest, most able, unflustered, bouncy, hunky, funny/serious, exuberant, passionate, caring/sharing, goddamned time-travelling geezer in the whole wide universe.

Davies gives him some great lines, in light and dark.

Jackie [in dressing gown]: There's a strange man in my bedroom [meaning the Doctor]!

Doctor: Yes there is!

Jackie: Anything could happen!

Doctor: No it couldn't!

And later, from the bloke in the building society ads, playing Clive, a hobby-researcher following the Doctor's antics via the internet, this chilling description of our Time Lord...

Clive: He brings the storm in his wake and he has one constant companion. Death.

Sends shivers down the spine. And I'm going to stand in the spaces where *Rose* was created and where the Doctor was returned to life.

Hello – as if by Tardis – here I am! Cardiff.

It felt very strange leaving the station and spotting Karl up ahead, beyond the barriers, with his son, Jack. I couldn't help grinning. Not out of sheer joy – though of course I was happy to see him – but because my muscles made me do it. It was involuntary. A mixture, I suspect, of embarrassment, happiness and self-consciousness.

They had both changed physically since I last saw them. Jack, now 15, was about a foot tall when we met last (sometime around the mid-Nineties, Karl assured me; and being teetotal his memory is far superior to mine), and Karl himself has filled out a tad, for reasons of internal organ failure that I won't trouble you with here.

As it quickly turned out, he was otherwise still pretty much the same Karl I had met in 1985. A whirlwind of thoughts, opinions and ideas, and still hooked on Lucozade.

It took mere minutes to reach *Who* territory from Cardiff station. That simple.

There's the Halifax that appears in the scenes of devastation post-Autons… Over there, the entrance to La Fosse… The Queens Arcade facia, outside which Jackie phones Rose and tells her she's about to do a bit of shopping…

Karl says that knowing the area as well as he does inhibits his enjoyment of *Doctor Who* – "I walked along there only last Saturday" – and the over-familiarity with the urban mundane fails to tally with the alien-heavy on-screen action. Doesn't feel right.

It made me glad that I don't live near Cardiff.

I picked up an ultra-cheap digital camera – blame that for the occasionally blurred nature of my website handiwork – from Argos, and we met up with Karl's wife, Catherine, and his daughter, Kate, aged nine. Until a week ago, I hadn't even known he had a daughter!

Kate had dreamed the previous night, she told me proudly, that she had found a magic hat. And when she wore the magic hat, she could talk to nuts. Not lunatic people, but actual nuts. Peanuts and their ilk.

I wished I could dream stuff like that, I told her.

And with that, the tour began.

Queens Arcade and Howells are practically next to each other, so we start at the latter, since that is where the show saw fit to start.

Except we're at the wrong end of the store. The shop-front before me (*pic 17.1*) is a tired, outmoded affair, whose first floor alternates crappy 'fashion' posters with what looks like panels of sticky-back plastic – the handiwork of Anthea Turner, I don't doubt. Above that, the sort of windows that depressed people stare out of.

I can't quite believe the poster on the very corner, which depicts a young woman leaning against a van, being attacked at the ear by a bloke who comes across as some sort of sex pest. Hardly an enticing advertisement for his outfit.

Before me, shoppers mill around; there's one staring at me in the photograph, presumably wondering why I'm snapping such a tedious scene.

Nothing tedious about it. If only you knew.

I need to find the classier end of the store, the end that was 'blown up' in *Rose* by the bods at The Mill, who produce all of *Doctor Who*'s computer-based special effects. It wasn't their most effective explosion, but their techniques would improve in leaps and bounds as the show marched inexorably onwards.

We walk down Wharton Street, where I instantly recognise the windows: large, black-framed panes set in creamy stone (*pic 17.2*). Rose ran past those, in which scene I can't remember. But she was here, on this pavement.

There's another entrance to the store here and I become distracted. Forget the explosion for now – it's time to enter Ladieswear.

Rose worked in Ladieswear in 'Henrik's', as Howells was known in the story. I have a screen grab in Fact Pack 3, which shows her walking past a section labelled 'Versace' and 'D&G', beside three white featureless mannequins in trendy outfits.

But that was three years ago, when the episode was filmed, and fashions change with the wind. Trendy today, tawdry tomorrow. If those mannequins walked down the street now, their progress would be followed by catcalls and derision. The colour aquamarine is in tomorrow, I believe, between 11.16 and 18.42, and woe betide the sucker who imagines blue will do.

What I'm trying to say is: those mannequins will have moved on. Shop sets are dressed and redressed. I'm hoping to find the Versace section, at least, because garish clobber surely never goes out of fashion.

Howells is part of the House of Fraser chain, and like every department store its ground floor smells of old ladies. Perfume and make-up. Young female staff caked in flan, applying further flan to women who believe they have multiple flaws to hide. Expensive pongs. Powders, creams and unguents.

"Cleanse yourselves! Your natural odours are repellent, your face looks like a witch's face and if you do not moisturise this instant you will crumble away like King Tut!"

I worry about this sort of thing. It's not great for the self-confidence.

So we scoot through the ground floor and up the escalator to Ladieswear on One. I'm aware that none of us bar Catherine really fits in here, and I fear we shall chance upon the Lingerie sub-section, me with my camera and distressed expression that might be misread as a leer.

I want to get in and get out, so lead our little group on a whistlestop tour of the first floor, checking out the label names.

Planet... Ghost... Ariella... Tigi... Ralph Lauren... Karen Millen... Untold... Diesel – for kids! Who buys their toddlers designer gear? But no sign of Versace. Perhaps I'm wrong about the garish thing.

We reach the top of a short flight of stairs and are faced with bras and knickers, a tidal wave of the fuckers. I suddenly feel like Father Ted. But I have to get through to see what's on the other side.

"After you," says Karl, and I dive among the lace and frills, looking neither right nor left but staring resolutely ahead, keeping my camera wrapped tightly in my fist.

"I'm not a pervert, you know!"

And I'm through, trying not to breathe heavily, which might be misconstrued. On the other side: just more racks and mannequins and store assistants with breasts. As far as I can tell, we've covered the entire floor area now, having found everything and nothing familiar. Ladieswear is ladieswear the country over, but no Versace or D&G.

Karl suggests we try upstairs, which we do, to find only furniture. Kate lunges at some bubble wrap and starts popping it, grinning. I feel like joining her. Lose myself in the blisters. But no, I have a job to do.

Down again, in among the ladies' things.

"I think we should just take a photograph anywhere and get out of here," I tell the Thompsons, feeling like the head of a snake with an increasingly restless tail, dragging these good people at speed around and around a tiresome department store.

So that's what we do. I find any old rack and pretend to look through it (*pic 17.3*), trying to eke some humour from the situation, but feeling too disturbed to do so.

There's one final quest before we can leave Howells and

breathe again. The lift. Rose got into a lift. It's pictured in Fact Pack 3, sandy coloured walls and two fire extinguishers. Quite a swish lift...

However, the one we discover on the ground floor (*pic 17.4*) looks more like something from Grace Brothers, framed by walls verging on vermilion. Good. Wrong lift. Must have filmed that scene somewhere else. Somewhere many miles from here.

Go-go-go!

And we're gone.

Phew.

That was the store that Billie Piper's Rose worked in, which you could just about tell, department stores being much of a muchness, but the thrill factor was low. Never mind, there is plenty more to see...

Black and blue clouds trundle over the city but the threatened rains are yet to come. The Howells corner that exploded is easily found, at the other end of Wharton Street. The BBC director made the building look taller, somehow, perhaps by not shooting the lowest floor, though the design remains the same.

I cross the road to stand where Rose stood to gaze at the destruction, on the corner of Golate and St Mary Street, beside 101 St Mary Street, which is currently To Let.

Now that's more like it. A fine edifice with tall ionic columns – the only type I can recognise, so in luck there – framing its windows and a sense of art deco. Impressive. I can only imagine the grotty facia back up the road was part of an extension, when the store directors were blinded by an architect's alleged vision of the future.

It makes a great shot (*pic 17.5*), finding the same angle that *Who* used, and pressing the shutter button. Doodle some flames at the top of the picture and I'd have a low-rent 'Snap!'

Back up Wharton, left into Trinity and we're once again at the Queens Arcade. The pavements are in the process of being re-paved, cordons blocking access, and back along Trinity Street there's a vast exoskeleton of girders in place: site of some imminent commercial opportunity for Cardiff's shoppers. The city is undergoing regeneration.

Catherine and Kate have made their excuses, and I couldn't blame them. Which leaves we boys, of the gender unremittingly eager for *Who*-based childishness.

We pass the front of La Fosse, where plastic Mickey went haywire, and consider adding the interior to our schedule, but I'm wary. Someone at the door with a lectern.

"Hello, we don't want to eat, we just want some pop."

Nah. There's enough here of relevance without that.

Indeed, practically within a triangle formed by the St John the Baptist Church, the Owain Glyndwr pub and the Queens Arcade, is where, Karl assures me, lovely Bernard Cribbens stood at his newspaper stand, to look up at the stars in the series four finale.

He and Jack try to decide exactly where, debating camera angles and landmarks that appeared in shot. While they do so, I think how hemmed in by all the commercialism the church looks; I doubt the shoppers even notice it. It's as if the mall were begrudgingly built around it because someone with ethics bridled at knocking it down, although the church sells merely spiritual concepts.

Despite its stature, that ancient building with its tower and stones feels to this visitor, well, forlorn...

I need a little history.

Cardiff Castle, which you can't really miss, was built by the Normans around the late 11th century, after they had conquered Glamorgan. The work was believed to be instigated by William the Conqueror.

One of William's relatives, Robert Fitzhamon, founded the first parish church of Cardiff shortly before the year 1100, and dedicated it to the Blessed Virgin Mary.

That's how St Mary Street, where Howells now stands, got its name.

With the town growing in size, at the end of St Mary Street a chapel of ease was built, dedicated to St John the Baptist. That's our church outside the Queens Arcade, which witnessed Auton mayhem and Bernard Cribbens. Built sometime during the 12th century.

Where does Owain Glyndwr fit in? He was the last Prince of Wales to actually be Welsh – born around the mid-14th century. In 1400, with Wales in English hands, Glyndwr instigated the Welsh Revolt against Henry IV. His men sacked Cardiff, their own town, in 1404, taking Cardiff Castle and the church in their stride. (The revolt was eventually stifled, Glyndwr went into hiding and was never caught. The man is a national hero, though I'm not sure what he'd make of his boozer.)

All that remains of the original St John the Baptist Church is part of the south choir arcade; the rest was reconstructed post-Glyndwr, in the second half of the 15th century, when the nave and tower were added.

That's the tale of that building. It's wonderful and indeed incredible that it's still standing. It just feels a touch incongruous to me, stuck there.

But hey – Karl and Jack have finally decided where Bernard Cribbens and newsstand were (roughly), and a money-shot is in order (*pic 17.6*), facing the Owain Glyndwr. Moments later, like three Mr Benns, we're back outside the Queens Arcade.

First, a shot down the road, where in *Rose* a red double-decker burned and citizens wailed as the Autons struck, which I recognise primarily from that Halifax logo screwed into a wall (*pic 17.7*).

The establishment beyond that is Sneakers, a sports shop with a poster of a football player in each window. The lads are trying to look moody but with those poses look exactly like they're auditioning for Subbuteo.

Whatever happened to Subbuteo? I used to love that game... Well, I used to love collecting the different teams, and the throw-in and (giant-sized) corner specialists, the cups and the advertising hoardings. Never got the hang of the game. Bit rubbish, really. Did anyone else have Forfar Athletic?

It's that window above Sneakers that gives the game away. Think: arched window in *Play School*. A trio of Auton brides – Autons in bridal gowns – smashed their way out of windows beneath that, so I snap there (*pic 17.8*) then ask Karl and Jack to play the characters, add a bit of dynamism to these perpetual still-lifes.

Unfortunately the pavement's being dug up and steel fencing has been erected around it, in case some gormless shopper falls into a hole two inches deep, to cry upwards, "I'm down here! I'm down here!" like Jeff Goldblum in *The Fly*.

But we make do. Karl and son dance exactly like robots from 1984, oblivious to the shoppers walking towards them – you can just see a toe appearing, right of *pic 17.9*. And they make me wish I were less self-conscious, because that looked like fun.

Reverse a few paces and we're back at the entrance to Queens Arcade, where my mind receives instant flashback to Jackie, phoning her daughter from within its curving façade, those enveloping arms welcoming one in to spend.

I've seen far less attractive mall fascias: that serif lettering – 'QUEENS ARCADE', lacking an apostrophe – and its vast arched window has a pleasing design, though I'm not sure it's so lovely a setting that I'd want take luncheon beneath it, as some are doing (*pic 17.10*). And, now I come to think of it, those steps up to the first level, on either side, look familiar, too. I'd swear the Autons ran amok where those diners now trough.

My main goal inside... Well, there are two. First the escalators, which Jackie descended, followed shortly by a madness of Autons, because they have a pleasing symmetry and smoothness. Second, the very first window that an Auton is seen to appear from – there, I shall find my own symmetry with the M&S frontage of my first chapter. I'm not sure which shop it was, but there's a screen-shot in Fact Pack 3 so I remain buoyed by hope.

The moment we're inside and down a level, I think: hello! This entire floor-space provided a battleground in *Rose*, where panicked shoppers ducked and fled, as the plastic peril loosed off shots with blasts from weapons concealed behind their snap-down wrists. Now largely empty (*pic 17.11*). And to my left, The Entertainer! Vivid red sign, 'Specialist toy retailer', and bright gubbins to boggle-eye the kids in its windows (*pic 17.12*). Three short Auton children emerged from there.

Behind us, the escalators we recently descended are revealed, from this angle, to be far more thrilling and historic than I had realised. It's them! Now they look somehow futuristic, twin silver slides into a world of make-believe. Get in! Leaving Karl with the camera, I sprint up the up and descend static the down, trying to play the Auton (*pic 17.13*), but dancing more like a robot from 1928, long before robots had been perfected.

Which just leaves the first shop window, containing original Auton vandal. And it wasn't here. Nothing matches up. There were escalators behind the shot, but not these ones here.

Karl has an idea, and at the opposite end of the floor we're by a dinkier pair of escalators and... is this the corner? I don't know. We're standing outside the Post Office, which is hardly renowned for its mannequins… But that was *Doctor Who*, messing with the mind, and maybe the architecture has changed since 2005?

(I love these mental machinations that accompany the trips, trying to fit visual facts with televisual fiction.)

You know, this *is* it! This *is* where that very first Auton appeared. He'd have been behind the window at the left of the Post Office entrance. Money-shot time!

As I walk in, a female employee is rearranging leaflets, as employees tend to do when there isn't enough work to go around. And I stand there, wondering whether to brazen it out: to squeeze behind her leaflet board and pretend to be an Auton while she considers me to be a tit.

"You alright there?" she asks helpfully, spotting my confusion.

"Yes, don't mind me!" I chirp and delve into the scene; hang her opinion of me. Unfortunately, I'm still laughing as Karl takes the money-shot, while I half-heartedly ready one hand as if to smash the glass (*pic 17.14*). Real Autons don't laugh.

Returned outside with relief, Karl points to the ceiling where empty grooves (*pic 17.15*) are evidence that an entirely different shop-front once inhabited this area. The very same shop-front from *Rose*, for instance.

And I think to myself: Karl's better at this than I am; he pays more attention to the details.

Already I've packed in more locations than I could have imagined in such a minor area, but there are more waiting. We meet up again with Catherine and Kate and walk north towards the Thompsons' parked car – through Cathays Park. Which is stunning.

Manicured lawns and flowers that grow in packs, bounded either side by vast, austere buildings lavished with statuary and pomp. The National Museum Cardiff, City Hall, the Temple of Peace and Cardiff University... (Plenty of *Who* scenes among that lot, should you wish to investigate). Formal gardens. Utter tranquillity. (I've just checked Google Maps and there's a far larger park, Bute Park, just to the west, which runs alongside the River Taff.)

I'm so glad to have been shown around the city today. Previously I had explored only the centre, and had been as disappointed as I am in my own home city by the proliferation of soulless All Bar Ones. Yet I spotted Cardiff Castle at the far end of the street while viewing Howells, found a 12th century church in among the chains, and have ended up in an area of sculpted horticulture and dazzling architecture – all within crawling distance of each other, given a stiff set of kneepads.

The keen-eyed *Who* fan may have read twice that 'statuary' back there. Yes, they used some of these carved creations at the end of *Blink* – the one with the Weeping Angels which I shall be focusing on tomorrow – when writer Steven Moffat cheekily suggested to the nation's children that any and all real-life statues might feasibly haunt their nightmares.

There's one from *Blink* at the end of Cathays Park, within the Welsh National War Memorial (*pic 17.16*). Inside a circular colonnade, the winged messenger of victory, holding aloft a sword, raised high above three figures depicting each of the armed forces.

But it's impossible to think of *Doctor Who* when viewing the memorial. The inscription around the inside reads: 'Remember in peace those who in tumult of war, by sea, on land, in air, for us and for our victory endureth unto death.' I have to half-circumnavigate the colonnade to be able to read that, and end up beside a flower bed of massed, vibrant red, like blood.

Two young women are sitting on the steps, catching an intermittent sun.

Cutting out of the park onto King Edward VII Avenue, there's another statue used in *Blink*: a winged woman holding a branch (*pic 17.17*). (I'm sorry, I didn't read the inscription and that's the best I can do in description: 'winged woman holding branch'. Perhaps that was the Temple of Peace?) And we're in the car and away, towards Bargoed.

Yet *still* there's one last *Who* site on offer, even as we drive along the M4 – up among the green-shrouded hills to our right, a fairytale concoction, Germanic overtones, with spires but no lengthy-haired princess (pic 17.18). Castell Coch, the folly built in the 1870s for the 3rd Marquess of Bute, which served as UNIT's German HQ in *Journey's End*, concluding series four. Martha walked among those hills.

But for today, I am sated.

…Almost.

I just couldn't resist it.

After a suitably large dinner, and not desperate to go to the pub for once, I ask Karl whether he fancies a walk.

"Let's drive up to where they filmed *The Green Death*," he suggests.

Fourteen Dachshunds raced in through the door and began tugging at the flares on my unfashionable jeans, a crane-grab dropped from the ceiling, clamping itself to my head. And a vision of Billie Piper appeared, beckoning suggestively with an index finger.

Still I made it to the car.

The Green Death, 1973, Jon Pertwee: The One With The Giant Maggots. If you were alive then, aged between four and 40, you know it. If you weren't, just think about it: *Giant Maggots*. Gross x 1,000,000 = Brilliant.

It was set at a colliery in Wales, a working colliery. Ogilvie Colliery in Deri. Karl's dad used to work there. He's mentioned the filming many times before, how the local kids were so excited that – Welsh accent – "*Doctor Who*" had come to visit.

Two years after *Who* filmed there, the colliery closed for good and Karl's dad had to move to a different set of mines, further away, to stay in work. In turn, those too closed, as would all the collieries in Wales.

So Ogilvie is long gone. But I wonder what's in its place?

Karl drives through the late evening as we're occasionally lashed by rain. Through Aberbargoed and up into the hills where resting sheep casually line the sides of the road. Off onto a side road and over speed-bumps towards Parc Cwn Darran, or Darran Country Park.

So that's what became of Ogilvie Colliery and the setting for *The Green Death*: a country park. Just one testament to the men who worked in those conditions remains, which we pass beside that narrow roadway into the park: a pit wheel, buried halfway into the ground, which once formed part of the winding gear that hauled the lifts up and down. An ominous, black spoked semi-circle, perhaps 12 feet in diameter, maybe more, sitting there, like a gravestone or a memorial.

While dusk descends with fervour we drive past it to catch the last of the light in the park, determined to stop on the way back.

And I'm blown away, even in the half-light. Actually, *especially* in the half-light.

We're in a bowl, valley walls seem to surround us, blanketed in trees. Green everywhere. No sign of human habitation to our right, where it is particularly dark, teeming, I imagine, with wildlife, shapes moving, unseen; to our left, street lights and the odd car headlight shift electric shapes through branches.

Before us, a lake. Moonlight plays in the ripples as all around stillness pervades. It's captivating. Unexpected. Just beautiful.

I take a moment to breathe it all in. Gaze up and around, listen to rustlings whipped around on the breeze.

The Green Death might as well have been filmed on the moon, so far from those scenes is this vision here.

Karl suggests we walk around the lake and we do so, passing wooden stations around the waterside, from which people can fish – indeed I yearned – hearing the 'splosh' and 'ffflllllsssssssshh' of a bird landing on the lake's surface. We reminisce about *Who* and our student days and, when we reach the far side, my friend begins talking about the demise of the mining industry and how it crippled these valleys.

Typically I don't remember the details, but I did gain a fractional understanding of what went on. The poverty that ensued, the loss of pride and livelihood.

We stop back at the pit wheel on the way out and, with Karl aiming his headlights onto that black-painted monster, I try to capture its essence on camera, amid a darkness like soup (*page 17a*).

I'm afraid I failed.

TRIP 18

Saturday, 16 August 2008

Doomsday/Journey's End

Southerndown Beach, Bridgend

It's the final day of my *Who Goes There* location trips, the end of a personal era, but I'm too excited to dwell on that. Today: a beach, a house that looks haunted even outside of *Doctor Who*, and a cemetery. That little itinerary pretty much sums up the appeal of this round-Britain conceit I've adopted.

How often would you wake up of a morning and announce, "Right, kids/the wife/partner/friends/me – I have a plan, and it involves a cemetery…"

There's just one potential downer. The weather. Television's meteorologists had promised imminent storms, which failed largely to materialise yesterday, but which have arrived this morning with a grim determination. It's tipping down, the reservoir a firmament in grey. I failed even to come prepared, my only jacket a flimsy cotton thing in childish red.

Still, nothing will quell my enthusiasm. Not today.

Today we're off to the beach!

Southerdown's sands rolled out the carpet for two of new

Doctor Who's most poignant scenes, each quite similar.

Doomsday ended series two, after a battle against the Daleks and the Cybermen, who also battled each other, such is the way of megalomania coupled with vacant emotions. *Journey's End* concluded the latest series, also following a Dalek war, aided by the returning Davros.

The fate of all human life on Earth is up for grabs in both stories, with the Doctor and his companions the only hope.

For those yet to witness the events, it's not giving anything away to state that both times David Tennant's Doctor triumphed. He has to – otherwise how would his young fans sleep in their beds, knowing that their hero is fatally fallible and that evil warrants victory? However, there were prices to pay.

At the end of both *Doomsday* and *Journey's End*, you have, essentially, the Tardis, the Doctor and Rose – there were other characters, even another Doctor in one case, though mere sideshows to the central event – on Southerndown beach, he and she saying their farewells. After all those death-defying adventures together. All that affection bubbling beneath.

That Tennant and Piper were going to miss each other as a consequence, after months of umpteen-hour days, night shoots and bonding, I suspect only tugged a further heartstring.

And by what name was the beach known in *Doctor Who*? It became a bay in Norway. A bay in Norway known as Bad Wolf Bay.

So we're not only off to the beach. We're off to Bad Wolf Bay.

And so we speed through the driving rain, wipers on stun, along the A473, skirt Bridgend, and find the B4524, which follows the River Ogmore towards the coast road and Ogmore-by-Sea. Dry-stone walls, fields and sheep at the roadside. And grey. Grey, grey, everywhere, plenty of it drinkable.

Annoyingly, across the Bristol Channel bright rays of

sunshine, like something from *Teletubbies*, coat the Devon coast in a kind of gold. Though it looks terribly inviting, I have failed to pack the microlite.

Anyway, weather isn't everything. I'm perversely looking forward to visiting a beach in the rain. Adds to the Britishness. Plus, it means we're unlikely to be troubled by other people – and there is little worse than other people on a beach, despite the general size of the available lounging areas. All those white bellies and youths snogging.

Karl follows a sign to the Beach/Traeth (in Welsh), then swings towards Dunraven Bay, which I imagine must be our Bad Wolf. He parks in a small car park overlooking the bay and a young man comes across to collect payment. Three quid! I feel like telling him to stick it up his arse and fuck off while he's doing it – that's a *Withnail* quote; I don't really mean it – but instead count out the three chunkies, smile and say, "Thanks". I'm so terribly compliant.

There's a funny little ruined fort on the grassy hill to our left and six other vehicles in the car park. What they're doing here, fuck knows. An information board states:

Sea: rough
Visibilty: poor

This reminds me of the sign featuring the car falling into the canal back at Bulls Bridge. Thanks heavens for statements of the bleeding obvious.

Another sign notes 'Danger – falling rocks' and yet another exhorts visitors: 'Do not attempt to climb the cliff face'. They have no worries with me on that score. I'd be likelier to climb the charts with a cover version of The Osmonds' *Crazy Horses* played on the kazoo.

There's a yellow and red flag flying, which I assume means no bathing – gutted – yet a bloke wearing a tabard-style towel, very fetching, is wandering around carrying a surfboard. God, I hate surfers. Always staring at the sun and shagging. This one at least doesn't have any hair.

Windborne drizzle spatters my face as I leave the car and make the start of the beach. The surface is covered in rounded oval rocks, some pebble-sized, mostly nearer cricket balls, and, as I stumble further, up to baby-seal-sized. Slippery when wet, they're a bugger to walk on and I wave my arms around to keep balance, like a demented traffic director.

Over to the left, I'm starting to see cliff walls, multiple strata in the brown rock-face, like a cream slice in stone, with slabs at their feet that must have broken away so very many years ago (*pic 18.1*).

An arresting sight.

When I'm down far enough, the magnificence of these cliffs becomes properly apparent. Vertical row upon vertical row, fiercely distinct layers, each one representing millions of years, I'd guess, and shades at this range: sandy colour, darker browns, strange splodges of white (*pic 18.2*). It's like nothing I've seen before. The Earth's formation, writ large in rock.

And this is where another *Doctor Who* story comes in. *Doomsday* was the second episode of a two-parter, its predecessor being *The Age of Steel*.

There's a brief scene at the beginning of that which finds Rose on this same beach, with the camera's back to the sea, framing her face against these strata. Very striking it was, too.

So that's a money-shot, right there: myself against the same backdrop. I climb onto a chunk of rock the size of a reasonable podium, using minute barnacles clustered on its surface as grip. And Karl snaps (*pic 18.3*).

Back off the podium, down at my feet, the surface is just weird. It looks like large cobbles. Large, irregularly sized cobbles that might form a particularly old road. Yet these are natural. Amazing. Tiny pools have formed in the larger gaps and seaweed grows between others, as moss might do on a wall.

I have to find out what was going on there, because it bewildered me at the time…

Google 'Dunraven Bay' and you're returned an awful lot of photographic sites, several focusing on sunsets. Hardly surprising for such a gorgeous place. But it means the hunt for facts takes patience – and some high-level geological know-how to translate.

For instance, on the subject of those 'cobbles', all I could find was this, and I'm not entirely sure what it means. It's extracted from the *Journal of the Geological Society*, July 2006, from an article by Huw T Shepherd.

Take it away, Huw: 'Limestone, swept from a foreshore pebble terrace at the base of these northward cliffs by storm events, were deposited among the shelly skeletal material of the shoreface, producing a matrix-supported lithoclastic conglomerate.'

Ahem. Is that my 'cobbles'? Is, as I suspect, 'shelly skeletal material of the shoreface' better known as 'sand'? Academics are wonderful. I'd love to know everything they know about just one specific subject area, but my head would probably fall off.

As far as I can tell, then, my 'cobbles' may be limestone that broke off the cliffs, became trapped in the sand and… er, that's it. (Yes, I can hear you sighing, Huw.)

He does go on – for many pages, actually, in his article *Sequence architecture of ancient rocky shorelines and their response to sea-level change: an Early Jurassic example from South Wales, UK*. For instance: 'However, the retrogradational snicking of the breccias and shelly limestone facics at Pant-y-Slade is in marked contrast to the progradational contact between the overlying conglomerate and calcarenite facics…'

My spellcheck just went mental!

There's also a snippet from *Geology Today*, by... hang on, it's Huw again! The ubiquitous bugger! (And *Geology Today* spell his surname 'Sheppard'. So someone must be wrong.) Anyway, that article, of which only the abstract was available, notes that these 'rockshore deposits' – is that the 'cobbles' again? – from the very early Jurassic period – that's around 200 million years ago, when ichthyosaurs and plesiosaurs swam – are among the planet's rarest sedimentary rocks. Fewer than 200 examples exist. Incredible.

If only I could be sure what precisely the 'rockshore deposits' are.

So I rather prefer this summation of the geology from a tourist website: 'The village of Southerndown is set back from the dramatic dry-stone cliffs surrounding Dunraven Bay, these are mostly formed by alternate layers of limestone and shale, which give the cliffs their unusually regular pattern.'

I understand that! Yay!

All fascinating stuff, but there's more. A ghost, shipwrecks, 'The Legend of Southerndown', a prophet of doom and a severed hand! Which I shall come to later... (Sorry.)

Back on the beach, I spot a cluster of huge chunks of cliff material that had broken away, sitting at haphazard angles, and recognise it from a *Who* scene. Featuring Rose again, I suspect, from *The Age of Steel*. I would blame Fact Pack 3 but I – cough – left it back at Karl's.

Undeterred, I take a photo for posterity (*pic 18.5*).

The view ahead, across the sea, takes my breath away (*pic 18.6*). This vista of angry, rolling clouds, like smog over Beijing, sea and breakers, the sky reflected in shallow surface water abandoned by the receding tide, rippling in the wind, while a band of gold pauses above the horizon.

I am *so* glad, that of all the locations I could have chosen from new *Doctor Who*, I chose this one.

Oh alright, I'll come clean. I'd planned to visit a different beach, Whitmore Bay on Barry Island, from *Last of the Time Lords*. It was Karl who suggested this might be better. He must surely be right.

I take shots of both edges of Bad Wolf Bay (*pics 18.7 and 18.8*) while getting my bearings, hoping to estimate where the Tardis and Doctor stood in *Journey's End*. Though it doesn't help that I've forgotten my reference material, I can just about recall the settings.

As pure luck would have it, I reckon the tide's out about as far as it was when the *Who* crew rolled cameras. The Tardis had landed in sand and was filmed with the left edge of the bay behind it, about where Karl is modelling in the photo (*pic 18.9*).

I get to play the Doctor, naturally, and he faced Rose perhaps 20 feet from the Tardis, with those scenes filmed mostly against the right edge of the bay. About where I'm standing in the photo (*pic 18.10*) – pulling my flimsy jacket around me in a vain attempt to block out the wind and incessant drizzle.

So they were here before us, the Doctor and Rose. Standing on this same beach, if not precisely on these same grains of sand.

It's a vastly atmospheric space. I wouldn't quite say oppressive, but I do feel comprehensively dwarfed by nature here. It's just Karl and I on this stretch of sand, the sea one way, those crazily paved cliffs the other, and above us, endless sky. It suddenly feels lonely here, just us in the universe. Moving.

I understand precisely why *Doctor Who* came to call.

We walk back towards the car and Karl points out how odd it is that these giant pebbles, battleship grey in colour, are like nothing in the geology around us. So where did they come from? Curse you, Dunraven Bay, you geological question mark (for those of us with a C in O-level Geology).

There are fossils easily spotted among the rocks and I snap a fan-shape etched in stone (*pic 18.11*), wondering whether it was once a fern, umpteen millions of years ago.

I used to love fossil-hunting as a youth, though I rarely found any. That and butterfly collecting, making Airfix models, reading, listening to Pink Floyd and watching *Doctor Who*. Such an innocent, introverted existence, stamped with the mark of the Seventies.

It's odd that, given my model-making endeavours, I could have told you so much about the Messerschmitt ME109E or the de Havilland Mosquito – made of plywood! – so long after the war, me being just a child and all. Kids these days would have looked at me funny and perhaps hit me.

Rather than zip away, since it's not yet even noon, we go exploring up in the hills. First, a strenuous climb up the steep grassy bank towards the top of the cliffs. When the sky becomes too close I develop vertigo and hand Karl the camera, so he can take a photograph looking down onto Bad Wolf Bay (*pic 18.12*). It shows clearly the effects of cliff erosion, and the sands, now a mirror formed of shallow brine, where the *Who* cast and crew set up just six months previously.

Funny to think that you could have sat up here and watched them.

Behind us is that little ruined fort we spotted when we parked, so we tumble down to that. Though it feels aged, with its fortifications and thick walls, red brick among the mortar suggests that looks may be deceiving. Only hints of magnificence remain, and the clearly once ostentatious, long-abandoned dwelling proves yet another mystery thrown up by this bay.

This, it transpires, is where the legend kicks in, with its ghost and its severed hand...

I've been trying to piece this together. The tale turns out to be a complex one, tarnished by retellings and the passing of centuries, but this is how I see it:

What Karl and I are looking at is, I believe, one of the unnecessarily grand houses that formed part of the Dunraven estate. Had we continued to follow the clifftops towards their apex, we should have come upon the few remains of Dunraven Castle, built on the site of an Iron Age hillfort that dated back to around 500BC. Vikings once settled in these parts and the Saxons are said to have burnt Dunraven's fort to the ground in 1050.

Enter our old friends the Normans, who assumed control of the region, and inevitably Owain Glyndwr, perpetual thorn in their side, who destroyed everything they built.

By the 1540s, that Iron Age site was occupied by a building known as Manor Place, owned by one Walter Vaughan, whom legend has down as a very naughty boy.

Vaughan, it is said, planned to start a sea-rescue venture, having lost three of his children to the waves. His well-intentioned idea brushed aside by the powers that be, Vaughan got the hump and turned instead to piracy. Legend suggests that he tied lanterns to the tails of his sheep at night, as they grazed the clifftops, thus luring passing vessels to their destruction in the bay. There, he and the infamous pirate Mat of the Iron Hand (being a hook) would plunder the beached treasures.

One fateful night, however, Vaughan (or possibly one of his gang leaders – it's hard to separate out the solid fact from salty tales hundreds of years old) spotted on the severed hand of a lost mariner, washed ashore, a ring he recognised as that of his only surviving son, who had been returning home from a mission by sea. Oh terrible fate. (Allegedly.)

Broken by the tragedy, the Vaughans sold up to the Wyndham family, successive generations of whom tarted the place up, until the ultra-grand castellated mansion of 1803 became known as Dunraven Castle.

During the Great War, this cod-castle was used as the Glamorgan Red Cross County Hospital, and during the Second World War – when Ivor Novello paid a visit – it became the Dunraven Convalescence Hospital, each time treating wounded soldiers.

During those wartime nights, several staff reported seeing a ghostly presence who left behind an aroma of perfume, reminiscent of the yellow mimosa flower. She became known locally as the Blue Lady.

You may also hear tell in Dunraven of the Cyhireath, whose hideous moans prophesied doom out at sea, though the noises are dismissed by less excitable types as being simply the crashing of the waves.

Dunraven Castle fell into disrepair and was pulled down in 1963, having been used for some time as a guesthouse. Evidently, you can still see the walled gardens up there.

And you thought *Doctor Who* was out there.

TRIP 19

Saturday, 16 August 2008

Blink

Fields House, Newport

Blink. Fabulous, terrifying *Blink*. New *Doctor Who*'s zenith according to the polls, and I would concur, yet it barely featured the Gallifreyan maestro himself. Which is some going.

Steven Moffat, the writer, had already penned two-parter *The Empty Child* and *The Doctor Dances* (a gas mask growing out of Victor Meldrew's face and a small, scary boy asking, "Are you my Mummy?"), and later *The Girl in the Fireplace* (robots under beds). *Blink* was his series three shot at petrifying the kids, and it worked like a doozy. Even I jumped. (Several times.)

I watched it again in the company of the Thompsons, on the Friday evening before Trip 19. Kate, nine, viewed the entire thing with a cushion armed and ready on her lap, which she hid behind when the going got tense, occasionally yelping; just as I used to do at her age, back in – erk – 1974.

The BBC website hosts a Fear Forecast page charting the reactions of a panel of youngsters to each *Doctor Who* episode. Amy, aged six, Harry, aged eight, and Samuel and

Adam, ten and 14.

The minute-by-minute analysis of their movements includes Samuel, in the very first minute, asking, "Can I swap and sit next to Dad?", all four jumping out of their seats, Harry covering his face and Samuel grabbing his father in minute 33, and Harry and Amy having to watch through a crack in the door two minutes later.

Using the Fear Factor Scale, which runs thus:

1. Mildly Scary
2. Quite Scary
3. Very Scary
4. Chilling
5. Terrifying

the children mark the episode. Samuel and Adam give *Blink* 5; Harry and Amy both go off the scale with 6 apiece.

Any old git who claims *Doctor Who* ain't what it used to be should really think again.

Blink's opening scenes alone verge on genius. Sally Sparrow breaks into an abandoned mansion to take photographs and begins peeling off wallpaper, beneath which someone has scrawled a warning – addressed to her specifically, mind – to beware the Weeping Angels. And to duck.

'Duck now!' As she does so, a rock whistles over her head to crack against the far wall. Yet out in the garden, from whence the missile came, is only a stone statue of an angel, covering her eyes with her hands.

How the hell, you think, can Sally Sparrow be reading a warning to herself, written umpteen years in the past and papered over probably before she was even born? All is revealed at the end, of course, when you can only marvel at how effortlessly Moffat plays with timelines without ever making your brain hurt.

That abandoned mansion, known in the story as Wester Drumlins, is in real life Fields House, a fucked place extensively featured in the television action. Detritus on every floorboard, walls holed and rotting, footsteps echo; a conservatory outside like a greenhouse sacrificed to the seasons, with distinctive patterned tiles on its floor. From the outside it becomes a towering vision of eaves, Dutch gables, brick and so many windows. Blue-framed windows, with drainpipes to match, through which actual Weeping Angels did look.

It's as if the architect constructed his nightmares in brick and mortar. As Larry, Sally Sparrow's fellow detective on the trail of this Doctor fellow, notes, the place looks like something out of *Scooby-Doo*.

Though I grew up with classic *Doctor Who*, so that era remains at the centre of my affections, I'm particularly excited about finding Fields House. Partly because of *Blink* itself, but also because it has such character. Such eerie character.

The show, both classic and new, has visited all manner of manor houses, resplendent and posh – Athelhampton House and Stargrove Manor among them – but I'm no fan of country piles. Plebs queuing to peek at a cost, rare blooms in the garden and the whiff of tie-and-jumpered nobility desperately trying to pay the gas bills.

Fields House, while offering roofs to the undoubtedly rich, doesn't look grand enough to have been inhabited by ladies with a capital L. More by someone with a slightly macabre sense of humour, I'd guess.

Elegant in its prime, in delapidation it is simply a wonderful location.

As to its possible origins, Karl makes an intriguing point as he drives us up, up and away from Newport city centre, climbing the side of a valley towards parkland and residential niceties where the houses grow in stature.

"All the people who worked in the docks lived down there," he says, motioning back towards urbanity and the River Usk. "All the people who ran the docks lived up here."

Newport, once a modest fishing port, made its name during the Industrial Revolution, when coal and iron from the South Wales valleys was brought in by canal and shipped out from docks there, which opened in 1842 and only expanded. Until the mines and steelworks closed, of course, and by the late 1970s the dockyards – and their dockers – had become redundant.

Lately however, Karl explains, Wales has been rebuilding. The miners and dockworkers have been replaced by IT workers and others in the financial sector. The money is returning, and with it the pride.

Perhaps the gentleman who built Fields House indeed once commanded some high office in the Newport Docks, wearing a hat and chomping on cigar?

I can tell you that Fields Park Road, of which Fields House is number 18, was opened in 1897 and, via the archive news reports held at the touchingly devoted www.newportpast.com, I can paint a vivid and curious picture of the later years of the 19th century.

For instance, that same year, 1897, Queen Victoria celebrated her Diamond Jubilee. Nationwide celebrations were held on 22 June, which was declared a public holiday. A military parade on the Newport marshes was followed by the United School Concert and Fire Brigade display, and bonfires were lit on the mountains around the city.

Victoria being an English queen, it's reasonable to assume that not everyone was leaping for joy, and whoever sums up each event on the website has written, wonderfully witheringly,

'Queen Victoria's Diamond Jubilee – muted celebrations in Newport.'

On the same day, the *South Wales Argus* reported that William Thomas had been collared by PC Rawlings, having been 'imposing on people' after drinking much brandy. The report continues: 'Defendant pleaded he was subject to fits. The Superintendent said he had not had any fits while in the cells. Certain people who had been watching the prisoner in the course of the afternoon said he always seemed to have a fit when near a public house.'

These are just a few of the my favourite highlights from the 1850-1900 section of Newport Past:

1854: Teetotalism campaign at Newport

1859: Mary Allart's Mysterious Telescope deception.

1864: Pressure to save 'Fallen Women' from final ruin.

1890: The fighting policemen of Newport.

1899: Organ grinders annoy the Mayor.

Within that same period, of a more practical bent, the South Wales Railway opened, the Royal Navy and Army recruited men to fight the Crimean War, soup kitchens were opened for the poor, and Newport saw its first drainage system, regatta, polo match, tramcar, electric lighting, telephone exchange, cab rides, and cheese, hide, fat, skin and wool markets.

It's alright, I know you're dying to know what 'Mary Allart's Mysterious Telescope deception' involved. I certainly am. Hold on…

The lady, who termed herself Madame having allegedly hailed from Paris, claimed to be in possession of a Mysterious Telescope, through which punters could witness a vision of their future partner.

Though I generally assume the Victorians to be suckers for that kind of supernatural tosh, the Magistrates were having none of it. Allart was hauled before them after being found 'drunk and incapable' in Commercial Street, and it was reported they: '...cautioned her that the continued practice of such deception would render her liable to three months imprisonment, and that they would certainly convict her as a vagabond.'

Into all that drunkenness and bewildering upheaval, courtesy of the Industrial Revolution, came Fields House, sited high up in the Newport hills quite purposefully, one imagines, to look down upon everyone else.

We find it fairly easily while driving around Fields Park Avenue, having spotting its roofs rising above treetops. Well, it's so darned recognisable (*pic 19.1*).

I'm already aware that it's going to be boarded up and therefore supposedly inaccessible. According to www.doctorwholocations.net, the place was abandoned many years ago, then some bright spark proposed turning it into flats in 2005.

I can find no confirmation of that, but I did come across a *Buildings at Risk Register* dated January 2004, which placed Fields House at category 3C, 3 meaning 'At risk' (2 being 'Grave risk' and 1 'Extreme'), and C meaning 'Slow decay'. Which is rather sad.

We have, I suspect, stumbled upon the rear entrance. The main drive, via which Sally Sparrow stole in, didn't look anything like this. Here, the building is but ten yards from the road. She had a noticeable walk.

There's a large wrought-iron double-gate here, supported by thick pillars either side, with bushy, overgrown hedges and trees in the garden and lining the boundary of the garden. The window frames on this side of the house are a sort of yellow ochre, and the drainpipes russet red. But it's definitely the right building. Architecture with a hint of mental institution and a smidgeon of Holland.

Had *Blink* been part of classic *Who*, filmed 30 years ago, this same site might well be hosting a glass-and-concrete high-rise by now, all traces of the original location long since annihilated and now buried. But it's not, that's one beauty of the new *Who* – and I've caught it in time.

We leave the car to investigate.

Opposite is part of the University of Wales, Newport, and I can't imagine its students are unaware of the televisual provenance of this place, right on their doorstep. I bet a few of them have nipped into those grounds for a quick peek, wishing they might chance upon Sally Sparrow. I intend to do the same. I'm just wondering how tricky it will be.

The main gates are locked shut, unsurprisingly, so I pose for a quick photo (*pic 19.2*) before taking my nose for a weak point elsewhere. There's a smaller iron gate just back up the road, framed by topiary with stubble, which leads through to the rear of the property.

Further grounds there, shrubs and trees, and a single-level room tacked onto the back of Fields House, with white signs in red writing, warning all to keep out, and that the property is protected by CCTV (*pic 19.3*).

I can't say I'm taken in. Nailing up a plastic sign warning that somewhere is over-run with surveillance equipment must be far cheaper than actually installing surveillance equipment, and I certainly can't see any.

This back gate, too, is locked, and the hedging around it too dense to shimmy through.

So we head down the hill, alongside more of Fields House's extensive grounds. There, the hedge is patchy in parts, growing around an unimposing metal fence. I make a mental note of this as we return to the car to check out the other side of the property.

Now we're in Fields Park Avenue, parked outside St Catherine's Nursing Home, which must offer less potential for irksome sightseers.

This indeed is Sally Sparrow's entrance (*pic 19.4*) – and someone security-minded has conclusively gone to town on it.

Over the usual steel-mesh barrier used to keep undesirables out, a sturdy wooden fence allowing no access to daylight has been fastened for good measure. A 'KEEP OUT' sign is just about visible. At either side is some raggedy barbed wire.

I hang my camera over what little gap there is, aiming towards the house, and take a picture (*pic 19.5*). The driveway, pitted and greening, is so long, and the trees that line it to the right so tall, that Fields House remains hidden from view. Still, that's the very driveway that Sally Sparrow crept along, on her way into *Blink*'s otherworld of shifting statuary... Trapped behind half of Colditz.

My adrenalin's up now, because I know what is required. Here again, I must stress that trespassing is illegal. Please don't do as I do, because I'm an idiot.

I can't help it, which is quite bizarre – and wrong – for one so eager to comply with authority. In fact, I'm so hyped up after all the (mis)adventures of this book that I'm now worried that I'll graduate accidentally to bank jobs.

Judge: PC Pendleton?

PC Pendleton: I apprehended the accused as he was leaving the bank, clutching a bag labelled 'SWAG'. He seemed rather excitable, your honour.

Judge: And what did he say to you?

PC Pendleton [consults notebook]: His first words to me were, "Well, I wrote this book, see..."

I sincerely hope it doesn't come to that.

All I'm thinking is: what harm can it do? Pop in, take a few pictures, pop out again?

Actually, swap the word 'pop' both times for 'leg it'.

So that's what I do.

Karl parks the car outside the scrawniest section of the hedge, back in Fields Park Road and – wait for it – keeps the engine running! – while I rip off my overly conspicuous childish-red jacket, launch myself out of the car, foot up onto the fence, barge through the hedge, nearly stumble, but in! Into Fields House's grounds! Into *Blink*!

Already I'm breathing heavily and wide-eyed.

I sprint towards the house, feeling like the advance party of a crap guerrilla army, and take a hurried snap of the ochre-framed section where chipboard has been nailed over the door (*pic 19.6*). No money-shot, it is however worth recording for posterity. Then I work my way round clockwise towards the front of the house.

What I'm really after is that conservatory with the distinctive tiling. That greenhouse-type glasswork provided the backdrop to many a *Blink* scene, became a kind of trademark of the house. Of course there's no guarantee it'll even still be there. If Fields House is to be turned into flats, the first thing to go will be the most easily dismantled.

Shooting from the hip, I snap a lovely circular bay that covers two floors, where ornate masonry detail divides the levels and the windows dominate, bounded by frames that look frankly in reasonable nick (*pic 19.7*) – but not painted blue. It's the glass in frames painted blue that the three Weeping Angels gazed down from. Want those ones.

And there! Blue frames (*pic 19.8*), further round the house! Not the right ones, but the right colour, which bodes well. Strands of ivy, seemingly unconnected to each other by the traditional stems, hang like streamers from the walls. How, I have no idea. And I don't care because I know I'm within a whisker of my goal…

The conservatory! It's still here!

I don't quite remember because all this happened so quickly, but I seem to remember chuckling audibly at this point, and quite probably talking to myself.

My first instinct is to look for the tiling, so I poke my head inside the conservatory – and yes, it's there too (*pic 19.9*), just as I remembered it. Russet and blue sort of cog-wheel designs on a bed of ochre. Could it have been carefully contrived to match the paintwork outside? Mind you, we had tiling like that in our hallway at Chardmore Road, in a property of roughly the same age, so perhaps those were just the colours of the Victorian era.

Next I look up towards the building and there they are: my three windows (*pic 19.10*). The *Who* camera panned across those, on the first floor, to discover an Angel in each one, staring malignly down on Sally Sparrow, biding their time.

I pull back, out into the garden, aware that there are tall properties surrounding Fields House with windows and residents, and that now I'm out in the open. They would never have recommended this sort of thing at SAS School. But I'm not planning on hanging around.

From this vantage point I can see quite how lovely the conservatory is: arched in design, multi-panelled, with the flat planes of glass forming the curved sides layered like fish-scales (*pic 19.11*).

A few delightful teas will have been taken in there, beneath that quaint canopy, while the sun baked the geraniums.

I'm on a mental stopwatch, aware that I'm running into the red – or that may just be paranoia – so everything's happening in a blur. I do however notice piled planks of old wood stacked haphazardly among the grass and ferns, as if demolition work has already begun inside Fields House.

Time for one last pic, of the side of the conservatory, as I head back towards the car, capturing the pleasing lines of its construction (*pic 19.12*), and though I do glance towards the door – trapped behind hardboard, bearing yet another sign in red-and-white – even contemplating finding a way inside would be a step too far..

I had wondered whether the *Who* designer's Doctor scrawl, that warning to Sally Sparrow, might still be visible in there… But no, I'm not that daring or daft. Might be genuine hazards lurking within.

So I bat back around the house beneath tree boughs, foot onto metal railing, grab a branch, surge through the hedge, and straight back into the passenger seat, engine still running, my door having remained open. And Karl and I spontaneously burst into laughter.

Bodie and Doyle we ain't.

TRIP 20

Saturday, 16 August 2008

Blink

St Woolos Cemetery, Newport

I very specifically chose a cemetery as the final location of this book, for reasons that I imagine are obvious. There's the finality of the graveyard mirroring the end of these travels, and there's my Mum.

There was so much, in my naivety, that I hadn't prepared for.

I thought that *everyone* got a gravestone, whether they were cremated or buried, or stuffed in a capsule and shot into space. They don't. They bloody don't.

Lilian Victoria Griffiths doesn't have one. My Dad has her ashes and seems to be guarding them, and that is his business. I totally understand. And I wouldn't dream of questioning him, because it was Lilian and Norman for all those 70-odd years and his is the right.

But I have nowhere to go to where I feel I could talk to my Mum still, imagine her presence, and I dearly wish there were.

I can stop whatever I am doing and I can think about her, and more often than not it upsets me, yet I never, ever want to stop thinking about her.

Naturally, it gets easier.

But it's not time that heals, as is so often stated, it's the familiarity with the trauma, and this can only happen over time. If I tried blocking out what had happened and allowed it to inhabit my consciousness only rarely, it might take me years to come to terms with it. So I believe it's best to let it in.

I Blu-Tack'd a photograph of Mum on the wall behind my Mac screen, so I can see her now. She's wearing a summer dress and a smile, in our back garden at Alton, so the picture probably dates from the late Seventies. For some reason, she's clutching a sombrero.

Look, I don't want to get morose on your asses, that's not my intention. But I did intend this silly little book to be some kind of memorial to her. She was *my* Mum, you know? She was everything I could have hoped for. And I can't stop missing her.

I just look forward to the day when the hurt has sufficiently subsided so that I can look back on the bigger picture, with gratitude, that of all the wombs of all the mothers in all the world, I was lucky enough to begin my life in hers.

It'll happen.

All of which sentiment might make these trips seem a touch frivolous, but they aren't. For one, they've distracted me. Yeah, it's only a daft television show, and yeah, I've been playing little boys, running around sandpits and quarries and behaving like a child scrumping apples, but I've been having a bloody brilliant time.

Sod what anyone else thinks. If you collect stamps or find battlefields fascinating, or if you ballroom-dance every weekend or dress up as Captain of the Enterprise – actually, that's a *bit* dodgy – good on you.

Life can be pretty shit at times, and it's our dumb, quirky

obsessions that can help to pull us through. Cast all the bad stuff to one side for a moment, allow a little breathing time to take stock.

Listen, I bet 50 Cent collected GI Joe dolls. Asked Santa for new uniforms every Christmas. Pow! Pow!

(Unless he somehow comes to read this, in which case: Mr Cent, I'm really sorry, I don't know what came over me... I... I just got carried away.)

Right, if you'll excuse me, I have a graveyard to visit.

St Woolos Cemetery is just at the bottom of Fields Park Road. You could walk it from Fields House in two minutes.

Since I've forgotten Fact Pack 3, containing all the maps, I am blissfully unaware of that, so we drive around for ages wondering where it is, past St Woolos Cathedral, St Woolos Hair, St Woolos Flowers and St Woolos Autos, until I tell Karl that I do remember looking at the cemetery on a map and thinking how vast it was. You'll *know* when you've found it, I tell him. (Rather appositely, that memory will come back to haunt me.)

"Right!" he says with authority. "I know where it'll be!"

We park off Bassaleg Road and step out of the car. It's 4pm and the rain is falling in columns, dampening sprits and outerwear. I'm all too aware that this is my final location visit, the end of the road, and I can't pretend that this is how I foresaw it.

Then again... Graveyard. Rain. Rain. Graveyard. Perhaps this is how it was meant to be?

We pass through the cemetery gates. Ahead is an office building, outside which is a noticeboard detailing opening times. I hadn't expected either. I imagined cemeteries would be open all hours, particularly since they seem to come into their own under the cover of night. But death, lest we forget, is a business.

It suddenly feels very official here, not the basis for a game of finding *Doctor Who* locations, and I start to become uncomfortable. I'm wearing ripped jeans – the only ones I packed – and that silly top previously documented. Karl's at least dressed in brown, which is almost black. I feel like a sodden rodent off to fancy-dress.

It isn't right.

So I urge my friend past the office as speedily as possible, in case someone decides to quiz us, and I really, really don't want to have to explain this one.

St Woolos Cemetery stretches out before us and to the right, as far as the eye can see. It goes on *forever*. Just like I'd remembered it in the car: vast.

And I think: I wonder where they filmed the *Blink* scenes? Hmm?

All I can remember of the screen grabs in Fact Pack 3 is a chunky cross. And, well, there are one or two of those.

I'm after the scene in *Doctor Who* where Sally Sparrow visits the grave of her friend, Kathy Nightingale, watched by a Weeping Angel. To explain confusingly: Kathy, though the same age as and contemporary to Sally, died in Sally's past. It's all in Steven Moffat's timelines.

Anyway, Sally visits this grave in a cemetery that isn't named in the show, but which is St Woolos in real life.

Had I some reference material to hand, I might have had a chance of pinpointing the right area. But I don't. Grave after grave after grave after grave, a sea of death documented in turf and stone. And the rain pours down.

I snap an establishing shot, otherwise out of ideas (*pic 20.1*), then one of the several asphalt roadways that criss-cross the plots (*pic 20.2*). There are so many different types of headstone. Crosses, obelisks, traditional slabs, some fallen flat, others leaning crazily where the ground has subsided, pillars, angels, scrolls... But where was Sally Sparrow?

In this area west of the cemetery office, I feel as if I'm warm, something feels right, but there's just no way of telling for sure.

The final location and I'm stumped. It feels like a failure. Pit-pat-pit-pat goes the rain on my scalp as the drips enter my eyes.

Clutching at straws I ask Karl to phone Jack, who I think might have pocketed Fact Pack 3 yesterday, as he helped suss money-shots in Cardiff. It's the flimsiest of straws. And we keep walking, past all these memories of people.

I take another photograph of St Woolos graves (*pic 20.3*), to feel less than useless. One bit of the graveyard does look like another to the casual observer.

Then standing on a roadway, staring towards its end, the dimensions of this place become yet more apparent. It's quite overwhelming. Slopes and banks and still more headstones previously unnoticed, way over there.

The weather, if anything, is worsening. Raindrops battering the leaves or dying on the ground. So we take shelter beneath a tree with long, low boughs, one of many that magnify the air of serenity in this place. So many different types of tree all around, and I can recognise only the firs. I wonder where Ray Mears is when I need him.

Karl gets hold of Jack, then Catherine, who describe a certain type of headstone and a tall fir in the background – see above – and the futility of their efforts becomes quickly apparent.

Once every few minutes a car drives past, and the gulf between their occupants' reasons for being here and mine is sandpaper to my soul. Grieving, decorating graves, tidying them up, ensuring someone isn't forgotten.

But surely many of these remains are. Disrepair. Headstones cracked and broken. I scan inscriptions. People here who died at the age of 81, 73, 43, 16... We are never safe.

St Woolos Cemetery was opened in 1850, and the Newport and St Woolos Burial Board was set up following the Burial Act 1853, to administer the cemeteries in Newport and St Woolos, Monmouthshire. This is the oldest public cemetery in Britain.

Sprawling, seemingly endless as this site is, it is still not enough. Our old friend, the *South Wales Argus*, of December 2004, reported a proposal to swallow up nearby playing fields into the cemetery, creating space for 3,000 more graves. Residents wrote to the council to protest.

Around 300 people a year are buried here and estimates suggest St Woolos will be filled in seven years. Then where will all the dead people go?

Everyone buried here had someone once, I think. At the funeral, friends and relatives gathered around a hole in the ground.

I fear I can picture them.

And I feel like a fraud. I just want this over with.

So we break cover and I kneel in any patch of grass, pretending to be Sally Sparrow, while wishing I wasn't (*pic 20.5*). Tacky. But done now.

Karl and I make our way back to his car, slump gratefully inside, wringing wet, as the rain vents its spleen on the windscreen.

After such a tense visit, there is at least an interesting addendum to our St Woolos story. During my travels around the internet, I discovered that the cemetery has been used once again by *Doctor Who*, for the 2008 Christmas Special.

Locations hounds, as I now consider myself to be, have taken various photographs of a section of the graveyard covered in fake snow. And there are others, elsewhere, showing Tennant beside co-star David Morrissey, whose costume raises one's eyebrow.

I won't give anything more away here.

I do have one hope: that lovely Sally Sparrow will one day return, played by Carey Mulligan, ideally as the next Doctor's companion. The character is Steven Moffat's creation, after all, who assumes control of the series once Russell T Davies departs prior to series five in 2010.

Can that really be right? 2010? It seems an eon away.

But as we know, time flies.

And that's it. It's now 5.13 in the morning (whoops) and it's all over.

Such a mad dash around the country, witnessing such varied and unlikely sights, dredging up so much *Doctor Who* history – plus the actual history of all those places, which I have found equally compelling – and the sensation is bittersweet.

I have stood where Jon Pertwee stood, and Tom Baker, Billie Piper, David Tennant, I have chanced upon Skaro, planet of the Daleks, shot at Bok (actually Dylan), and talked my way into *Pyramids of Mars*.

I realised, as I drove around England's backroads and was chauffeured towards Wales' beaches, how bloody gorgeous these countries are, and how much I am missing when I sit on my sofa, unmotivated to move and discover. I hope the experience changes me.

By Christmas I shall have a tiny daughter. I'm proud and grateful that Sinead will be her Mum and Dylan her half-brother, because, as if I required reminding, I only need think back to Binnegar Quarry, Betchworth, East Hagbourne and Aldbourne, to remember how kind and devoted, and what damn fine company those two people are.

Yes, everything's going to be alright. Forever.

DOCTOR WHO 50TH ANNIVERSARY SPECIAL

Note: To view the accompanying picture gallery, visit the Who Goes There page on www.nickgriffiths.co.uk and click the 50th Anniversary Special link.

This may seem irrelevant to a book revolving around *Doctor Who*, but I was a terrible nerd as a child. Naïve and nervous, a public-school youth in a tweed jacket, desperate for adventure but fearful of the consequences.

I had precious little contact with the opposite sex – the school being boys-only and I being effectively an only child (my four far-older brothers having long since left home) – I was a member of the school Science Society, the Airfix Modelling Club and soldered electronic components to printed circuit boards on certain afternoons off.

I'd been hooked on naff rock, wore a faux-leather jacket with the Rush logo *felt-tipped* on the back. I'd had teenage acne that gathered in gangs and a greasy centre-parting. I played *Dungeons & Dragons*, even painted the lead fantasy figures, and to this day I will gaze longingly at the box of any role-playing game, wishing I had 1-5 friends who'd be willing to play it with me.

I also happened to love *Doctor Who*.

As I remember it, I was a cipher of a child. No personality, nothing to recommend himself, a drone. Studying hard to avoid parental reproach and to build bridges towards the future.

I attended a school reunion in November 2010 and mentioned this to one fellow former pupil, who assured me that I was wrong, that I did actually have a personality, and I have no reason to disbelieve him. But that's how I remember it: subsumed by the old-school public-school system.

In 1985 I went to college (King's College) and London. From suburbia to the big city. At least I was trying.

I had managed to have sex with a girl during my A-level retake year at a tech, I'd even managed to converse with her without stammering, so the gender relationship side was no longer hopeless, but, come on – I was going to be studying Electrical & Electronic Engineering!

Top choice, Casanova.

There was one fellow student on that course who stood out among the heads-down grey of lecture life. He wore a green and white jumper with a huge red Welsh dragon on the front, he spoke his mind and had a reputation as a womaniser. I clearly recall thinking that I'd prefer to be like him: the no-fear approach.

When one afternoon he spoke to me, I was amazed that he'd given me the time of day. Yet somehow we became mates and spent most of the second year of the course together in the Nell Gwynne pub, off The Strand, drinking away our grant money and playing the fruit machine as my rebellion kicked into gear.

His name was Mal.

Fast-forward almost 30 years. Mal lives in Wales with his wife, Jan, and two kids, Emily, 20, and Jamie, 15. He's had two heart attacks – at least, I may have lost count – and still smokes. Having cocked up that original Electronics course, he retook his exams later, went as far as gaining an MA, and is an expert in computer networks who works long hours all around the country.

Mal will be my chauffeur-cum-Welsh tour guide for this commemorative location hunt, in honour of the *Doctor Who* 50th Anniversary. It should be interesting.

I've planned to meet him in the centre of Cardiff, after his work. Cardiff is, of course, the hub of the *Doctor Who* universe, where the show has been made since its rebirth in 2005. As a consequence, the region is chock-full of juicy locations, though by all accounts the location managers are running out of options and several places will have been sighted on telly on more than one occasion.

I've taken the train up from Cornwall, where I live by the sea, nursing a debilitating malaise, the result of way too much cider the night before, followed by vodka into the wee hours.

Why I do it to myself, why I can't grow up, I don't

know. Perhaps it has something to do with my uber-square upbringing.

It's not the best foundation for a location trip and I wouldn't recommend you do the same.

Jan appears first, as I nurse a barely-diminishing pint and my battered constitution outside a city-centre hostelry, keeping my head down so the scary, scrapping pissheads of a Friday afternoon don't catch my eye.

I haven't seen Jamie in half a dozen years so fail to recognise him and instead mistake him for Emily's boyfriend, which goes down well with both brother and sister.

There's a bloke lying on the ground outside an office doorway, arseholed, and it's not even five o'clock.

Mal appears. He's wearing trousers I'd describe as 'slacks', such is his fashion sense, and having pointed this out to him he proudly shows off his green suede shoes, as if those somehow make up for it.

There's actually a dual purpose to my visit to Wales. Besides the *Who* pilgrimages, I'm here to take the Suicide Seven Wing Challenge: a Man v. Food-style battle against the hottest chillies available to humanity, which takes place in a Cardiff eatery.

Jan asks if I'm planning to have a go this evening. Since my insides already feel as if they've gone ten rounds with Mike Tyson, I am not. Instead, Mal and I head off to a boozer in Aberdare, where I order a chicken phall from the local Indian restaurant and perhaps mercifully receive a mere vindaloo.

Where Friday had been sunshine and shades, Saturday morning is bastard drizzle and a canopy of grey. This is more the weather I associate with Wales. (I've visited the country on several occasions and fail to recall a time when it did not rain heavily – actual inhabitants of Wales may find this observation irritating.)

Though seeking locations used in *Doctor Who*'s 50th

Anniversary episode is the obvious choice for this celebratory chapter, the elephant in the room can't help pointing out that I have not actually seen the episode, since it doesn't air until November 2013.

The original *Who Goes There* chapters were all about seeking a 'sense of *Who*' – visual and ethereal links to the past, of familiar sights and lingerings in the air, from when the *Doctor Who* cast and crew trod the same ground.

Filming of the 50th Anniversary episode has wrapped, the cast and crew were there... but where exactly?

Thank goodness for the Internet and for my fellow location hounds who work tirelessly throughout the filming season, following Twitter tip-offs to suburban alleyways, abandoned buildings and city-centre landmarks, to report sightings of Tardis, monsters and the Doctor himself. It's perhaps over-romantic to picture them in collars-up raincoats and Raymond Chandler hats, drifting back home to smoking dames, even if that's how I like to think of myself.

And thanks also, once again, to doctorwholocations.net, who combine all that knowledge in one webpage.

So I do know where to go, with often photographic evidence of the *Who* crew in situ; I just have to track these places down.

Readers of the original *Who Goes There* will remember my Fact Packs: notes and print-outs for each location I plan to visit, to facilitate my mission.

This time around, well, I've become rather addicted to this book called *Brazilian Adventure*. Not by Willard Price, fans of 1970s youth literature, since he didn't centre one of his *Adventure* series in that land of classic lady-depilation. No, this is a 1933 hardback by Peter Fleming, whom I discovered, only well into the book, was the brother of James Bond's Ian.

Well, *Brazilian Adventure* is Brazil-liant! How I came across it, I do not recall, but I do remember reading the Amazon reviews promising one of the funniest travel books ever. And it is.

Fleming is drier than desiccated coconut, prone to withering put-downs in Edwardian tones, to self-deprecation and to brutal honesty, as well as gigantic snobbery.

'Sao Pãolo,' Fleming states, 'is like Reading, only much further away.'

I utterly love him. (And can't help seeing myself in him.)

Plenty of Fleming's writings have struck chords with me, none less so than this brief excerpt: 'Certain people, of whom I am one, thrive in an atmosphere of uncertainty. It is not that we have the gambler's spirit... We are not so dashing. If we take risks, we take them because we are lazy. We delegate our responsibilities to fate. In any situation, the more you are obliged to leave to chance, the less you are obliged to do yourself.'

In that same spirit, I bid 'Balls!' to the Fact Pack, pick up Mal's laptop and dongle, a pad of A4 donated by Jan and climb into the passenger seat of his – hello! – Mercedes, and we're off. Into the drizzle.

GELLIGAER COMMON
22 June 2013

First stop, being nearest to Mal's home base in Llwydcoed, is Gelligaer Common in Fochriw. Yes, good luck with the pronunciation. That's roughly Geth-li-gare and Foch-rew.

There, according to doctorwholocations.net, filming took place on 4 April 2013, involving the Tardis, a low-flying helicopter and Jenna Louise Coleman on a motorbike. If that doesn't send your temperature racing, nothing will.

Mal hangs a right towards Merthyr Tydfil past a noticeable though grim-looking Kingdom Hall of Jehovah's Witnesses, which he explains used to be a hotel. I'm hardly surprised that potential hotel guests gave the monstrosity in the middle of zilch a wide berth, but am mildly shocked that Jehovah's Witnesses really do get everywhere.

Admittedly there is not a soul to be seen, but perhaps they all emerge at some set time each day, like something out of *The Stepford Wives*? My upstairs neighbour's Dad was a Jehovah's Witness and he told of being obliged to knock on people's doors come Sunday, proffering magazines no one wants. I went off him after that.

We pass through green. Lots and lots of green – one could never accuse Wales of being infertile – beneath a firmament of grey. I am reminded of Richard Llewellyn's novel, *How Green Was My Valley*, to which the reply must have been, 'Very, very, very green.'

Clearly the perpetual rain has its uses.

However, there is a blight on the landscape, which Mal will return to time and again in this region of his country: open-cast mining. They're planning to open a mine not far behind his house, which he is fervently against.

'Look across there,' he says, pointing to our left towards one of many hillsides.

The ground looks as if it's been charred, like a farmer's field after the burning of the stubble.

'That's what open-cast mining does,' he says.

The hillside has been robbed of all its nutrients, leaving it barren and desolate.

Gelligaer Common, it turns out, is bloody big. Since we're looking for a comparatively tiny area, I fire up the laptop and seek photographic evidence of where the *Who* crew had filmed. But the dongle is inefficient amid this sprawling, barely-populated landscape and I'm left staring at a tantalisingly-thin, rectangular section of just-sky while the remainder of the image refuses to load.

Irritated, I spot some GPS coordinates on doctorwholocations.net and Mal loads them into his satnav. And we're off... again.

Except there's a horse in the road. Yes, a horse.

It could easily have been a sheep, since there is no shortage of those in evidence, but this happens to be a horse. It's brown and not terribly large, though large enough to cause damage. There's a stand-off vaguely *OK Corale*-style, as it stares at us and we stare back, before it ambles off to find something more becoming with which to occupy itself (grass-chomping? horse-sex?).

During the stand-off, the rest of the Gelligaer *Who*-filming image has at least cranked itself into view. And it doesn't leave much to go on. There's a common, stretching in every direction, a few clumps of grass, sky, and – the sole feature – a crappy path comprising parallel dried-mud tyre tracks. It's like gazing at a *Where's Wally?* puzzle when the illustrator has forgotten to draw in Wally. We have as much chance of finding that particular scene as I do of building a rocket from dustbins and challenging Richard Branson to a race to the moon.

Undeterred... Actually, that's not true. I was enormously deterred, though I had no choice but to continue.

Enormously deterred, we drove on until we hit the coordinates on the website: 51°43'15", -03°18'04". Since we weren't sure about that -03° – Mal's satnav failing to allow negatives – we were effectively clueless.

I referred myself back to *Brazilian Adventure* and felt heartened. This was exploration, Fleming-style.

There were sheep everywhere, bleating insanely. Sheep shorn so badly, they looked as if they had charged blindly into Edward Scissorhands (pic 50.1). Bald patches and grimy dreadlocks competed for space on the same beast, bits hung down, bits flapped around. If Mad Max did farming...

I imagined the shearer must have been having a laugh until Mal pointed out that these were wild hill sheep and that their wool just sort of falls off when it feels like it.

A single ribbon of tarmac cut through these rolling, desolate, godforsaken hills (pic 50.2), populated by more sheep, which we followed hoping to spot a mud-track.

Eventually Mal swore that he had seen such a track, off to our left, but since there was no room to stop the car we carried on driving for a good half a mile before finding a lay-by.

Gathered tufts of spiky grass and boulders that looked as if they had been shunted there by hand sat among the mulch and ovine half-lives. It wasn't inviting.

I opened the door to be greeted by a cacophony of buffeting winds as the door was flung back towards me by an invisible shove.

'Blimey!' I said. 'It's windy out there!' (This is the trouble with luxury cars – they're too well-built to register the exterior weather conditions.)

Released from the car by pure willpower, I realised I was underplaying the situation. Outside the sanctity of the Merc, it was blowing a fucking gale. To prove as much, I tried standing on a rock while Mal snapped a picture (pic 50.3), leaning forwards into the maelstrom to avoid being launched backwards.

What now? The trackway we sought was a good hike back down the road and everywhere looked the same.

Gratefully I returned to the car and sought refuge in the laptop. Peering closely at the single image to hand, I spotted a tiny telegraph pole, off to the left of the image, and some tiny white buildings over a ridge. Nothing matched with the reality out there.

So we moved to a new lay-by having noticed black and multicoloured wiring lying tangled by the verge (pic 50.5). Had this been dumped there by the BBC, I wondered?

But it occurred to me: of course it bloody wasn't! As if the BBC wander around littering the country willy-nilly with every discarded length of electrical cable.

However, we were desperate.

Desperate enough to start wandering off into the hills

(pic 50.6) in search of anything that looked like anything.

Heading into the wind was almost unbearable, forcing clothing to encase and flap around the body; we looked like we were skydiving. I blundered upwards towards a peak, aiming for a vantage point, head down to avoid treading in shit.

And there was shit everywhere. The further I staggered towards the interior (pics 50.7-50.8), the larger the shit got, until I came upon Shitmageddon (pic 50.9): triple heaps of piled poo, in varying shades of doom, lying there like the Pyramids of Giza – but that isn't Giza and that's no tomb of the Pharaohs. Lord knows what kind of creature blew out that horror-show, but I couldn't help wonder whether there was a curry house out there somewhere on the moors.

Mercifully, if there was any malodour, the stench was 20 miles away on the wind before it could reach my nasal passages.

I turned and looked back (pic 50.10). Mal had disappeared, no doubt back to the car. There were horses now visible among the sheep, which might have partially explained Shitmageddon. What they did all day, I had no idea.

Though I was freezing cold, despite it being summer, I carried on upwards, compelled by Fleming's spirit of adventure and by a dedication to my readers. In my head I'd long ago given up hope of finding the spot where the Tardis had been sited, or where Coleman had dismounted her steel steed.

For a start there wasn't a single sheep or horse visible in that image from filming, which alone suggested we were miles out. Equally, you could hardly have had Coleman dismounting her motorbike and stepping inevitably into a smouldering pile of sheep-do.

Still I carried on, bullishly pressing towards a ridge that never seemed to get closer, muttering to myself. As I did so I disturbed a bird that rose up all a-fluster before me, wheeled in the buffeting air and was off like an ungainly glider in a wind tunnel.

It resembled no bird I had witnessed in real life, bulky and brown with a distinctive long, downwards-curving beak. Thanks to my nerdy childhood, I recognised it from my PG Tips picture cards book of British Birds. It was a curlew.

I had seen and recognised a curlew – I was Bill fucking Oddie! Amid the grimness of the surroundings and the ignominy of my failure, I felt a surge of pride.

Then it started raining.

To cut a long story short, I did finally reach the top of the ridge, where I discovered a view (pic 50.11) that was purest green. No longer Oddie, I had become Lord Percy.

Happily it was impossible to trudge disconsolately back to the car, as the gale-force winds were now blowing the rain into my face, which felt as if I were under attack by kids with pellet guns, so I had to urge myself into the elements, cursing all the way.

White noise was buffeted into my ears and partied like hippies strung out on acid around my eardrums. Such was the bizarre cacophony I felt, as though I had wandered into an episode of Jon Pertwee's: one of those where the hirsute BBC sound bods went mental with new-fangled synthesisers.

The situation could barely have been much worse had I come under attack by Sea Devils.

When, some months later, I finally crawled on my hands and knees back to the car, wrenched the door open and launched myself inside, breathing like someone drowning, Mal, smoking, had the laptop on his lap. 'This photo we've been looking at,' he said casually. 'It's from 2009.'

It was, in fact, a location image from David Tennant's *Tooth and Claw*. Nothing to do with the 50th Anniversary Special.

Wrong area, wrong picture, wrong story, wrong year.

Somewhere up in the clouds, Peter Fleming smirked down at me.

Look, it really wasn't as bad as it sounds.

One expanse of common looks largely like another. Especially when it's Gelligaer Common.

Did I get a sense of an other-worldly, barren landscape, of the type so admired by producers of *Doctor Who*? You bet I did.

I went as far as imagining I was in an actual episode of the show, albeit one filmed 40-odd years prior to the one I was researching.

Research post-visit revealed a rich history behind Gelligaer Common. Megalithic tombs, Roman forts, Christian burials, iron age and bronze age workings, even links to King Arthur.

The Campaign for the Protection of Rural Wales website has a pulled quote that caught my eye: 'Only the curlews and skylarks remain to enhance the stillness of the place and the feeling of peace with the world.'

I'm not sure about 'stillness' and 'peace with the world', but I can certainly vouch for the curlews.

'Where next?' I ask Mal, having allowed him to plan our route. (Well, he has the local knowledge.)

'Neath,' he replies.

'Ivy Tower?'

'Yeah.'

A big stone tower covered in ivy, then. 'We should be able to find that,' I suggest.

'Maybe,' he replies.

IVY TOWER
22 June 2013

Mal's quickly back on the subject of open-cast miming...

sorry, typo: I meant mining, though open-cast miming would have been easier on the ear.

It's a necessarily emotive subject.

Just to our left, that great warehouse affair is actually a pit-head that was closed down only a few months ago, he says. Having devoured the mineral riches in one stretch of land, the mining companies slide off to find another. This insatiable draining of the earth's natural resources will only cease, it seems, when the crust is but a husk.

This region is riddled with mines. All the flattened conical hills evident on every side are slag heaps that have been levelled off. This is to avoid a repeat of the heartbreaking 1966 Aberfan disaster, in which piled spoil from a colliery slid downhill at an alarming rate and buried a junior school, killing 116 children and 28 adults.

'They ran coach trips from Merthyr to [Margaret] Thatcher's funeral [in London],' says Mal. 'Not to pay their respects. To check she was dead.'

Thatcher, when she was Prime Minister, fought an acrimonious battle against the National Union of Mineworkers and is hated for being seen to destroy the country's mining industry.

Since he's so against the open-cast mining on his doorstep, I wonder whether Mal wouldn't wish her back. But he's already off on 'Valleys boys on steroids fighting in Cardiff' so I let the thought lie.

The rain's tumbling so fast the wipers require double-speed to keep up. We're on the main road towards Neath, in a valley as verdant as the average rainforest.

Occasional thin, wispy individual clouds linger among the trees barely above car-height, like something out of a Postgate/Firmin production.

It feels like November out there.

I'm looking forward to Ivy Tower, perhaps more than any other location in the itinerary. Why? Because of the name. 'Ivy Tower' is so evocative. Plus there are some great shots of the tower on doctorwholocations.net, including an official BBC one of a Zygon filming, and I've always had a soft spot for a Zygon. Though they've battled the Doctor only once, their design was a masterstroke, their longevity in hearts and minds only aided by appearing during Tom Baker's golden period.

While discussing the gem that was 1975's *Terror of the Zygons* in my *Who* memoir, *Dalek I Loved You*, I began thus:

Terror of the Zygons
If the makers of new Who *don't one day bring this lot back, they are missing a trick…*

They're just so… orange. And lurid. And suckery. The way the actor's body is encapsulated inside that foetal structure and given extra looming height by that grotesque bonce. The Zygons are a work of genius and if I'm not exactly going to see one, I will be visiting where one strode about.

We begin winding uphill as we approach the coordinates plugged into the satnav, passing a GNOLL ESTATE COUNTRY PARK sign. The road is potholed and there isn't much screaming 'country park' – and I should know because I've been to one.

Bereft of Things To Do when I was a youth, my parents would very occasionally drive many miles to the Wellington Country Park, where I would go fishing, in an (often successful) attempt to land the world's smallest ever perch.

It struck me that if one did not enjoy fishing, there was bugger all else to do at the Wellington Country Park (though it's feasible that I did not fully explore the options).

As we round a bend and spy NEATH DOG GROOMING, the satnav announces that we have reached our destination. Which is news to me, since I had then and fiercely maintain zero intention of ever visiting a dog-grooming parlour.

But what's that through the trees? Could it be a stone tower covered in ivy? It is! That's Ivy Tower!

Except it's on private farmland, which may prove problematic. So as we drive into the farm I begin dusting off in my head the old 'See I'm writing this book...' speech.

There's a 4x4 parked in the driveway. Printed on its rear spare tyre are the words: 'Rhys Davies Young Farmer of the Year'. This is Gellideg Farm and we are in the presence of farming royalty.

I exit the car, grateful that the rain has ceased, and gaze across at Ivy Tower (pic 50.12), dwarfed under a bruised sky. It's all rather exciting.

Researching after the event, I discover that Ivy Tower was built by a well-heeled family named the Mackworths, who owned the Gnoll Estate, in the 1700s (around 1740 or 1780, depending upon which source you consult). Back then it was known as The Belvedere, presumably to lend it an air of grandeur, and housed a ballroom to wow visitors.

The wow factor has been diminished by the passing years, as all that's left is an albeit solid-looking ruin, which looks from a distance like a bit of Stonehenge. Not that I'm averse to a ruin, as an avid fan of *Time Team*, so I'm eager to see the construction close-up.

There's a porch outside the farmhouse. Clutching my notebook to aid location-hunting authenticity, I rap on the door and listen, mildly terrified. I hate those situations (the sort of situation in which I have to address a complete stranger).

A dog barks, there's movement inside and a woman shortly appears at the door, looking understandably suspicious.

'Hello,' I say. 'I'm writing this book, see, about *Doctor Who* locations. That's one over there, isn't it? Ivy Tower?'

'Yeeees,' she says, all wary.

Further garbled explanation later, and the lady has

warmed to us ever so slightly. I can tell she thinks we're with a tabloid, as when I ask whether she spoke to David Tennant during the filming, her reply is barely monosyllabic.

However, when I enquire whether we can traipse through her sodden field to look at the tower close-up – which only an idiot or a genuine location hunter would want to do – our authenticity begins to emerge.

'Well, you can,' she says. 'Only there's a bull in the field.'

'A bull?'

She nods.

I am reminded of the bull scene in *Withnail & I*. Withnail hurdling a dry-stone wall then sparking up a fag, while Marwood runs at the snorting beast, shouting. 'A coward you are, Withnail. An expert on bulls, you are not.' It occurs to me that I am Withnail.

I glance at Mal, hoping for ideas.

He shrugs.

'Will it run at me?' I ask.

I'm hoping she'll chortle 'Nooooo!' Instead she says: 'I'll ask my son.'

If the Young Farmer of the Year needs to be asked whether he'd step into a field with this bellowing monstrosity, what hope do I have?

Rhys Davies, Young Farmer of the Year, appears. 'Would you go into the field with the bull?' asks his mum.

The Young Farmer of the Year grins. 'Well, I would,' he says. 'But I've got a stick.'

I mentally tot up my own sticks and feel queasy when the calculation fails to rise above zero.

I'm making light of this, but I was genuinely scared. I lived in London for 25 years, where bulls are frankly scarce.

My sum knowledge of these charging horns on legs comes from television and film, in which these bellowing carcasses of malevolence paw the ground then charge with horns akimbo, to lance some hapless Spaniard decked in finery through his penis, tossing him in the air like he's a rag doll.

What are the chances, I wonder out loud, panicking, of us crossing the field towards the tower without being spotted?

A deafening silence speaks volumes.

The thing is, I know I have to attempt this. Because we're here now and I can feel the drama building. On the other hand, bulls can be properly dangerous and I know bugger all about handling one.

I peer across the field, trying to spot the beast but it's clearly gone into hiding, waiting, biding its time.

'You could always take cover in the hut (pic 50.13)?' the lady offers.

I gaze at the corrugated iron/wooden shack plopped between us and the invisible bull. It's not what you'd call solid-looking and I wouldn't be surprised if at least one madman (staring eyes, lengthy grey beard) was shacked up inside it.

'Could we skirt around the field?' asks Mal, clearly thinking the same.

I can see his plan. There's a wire fence along the perimeter, which seems to skirt around the back of the field and Ivy Tower itself, potentially allowing us to sneak up unseen.

'You could,' comes the reply.

It's a plan. It's all we have.

I let Mal lead the way.

Well, it was his idea.

Staying the other side of the fence from the bull, we began working our way towards the tower some 100 yards away. I snap a quick long-lens shot (pic 50.14), so there's something in the camera at least, should I be gored to death.

Breathing heavily through a mixture of adrenaline and fear, I keep checking for signs of the bull. All that appears are two horses (pic 50.15). The white one stares at us as if we're idiots.

Suddenly Mal climbs through the fence, into the bull bit of the field. Has he taken leave of his senses? Should I do the same? Will it gore him first, since he's in the lead? Assuming yes to the last one, I follow his example.

I'M IN THE BULL FIELD.

Long wet grass drags against my shins and my socks are already damp as my trainers weren't cut out for this sort of thing. The closer we get, the more the contours of the field hide whatever is at the base of that tower (pic 50.16), which is disconcerting. I'm treading as quietly as I can; it doesn't seem quiet enough.

How sensitive is a bull's hearing, I wonder. Unfortunately, the Young Farmer of the Year has fucked off back indoors so I can't ask him.

When we reach the corner of the fence, where it turns a right angle to head towards Ivy Tower, we're perhaps 25 yards from the tower/bull. If the bull charges, I need an escape route. Having always been useless at athletics jumping events, I know I'd get tangled in the wires if I tried to leap the perimeter fence, leaving the bull free to lance my penis then toy with my limp carcass.

My eyes alight on two sections of wooden fence (pic 50.17), low enough that even a donkey like myself could navigate them at pace. Reassuringly, Mal is still ahead of me (pic 50.18) and the goal is very much in sight (while the bull is not).

Incredibly, I am still alive. The realisation buoys my confidence and the next thing I know, I'm striding – well, stalking precariously – towards an entrance to Ivy Tower (pic 50.19), having handed Mal the camera. I have taken the initiative.

And there I am: the money shot. Me at the tower itself (pic 50.20).

I can't pretend for a second that either *Doctor Who* or *Zygons* were crossing my mind. I was far too terrified to worry about television. That bull could have appeared in front of me at any second.

I snapped some shots inside in quick succession (50.21-50.23), fully expecting to see a head with steaming nostrils appear in one of the doorways, and am hugely relieved when it does not. Which nevertheless begs the question: so where is it?

Hopefully it's giving nothing away, since I'm writing this after the event, to reveal that I did not die.

I did look back over my shoulder during my escape from Ivy Tower... Sorry, let me capitalise that... during my Escape from Ivy Tower – Hollywood producers, please contact me via my website – to spy a bunch of grazing horses and, in the middle of them, the bull.

As I spotted it, it looked up and saw me. I can't tell you whether it chased after me, because I was running too fast to bother to look back.

I assure you the pile of lightly aerated poo (pic 50.24) has nothing to do with me. I imagine it to be pure bullshit.

Only some time after the event was I able to calm down sufficiently to consider Ivy Tower and its *Doctor Who* connections. (I knew those photos would come in handy.)

As suspected, the building, even dilapidated, is pretty astounding. The stonework is a thing of beauty, completed by its veils of clotted ivy. It's the sense of history that really captures the imagination. This circular construction, perhaps 15 metres in diameter – it's not wide, so hilarious to imagine people waltzing around it ballroom-style – is just so *solid*.

An archive photograph shows windows and castellations and we learnt chatting to the farmer's mum that on a clear day – which this was not – one can see as far as the Mumbles, some dozen miles away at the far end of Swansea Bay.

I've no idea what role the Tower plays in the 50th

Anniversary episode, but I've seen photos of a Zygon striding around it. David Tennant filmed here, as did Joanna Page (*Gavin & Stacey*) in an elaborate dress that had people guessing she was playing Elizabeth I. A tent, the like of which used to be pitched at jousting tournaments, was sited in front of the tower. What that all adds up to, I have no idea.

I'm hoping the Zygon was using Ivy Tower as a disguise for its spaceship, which would be really cool.

The positive aspect of seeking out locations not yet seen on television is that when they eventually are, I can point at the screen and declare proudly, 'I've been there!'

A final note on Gellideg Farm before we leave.

The lady who kindly allowed us to walk across her land admitted to us that she had indeed worried we were tabloid hacks and talked of being hassled by the press during and after the filming. Please bear in mind that the farm is private land and one can only handle so many location hounds. So please respect their privacy.

CWMDARE STREET & GLADSTONE PRIMARY SCHOOL
22 June 2013

Driving back down the windy hill, I spot a gate to our left and signs of water, so we park up to investigate and are greeted by the most gorgeous, tranquil reservoir (pic 50.25). This must be part of the Gnoll Estate Country Park. I'll Google it now...

According to its own website, Gnoll Estate Country Park is set in 230-acre grounds and offers four duck ponds – I know, calm my racing heart – two 18th century 'cascades' (a bit like weirs), a couple of follies, formal gardens, bowling green, tennis court, a selection of old buildings and a 'Ha Ha' (being a sunken fence, not a euphemism for a lady-part, which seems a shame).

It also incorporates, being part of the Mackworth legacy, Ivy Tower. And I've found some new information here.

The ground floor, as seen in my photos, formed the caretaker's room; dancing and banqueting took place on the floor above, being 8 metres in diameter.

This bit's interesting: 'The gamekeeper of the Estate would have resided there until 1920 when it was destroyed by fire.' Odd how there were no signs of scorching. Nonetheless, the remains are Grade II listed, which presumably means they couldn't paint the exterior pink without first asking permission (another shame).

We did have the Mamhilad Park Industrial Estate on the itinerary, but the name hardly compelled me there, plus it's nearly 4pm and I still have the Suicide Wing Challenge to undertake. So we save that thrill for tomorrow and slot in the nearby Cwmdare Street and Gladstone Primary School.

The laptop dongle's playing up; I could learn Hungarian then try it out on an old Hungarian couple, both short, one named Igor, in the time it takes to download a single image. However, I do recall seeing photographs of a motorbike, playing an anti-gravity bike in the story, speeding in through school gates. So school gates will form part of my quest.

This is also where the

I M FOREMAN
Scrap Merchant
76, Totters Lane

and

COAL HILL
SECONDARY SCHOOL
Shoreditch
Chairman of the Governors: I. Chesterton

signs have been spotted, so no doubt Gladstone Primary is playing Coal Hill Secondary. I've also seen a fan-video from the filming, in which a copper walks down a street, past the I M Foreman sign. Naturally, I can't recall any detail from the background and the chances of me being able to watch the video again via the dongle were smaller than an ant's John Thomas.

Those signs, of course, appeared in the very first *Doctor Who* serial, known popularly as *An Unearthly Child*. Coal Hill was William Hartnell's Doctor's granddaughter, Susan's, school; the scrapyard at Totter's Lane was where she said she lived and where the Tardis was kept.

All of which led to teachers Barbara and Ian discovering the ship, the Doctor and hence time and space. So the appearance of the same signage in the 50th Anniversary Special is of major significance and should cause a few damp patches on the sofas of watching Whovians.

Frankly, I'm so excited about the prospect of a multi-Doctor anniversary special that I may take precautions and wear a nappy.

The journey towards Cardiff takes us past the necessarily unattractive Port Talbot steelworks, a sprawling industrial smudge of warehouses, towers and chimneys.

'Is that your arse or the steelworks?' enquires Mal, as a ripe, indefinable odour seeps into the car. It's as erudite as our conversation becomes on that leg of the journey.

On the bright side, there is a bright side – or at least bright spots: patches of blue sky peeping through the cloud cover. Even the sun is in danger of showing its face.

Past Aberkenfig, Pencoed and Pontyclun – great names, which I can just about pronounce; happily we don't pass Rhosllanerchrugog, let alone Llanfairpwllgwyngyll-gogerychwyrndrobwllllantysiliogogogoch, as we enter the outskirts of the Welsh capital.

A maze of back-streets coax us towards our goal. Mal's

student daughter, Emily, lives around here somewhere and there are nigh on entire streets with To Let signs outside as the student population disappears off on its holidays. According to Emily, the estate agents rarely bother to take the signs down, such is the continual turnover.

It's not a vastly appealing area, 50s-looking dwellings all in a row, and reminds me of my own student-digs street in Tottenham. (My flatmates used to throw darts at my Duran Duran poster on the lounge wall, which sums up how well we took care of the place.)

Mal, handily, knows where he's going and stops the car before I'm even aware we've arrived. We've actually parked (pic 50.26) on Cwmdare Street and I take a picture of the sign to prove it (pic 50.27). That's one of the downsides of location hunting – you're in danger of taking some incredibly mundane photos.

I remember an image on doctorwholocations.net, of the street full of traffic cones, closed off to cars. Looking down it now... well, it's a street.

To my right, unexpectedly, is Gladstone Primary School – I'd had no idea the two were adjacent, all red brick and education. I'm looking, remember, for a gate, so zip towards the main-road traffic I can hear. I end up circumnavigating the not insubstantial building.

First up is the 'Childrens [sic] Entrance / Exit' (pic 50.28), which is far too small to accommodate a speeding anti-gravity bike, but a sign helpfully points to a 'Visitors [sic] Entrance' around the corner.

This second façade of the building is pretty impressive and surely Victorian, all brick, glass and architectural noodlings. More friendly than austere.

I didn't know then, but I was walking down the street our policeman actor would walk up (pic 50.29), having turned out of 76 Totters Lane, and down the end there, by the Visitors' Entrance, is where they temporarily hung the Coal Hill sign.

Unfortunately I'm so childish I'm stood chuckling to

myself at the sign beside me promoting Slimming World in – wait for it – Fanny Street. So amusing do I find this that I take a photo (pic 50.30). Clearly you had to be there.

Round the next corner, and if the dongle had only worked properly I'd have been aware that I was in Totters Lane itself, slap bang in the genesis of *Doctor Who*. As it is, I'm hell-bent upon finding a wide enough entrance to accommodate a motorbike.

On this third side of Gladstone, I did find what I imagine to be that gateway (pic 50.31), offering a good view of the playground in which the *Doctor Who* crew were pictured filming (beneath a strange old clock, according to the location pics).

Incidentally, it did strike me that I was fortunate to be scouting this particular venue on a Saturday. You definitely don't want to wander round a primary school taking furtive snaps through railings during the week.

(I did find a third entrance, the one with the nicest gate (pic 50.32), on the fourth side of the school, but by then I was fairly convinced I'd successfully tracked down my goal, and was experiencing gate fatigue.)

As a *Doctor Who* location about which I knew precious little, I can't pretend it excited me hugely. However, there are enough recognisable landmarks that it's another I'll enjoy when the story airs.

It's got to be worth a visit afterwards, to say you've walked down Totters Lane, and seen Coal Hill Secondary (bearing in mind you don't want to get accidentally caught up in Operation Yewtree).

INTERLUDE:
THE SUICIDE SEVEN WING CHALLENGE

In common with many of my generation, my concept of a curry was a sultana-based urging never again to eat a curry, served by dinner ladies (never dinner gentlemen, for some reason). At least one of the sultanas would have a stalk in it, leaving you chewing wood (which, depending upon your sexual orientation, makes it sound even less appetising).

Curries were for people who talk to you at bus stops.

For that reason, it was a good few years before I could be cajoled into a proper Indian restaurant, and that night the flavours of my chicken korma were a revelation.

I've no idea why – perhaps an addictive personality – but I've craved spicy heat ever since and fairly swiftly worked my way up the Scoville Scale of capsicum/chilli heat, straight past madras and into vindaloo.

These days, without fail, I order the phall, the hottest on the menu, and dabble regularly in the kitchen with the bhut jolokia naga chilli – aka the ghost chilli – among the hottest in the world. My Chinese/Thai fish-broth fusion laced with naga mash is angelic in its combination of freshness, flavour and stupidly intense heat.

All of which goes some way towards explaining why I actively wanted to take on the Suicide Seven Wing Challenge.

The remainder of the explanation lies in Adam Richman's *Man v. Food* show, in which the genial American seeks out food challenges. I found the programme gross, even offensive, featuring one man attempting to eat enough food to satisfy two dozen... until I discovered that Richman is a massive Spurs fan.

Then I began watching *Man v. Food* weekly and became obsessed with his occasional chilli challenges, in which he attempted to eat, for instance, what were claimed to be the world's hottest chicken wings.

His grotesquely sweating features; the evident oral agonies; the ridiculous rituals he was obliged to endure in order to succeed... None of that put me off.

In fact, it only inspired me.

So here we are in the Sizzle and Grill Steak House (pic 50.33), a quaint-ish little eatery on Cowbridge Road, calling itself 'The Home of *Man V Food*' (it isn't – that would be the Travel Channel).

I'm accompanied not only by Mal but by his daughter, Emily, and by her boyfriend, Dai, who came purely to watch me suffer.

Besides my wings, the menu offers the 69oz Challenge Mixed Grill (steak, two gammon, two lamb chops, three pork chops, half a chicken, four sausages, two eggs, mushrooms, peas, chips and – for the lady? – a side salad). Mental.

Eat the lot in under an hour, the meal's free and you win a T-shirt.

No? Perhaps one might tempt Sir with the Baby Burger? ('This is not a small burger; it weighs the same as a baby.') Or the Wing King Challenge: 75 – 75??? – chicken wings, their bones stripped clean in under 30 minutes, no toilet breaks, and you're forbidden from attempting the challenge twice in one year?

Still no? Then consider the Suicide Seven Wings Challenge ('Over 18s only').

'Seven Chicken Wings soaked in probably the hottest marinade ever. We used a blend of smoky paprika, tomatoes, honey, white wine vinegar and the famous and rather hot Naga Bhut Jolokia chilli or as the Americans call it Ghost Chilli.

'It measures a staggering 279,315-1,578,548 Scoville heat units. To put into perspective the Jalapeno chillies are a mere 3,500-8000 Scoville units.

'The deal is eat all seven wings and you will receive a T-shirt and your name and picture will be displayed on the wall of flame; however if you fail your picture will be displayed on the wall of shame. For our part we will supply you with glasses of milk or yoghurt and we have a few ice lollies available should you need them. All we ask is that you sign a disclaimer (yes it's that hot) proclaiming that you are an IDIOT (pic 50.34).'

I'm suddenly quite nervous. Not as nervous as I was with the bull, but nervous enough. If I attempt this, I look like a macho prick. If I fail it, I look like a macho prick.

It doesn't help that I have an uninvited audience and that the waitress has suggested I sit at the table next to them, since the dish, she explains, has a certain odour.

Nor do The Rules help.

1. NO CUTLERY
2. WINGS MUST BE EATEN WITH FINGERS
3. NO NAPKINS (DESPITE NO. 2)
4. NO DRINKS WITH MEAL
5. TIME LIMIT: TEN MINUTES
6. IF COMPLETED, WAIT A FURTHER FIVE MINUTES BEFORE BEING ALLOWED BEVERAGE OR NAPKIN

People have been jailed for torture for less.

But it's too late now.

My plate arrives. I gaze at it in horror (while Mal and family beam at it laughing). The wings, which are full-sized, not chicken-shop fare, are barely visible beneath great dollops of the sauce. It occurs to me that the Sizzle and Grill staff are intent upon me failing.

I'm focused purely on the first bite. If that's too hot for me, I'm finished, because the heat intensity will only build as the pores in my mouth are flung open in the desperation for air. If it's not, I have a chance. A slim chance.

The waitress starts the timer. I take the first bite.

It's nothing I've not experienced before, possibly even below my maximum. Is it tasty? No, it isn't. It's quite unpleasantly dry in flavour – I'd guess it's laden with homemade chilli powder, ground from dried naga – yet gloopy in consistency. Hell, it looks like diarrhoea.

By wing three (pic 50.35) I'm crying, or at least my eyes won't stop leaking. My nose is running in sympathy. According to my good friends watching, my face has turned purple.

They keep asking me questions. I can't reply because:

1) My mouth has gone numb;
2) I've only got ten minutes in which to devour this stuff.

So I keep going.

I'm inside my own head now, cursing myself for ever having considered this lunacy. Like the form says: I'm an IDIOT. But I'm there, I'm only ever going to do this once, and I'm bloody competitive.

Then I hear the door open. Other people are entering the Sizzle and Grill 'The Home of *Man V Food*' (it isn't).

An audience of people I know is bad enough. Strangers seeing me like this – like I'm some form of self-loathing coprophiliac – is far worse. Plus they're either going to wonder why I'm sitting one table away from my party or they'll think we're unconnected and that I have no friends – in which case, why am I sitting right next to them? Which all leads to this conclusion: I am a sad weirdo.

So I keep going.

There are just two wings left now. Had this been a more usual six-wing dish – whoever has seven wings? – I'd have just one left. As it is, I have two. And that's two more suicide wings than I ever want to see again.

The crashing heat in my mouth has set in so I'm enduring pain; I'm chewing on bits of gristle and fat, obscured beneath the piled devilish glop. I start hunting for virgin chicken, deep within the wing, untainted by heat or that unpleasant taste. And I begin to push sauce beneath my growing pile of gnawed bones.

Is this really worth it, I wonder? Why don't I just give up? Save some iota of dignity. It's severely tempting.

The waitress appears. 'You've got two minutes,' she says.

So I keep going.

I strip the last wing as the waitress reappears. She regards my plate with a dubious air. 'You've got to finish the sauce,' she says.

The plate's still lined with a thick pool of the stuff that I've been unable to eat, given the no-cutlery rule.

'What with?' I ask. (Actually, it was more like, 'Ot ith?' given my numbed gob.)

'Your hands,' she says.

That's it then. With the needle already flickering well into the red of the dignity-ometer, I'm about to hit rock bottom.

I overhear the new table – two blokes, two women – discussing ordering The Orgasma burger. At least I needn't worry unduly about their opinion of me, I think, as I scoop up... primordial soup and force it into my filthy cakehole with crooked fingers.

Christ, if only my parents could see me now. (Luckily they're dead.)

Determined not to fall at this final hurdle, I scrape up as much of the sauce with my fingertips as I can, aware that the clock is ticking, leaving white ceramic track marks in the horrendous goo.

The waitress reappears. 'Time's up,' she says, already inspecting my plate. It's hardly clean, I realise, but I'm done.

'Have a heart,' I plead with her. (It came out more like, 'Ab a dart'.)

She half-smiles. 'I'll ask Chef,' she says.

'Chef', I think, 'can fuck off'.

So I sit there, waiting, while Mal, Emily and Dai stare at me.

I must look like a right picture. There's nothing I can do about my fingers (pic 50.36), which are caked with a thick, reddish-brown mess, like I've recently conducted a dirty protest. My lips are burning like hell and I can feel the stuff all around my mouth. I dare not wipe at it: if this goes in

314

my eyes, I'm in casualty.

And after all that, my fate lies in the hands of Chef. If he says 'No', all... *this* would have been in vain.

I suddenly realise I've never wanted anything more – I want my photo on the Wall of Flame! I demand to have that T-shirt!

Did I win it?

Of course I did (pic 50.37)! Only the sixth or seventh to do so, I was told afterwards. (Glad I hadn't enquired about the odds before I'd started.)

Would I take on a suicide chilli challenge ever again?

No, I bloody well would not.

My stomach felt as well as could be expected (i.e. not terrible) after the event, particularly once I'd flooded it with the free milk provided by the restaurant. I thought I'd got away with it.

Then around two that morning, it started. Like someone had lit a fire in my belly. Not the proverbial kind; an actual fire. It doubled me up in pain and kept waking me up throughout the night.

I lay there hatching ways of destroying my bastard 'I Had The Suicide 7 Wings and Survived to tell the tale' T-shirt, a physical manifestation of the wanker I am, until mercifully, around 6 or 7am, the burn finally fizzled out, absorbed by my distraught insides.

How Adam Richman copes, I have no idea.

MAMHILAD PARK INDUSTRIAL ESTATE
23 June 2013

This section need not detain us at length, involving, as it does, an industrial estate. I'll be frank: I'd wondered whether to even bother visiting the place and did so more for completism's sake than for the potential thrills.

If Cwmdare Street had hardly floated my boat,

315

Mamhilad Park Industrial Estate would hole the craft below its waterline; the boat would then sink and became inhabited by a conger eel named Colin. Sadly Colin found the ambience all too demoralising and one morning blew his brains out with a rusty shotgun. Unlike wasps, which (allegedly) serve no useful purpose, the conger eel keeps down the populations of... er, stuff that conger eels eat. The undersea eco-system collapsed, leading to a sushi shortage. The aspiring middle classes went on the rampage, riots broke out and everyone died.

Welcome to Mamhilad Park Industrial Estate.

If they ever need a marketing tagline I'd suggest: 'Where the fun begins and ends. Quickly.'

Conversely, the journey there was rather interesting.

Following Mal's by then traditional monologue about slag heaps (e.g.: 'That's a slag heap. It's amazing; most of Wales is a slag heap'), we hit the Head of the Valleys Road, where the incessant loom of the Brecon Beacons hovered to our left. Mal maintained that he used to swim in the natural reservoirs as a kid, until accidents happened and the reservoirs were filled in. (Strikes me as a tad excessive – should we fill in the oceans after seamen drown?)

Then we're atop a hill and heading down into Blaenavon, World Heritage Site. From our vantage point, Blaenavon looks – with apologies to Welsh people if this sounds patronising – like something out of *Ivor the Engine*. Industrial yet somehow quaint, typically Welsh and noticeably steam train-y.

The National Coal Museum ('Big Pit') is here, allowing visitors a 300ft descent into the former colliery, as well as the Blaenavon Ironworks, Community Heritage Museum and Blaenavon Heritage Railway (the aforementioned steam trains).

The Heritage Railway travels at the highest altitude of any standard gauged preserved railway in England and Wales (I had to copy that sentence directly from the website, as I'm not entirely sure what it means), and the highlight of its family events is December's Santa Special, shunting wide-eyed youngsters to Santa's Grotto (which – respect to the devisers – happens to be in a pub. Win-win!).

As we drive up and out of Blaenavon among shivering stone cottages seeing out the present, Mal notes that properties in the area are going for a song, yet no one wants to buy them. 'Why would they?' he adds.

Through an area devoid of dwellings – where it was too dangerous to build as areas of ground would collapse into the disused mine workings – we're heading along the A4043 towards Pontypool and Griffithstown, where Mal grew up.

It's here that he starts going on about 'the world's longest railway sidings' and secretive wartime bomb-making, via the steel and ironworks nearby and in Newport. The area here is indeed very flat, ideal for railway lines.

Googling leads me to Royal Ordnance Factory Glascoed, the location in a valley between Usk and Pontypool chosen for its quiet seclusion and away from major cities targeted by bombing raids. During the war, its dedicated 17-mile rail network chuffed in and out some 13,000 workers daily. Which is quite astonishing when you consider the unassuming tranquillity and utter lack of industry here today.

Fascinating as that was, I find myself more deeply entrenched in David Hughes' delightful 'Reminiscences of Old Pontypool: Personal Memories of Pontypool in the 1930s and 1940s' blog. Among its myriad gems comes this: 'It's not widely known that, during World War II, two fleets of ships were built in Pontypool: aircraft carriers, battleships, cruisers, destroyers and submarines.'

My eyes, however, alight more readily upon 'Murder Most Foul in Pontypool', concerning the unsolved murder of 59-year-old bachelor, William 'Dripping' Lewis (so-named given his love of dripping – saturated animal fat, also a favourite of my Dad's – sandwiches); on 'Pontypool's Secret Society', a wonderfully *Just William*-esque tale of schoolboys, Quaker Oats and secret passwords; and on 'Climbing the Mountain with the Help of Watkins the Tinsmith', which I'll leave for you to discover yourself.

As noted in the original *Who Goes There*, it is precisely these tangential discoveries that make *Doctor Who* location hunting the joy that it is (for me, at least). If the location itself fails to live up to expectations – or succeeds in living down to them – hunt around the Internet for tales of the local history. (Some *Who* fans are far too narrow-minded to do so and will be whingeing and sweating as they read whole paragraphs of this book not remotely devoted to their beloved show, if they've even made it this far. To them I say: Get a grip. And also: Calm down, here comes a *Who* bit...)

The frustrating aspect of this particular location visit is that the filming of the 50th Anniversary Special at Mamhilad clearly was rather special. On the *Doctor Who* Locations website, according to *Who* location hunter par excellence, Dave Edwards – many of whose great photos you can see in the *Who Goes There* files on my website nickgriffiths.co.uk – when he arrived on the scene after dark: 'I saw what appeared to be a circle of girders surrounded with what looked like mirrors(?) with a huge light hanging over the top. Lots of flashing lights and huge flames burning then an almighty explosion that rocked the ground!!! My colleagues who were closer than me to the explosion... to put it bluntly **** themselves!!!'

Furthermore, the 50th was by no means the *Who* crew's first visit to the industrial estate. According to moviemaps.org, the following stories were also filmed there, often behind closed doors: *The Impossible Astronaut*, *Day of the Moon*, *The Eleventh Hour*, *The Beast Below*, *A Christmas Carol*, *The Satan Pit*, *Voyage of the Damned*,

The Satan Pit and *Planet of the Ood*.

What a shame that from the outside, in the cold light of a dull day, the Mamhilad Park Industrial Estate looks like this (pics 50.38-50.40).

MOD CAERWENT
23 June 2013

Hackles should immediately be raised here, too. The prefix MoD is rarely wont to infer: 'Please, come inside, have a look around. Would you like a cup of tea? What, those old files marked "TOP SECRET"? Have a look if you want but I doubt you'll find much.'

So I wasn't expecting to gain any access, though I was aware, having researched photographs of the place, that the building itself is pretty cool-looking. So I was anticipating a drive-by shooting. (Of photographs, not military personnel, Mr MoD, sir.)

Which is perfectly acceptable because the following and final destination of this commemorative trip is, like Ivy Tower, a jewel in its crown: Chepstow Castle. I've seen some fabulous photographs taken of the filming inside, featuring both David Tennant and Matt Smith, and a wandering Zygon, and for once should be able to pinpoint the same hallowed ground upon which they stood. And then stand on it myself.

Twitter's place in location hunting should be mentioned here. I came across a handful of diehards during my research of the filming, who posted pics, and others who noted signs of filming in their area.

@David_Tennant, no less, posted on 11 April: 'Filming for *Doctor Who* 50th Anniversary episode was at MOD Caerwent, Wales today. Private property so no reports if David Tennant was there.' (Evidently @David_Tennant is not the man himself, unless he's very easily confused.)

Replies to this tweet include: 'donna noble says the bees are disappearing to agatha christie' and 'my daughter's boyfriend had never watched *Doctor Who* before, but he did say that if you wear Converses you're ok!' This being the sort of thing that provides ammunition for those who dismiss Twitter as pointless.

With those people I would disagree wholeheartedly. Firstly, it is a lightning-fast and pithy means of communicating, so ideal for the location hunting lark; secondly, all sorts of people are on it. For instance...

Despite there being hundreds of photographs from the 50th filming, and of the locations themselves, across the Internet, I've seen none of Billie Piper's Rose in action. How? Why? (Don't get your hopes up – I can't necessarily answer those questions. But I can point you towards the account of @louiseeastell, who on 19 April posted: 'At the bbc being Billie pipers double...on set with her, David Tennant and co. omg. Can't quite believe it!' Followed, one hour later, by a photograph of herself in a costume, alongside an old BMW with the registration plate R16 WHO.)

So Piper was filming indoors, presumably the reason for the lack of pics. As to the costume – if indeed it is a copy of Piper's – that is best described as 'serving wench'.

We aim for Caerwent via Usk, the residences bordering the route becoming increasingly expensive the further we travel. Usk itself is like a scene from *Midsomer Murders* (less the murders): the dreamy River Usk running through a pristine, historic village of hanging baskets, indie shops, a clock tower and Quality Family Butchers.

The sun emerges, incredibly, as we arrive, so we stop at the Nags Head where the landlord is an Englishman, and order tea and teacakes, then sit outside to eat them.

Even for a Sunday, the air is unnaturally quiet, and I am reminded of my time in East Hagbourne, where *The Android Invasion* was filmed. Idyllic as Usk is, it's all a little too clean-cut for my tastes.

As we departed, so did the sun, popping its clogs as ashen-grey cloud rolled over the heavens and the world descended into gloom (slight exaggeration).

Usk, posh little Usk, leads a charmed life.

Via the A-roads 449 and 48 we approach Caerwent. The MoD building is instantly recognisable from the road, despite being set back several hundred yards across field and grazing land.

You'd have a job mistaking this cluster of red-brick monoliths (pic 50.41) for anything else.

Mal parks by the roadside and I exit the car to take photographs, my ears catching the incessant scream of highly revved car engines. Sounds like banger racing or similar, though no vehicles are visible to me. What they're doing in these parts, hell knows.

Thanks to a decent telephoto lens (Mal's), I can capture details without having to ask the Ministry of Defence to let me in (pic 50.42).

These vast buildings comprise what is more properly known as the Royal Navy Propellant Factory, manufacturing explosives and storing ammunition since 1939 (until 1993).

In 1967, the Admiralty handed it over to the Americans, whence it became United States Arms Depot Activity (the Activity bit seeming a bit spurious) Caerwent. Along the road beside which I was standing, by night, so as not to disturb the locals, convoy after convoy of lorries brought in shipments of weapons and ammunition.

If you're wondering what they did with it all – as I currently am – in 1990, 12,000 tonnes of it went off to the Middle East to murder and maim people in the first Gulf War.

The last weapons left the place in 1993, when it became a store for railway locomotives, as well as being used for the training of army personnel and cops, and, er, animal grazing – hence the inevitable sheep in my shots – and, wait for it, car rallying.

As architectural structures they're impressive. Corrugated roofs (is that asbestos?) topping sheer planes of brick, with those desolate broken windows a testament to the decay and disuse.

The most striking shot (pic 50.43), of the main building, noticeably taller than the others, with its blackened orifices, looked to me like the head of a one-eyed teddy bear hooked on junk.

As the target for a *Doctor Who* location hunter, the appeal of this site is purely visual, given the aforementioned security restrictions. (I can find no insights whatsoever into what was filmed here, by whom or precisely where.)

But hey, it was on the way to Chepstow so why not?

CHEPSTOW CASTLE
23 June 2013

You can't beat a castle in *Doctor Who*, so I'm delighted they included one in the 50th Anniversary special. One of my favourite photos in my treasured *Radio Times* Tenth Anniversary Special magazine features Elisabeth Sladen, one arm outstretched, other fist clenched in fear, creeping flat to the stonework along a castle wall, unaware that watching her from above is the Sontaran, Linx – a publicity still from *The Time Warrior*, her debut story.

That's Peckforton Castle, which cheats a little in that it was built in the mid 19th century in the style of a medieval castle (and nowadays hosts wedding and conferences – not that I wouldn't mind going there).

Chepstow Castle is the real deal – construction began in 1067, making it the oldest surviving stone fortification in Britain.

Despite this, Mal won't come inside with me. He's been there before, he says, and once was quite enough. Though I could do with the company and someone to snap me standing where Tennant et al stood, I sort of know what he means.

I remember my parents took me several times to see Lord Nelson's flagship, the HMS Victory, in Portsmouth. By the fourth or fifth time I was weeping inside.

Specifically, I'm seeking an expanse of grass. A medieval-style tent (somehow reminiscent of the roundabout in *The Magic Roundabout*) was pitched on that, alongside the Tardis; Tennant and Matt Smith were pictured wandering about it, dressed in natty matching grey fur-hooded anoraks; and a Zygon with a pert bottom strode across it.

I want that grass. Which surely can't be hard to pinpoint in a castle, castles being mainly noted for their stone?

We arrive in Chepstow post-lunch, not that we've eaten any. The town, says Mal, 'is Wales but it isn't Wales. Lots of people in Chepstow consider it to be England.' If he's right, we should point them towards a map.

Our quarry is easily found – it being very large and almost 1,000 years old (plus there were signposts) – and we halt in its car park close to a selection of pleasant looking eateries, as our stomachs rumble. To call this spot twee might only be a touch harsh.

The castle is right behind us, so I turn around. There it is!

I'm not what you'd call an expert on castle terminology – indeed I only know about ramparts and I'm not even sure the ones atop this tower come under that classification – so don't expect me to describe the architecture with any degree of finesse.

What we have here (pic 50.44) is a castle.

Hang on, I'm going to have to consult some experts...

So that fat tower on the left is the Marten's Tower and

on the right, the main entrance is contained within the Outer Gatehouse. The areas of enclosed lawn, the courtyards – including the one I'm after – are known as baileys. Chepstow has three: Lower, Middle and Upper, though I didn't know that at the time of the visit. Which one the *Who* crew filmed on, I would have to work out. (You'd imagine, for practical reasons, they'd choose the largest. I'll be bearing this in mind.)

...Sorry, I've just found a link to TripAdvisor, where people have actually reviewed Chepstow Castle. I had no idea you could review castles, nor why you'd want to.

The place is ranked #2 of 13 attractions in Chepstow (beaten by Tintern Abbey, since you asked). There are some crackers among the reviews.

Here's one moaning about the admission price for the castle and noting that the Chepstow Museum is free to enter, adding, 'Why bother to go into the castle when all the info about it is in the museum.' Erm...

'Unfortunately we got there at closing and we were not able to go inside...'

'Good family afternoon out, but no café :('

'The approach, parking and public convenience were poor. stuctures need maintainenace [sic].'

'The castle is a little smaller than others around.'

And perhaps my favourite: '...having visited several castles since, it's not a lot different to the others.'

Ah, the British public. Don'cha luv 'em.

So while Mal disappears off to track down some lunch, I head inside. Admission is £4.50, which doesn't strike me as steep. Entry, inevitably, is via the gift shop.

The trouble with having a four-year-old daughter is that half of this tat becomes buyable. There's a *Princess Creativity Book*, princess action figures and tea towels. Maybe not the tea towels.

I linger far too long, taunting myself and my ailing

wallet, before summoning the strength to break free of the gift shop's tractor beam.

As I exit, a trio of young girls dressed in medieval garb pass me (pic 50.45), which is briefly disorientating. Then it occurs to me: wherever there is clustered history there will be historical re-enactors. Those three kids could be at home playing with Barbie or watching *The X Factor*, but no, they've been forced into felt while Mummy and Daddy are nearby, calling each other Ethelred and Gawain, knitting socks from wool soaked in sheep's piss.

I've emerged straight into what I can now correctly identify as the lower bailey (pic 50.46). Someone has erected a bloody great big awning, which definitely isn't contemporary with William fitzOsbern who ordered the place built. FitzOsbern was essentially toadying to his King, William the Conqueror, who used Chepstow as a handy stopping-off point from which to raid the irksome Welsh.

Is this the lawn on which Tennant and Smith stood? It slopes rather noticeably, which wasn't on my checklist, and neither is it all that large.

I don't have a laptop with me, to compare photographs, though I do have a set of printouts... among which I have handily failed to include the Chepstow pics.

Can I at least imagine the *Who* crew filming here? To be honest, I'm not sure I can. It feels too small to accommodate tent, Tardis, actors and film crew. So I go off in search of a greater expanse of green.

Hanging a right into the interior, I come upon a balcony and am stunned by the view (pic 50.47). A wide, mud-banked river (the Wye) stretches far downstream and hangs a sharp right (pic 50.48) beside the castle (hence its original Norman name, Striguil, derived from the Welsh word of 'river bend'). Across the river is a sprawling white property that must be worth a bomb.

Equally unexpectedly, there's far more castle than I'd imagined, high atop cliffs. The furthest section (the Great

Tower) looks as though it's missing a good smattering of the original stonework, whether to some pesky war or to the ravages of time and neglect.

I linger a while, taking in the scene, which is worth the admission price alone. It's quite incredible that anyone had the audacity to build this structure from that material right here, on the top of a bloody great sheer drop. That said, it was all very well of Billy fitzOsbern to have the idea – he didn't have to physically build the thing. I've been quite petrified merely looking down from the safety of a several-feet-thick balcony. Imagine being the bloke hauling the latest boulder to the top of the Great Tower.

Mal calls: he's ordered lunch. I need to step on it.

Leaving the balcony I spot engravings in the stonework (pic 50.50). How old these must be, I marvel. Those initials, cut deep into the rock – C.H. G.E.L. – might have been carved there almost a millennium ago, perhaps by star-crossed lovers. Then I notice LFC (Liverpool Football Club) carved beneath and stop marvelling.

Though the wind was howling outside, walls this thick really keep out the cold, and despite their harsh stoniness, inside feels almost cosy.

Though I'm here for the grass bits, and I now have as long as it takes to cook a roast dinner, I still feel compelled to do a quick tour of the interiors. I find a crazy little room (pic 50.51) with light penetrating through two windows, giving the space a ghost-faced hue. Then I head downstairs (pic 50.52) beneath some gorgeous arched stonework to discover the cellar.

A cellar's a cellar, though Chepstow's is larger and older than most; however, I find myself sharing the room with another visitor.

It's always disconcerting, when attending a museum/gallery/exhibition to become aware of someone beside you. The awareness quickly becomes acute. Suddenly you start worrying over how much time one should reasonably spend inspecting an exhibit. Leave too soon and clearly you did not appreciate it enough – perhaps did not even understand it! – linger too long and you're stuck staring at something potentially really boring.

So I become trapped in the cellar for ages while the clock ticks and this other bloke won't go away, trying to look suitably interested in a notice on the wall describing the cellar, which is really boring.

Gratefully, when finally outside again, I discover the second area of grass (the middle bailey, as we now know). Two things concern me:

a) It's inhabited by historical re-enactors (pic 50.53);
b) It's even smaller than the last bit of grass.

One of the re-enactors is teaching members of the public archery, while others sit around chatting. They've pitched variously colourful medieval-style tents – and a 70s-style beach windbreak (pic 50.54). How that fits in with sackcloth garments and eating swans for dinner, I have no idea.

This definitely is not the place where *Who* filmed. The walls around aren't high enough and the green area is too tiny. Which makes me think I'd already found my goal, the moment I walked into the castle.

I have to keep going, just in case.

The final stretch of grass – anyone? Yes, the upper bailey – is piddling in size and cut through with a tarmac path. It was so pathetic, I didn't even photograph it. I did, however, photograph inside the Great Tower, which was quite spectacular (pic 50.55).

That is a castle tower. It *looms*. It oppresses. It impresses. It speaks in wind-blown whispers of riches and power. What stories its walls could tell. Of banquets and kings with gloved fists and ladies in finery.

It's just a shame that big arch in the wall at the end looks like a pissed Pacman ghost.

Mystery solved, then. All that's required is to retrace my steps to the lowest courtyard where, all other options having been exhausted, David Tennant, Matt Smith, the Tardis, a tent that somehow resembled the roundabout in *The Magic Roundabout* and a pert-bottomed Zygon once stood.

Perhaps, I think, if I look at the ground from a different angle, it will seem more familiar? So I do, from the top (pic 50.56).

Compare my photograph with the one from doctorwholocations.net accessed via this link: http://bit.ly/17Hv5fY. See that door with the descending steps behind the Zygon in a deckchair? That distinctive window above it?

THAT'S IT! (As Charlie Brown used to say.)

Exit from the castle, inevitably, was back through the gift shop.

Reckon I withstood a second visit (pic 50.57)?

I've since seen further photographic evidence from the filming at Chepstow and also in attendance were John Hurt (another Doctor, provenance uncertain), companion Jenna-Louise Coleman and Joanna Page, among others. All the main characters, bar Piper. So this was a major scene – perhaps the denouement?

And I wonder about that recurring tent, present both here and at Ivy Tower, as each time was our Zygon friend. Disguised spaceship?

Though the scripts themselves don't stand up to forensic analysis – like I cared as a kid – *The Three Doctors* and *The Five Doctors* were among the most exciting when they aired originally.

The Three Doctors because I had never had the chance to see William Hartnell or Patrick Troughton in the lead role; *The Five Doctors*, because it meant the return of Jon

Pertwee, whom I adored.

***

Come on, hands up, who's dying to see David Tennant back in his brown pinstripe? A sea of hands, from Washington DC to Washington, Tyne & Wear!

It's going to be completely brilliant. (Unless Moffat gets too nerdy on our asses... but I refuse to contemplate that.)

At the very least, when they play the Ivy Tower and Chepstow Castle scenes, I'll be nudging the wife (busy reading a magazine): 'I've been there! I've been there!'

Selected bibliography

General
http://www.doctorwholocations.net/stories/dw08

Gelligaer Common
http://www.cprw.org.uk/magartcl/gelligaer.htm

Ivy Tower
http://education.gtj.org.uk/en/item1/36160
http://www.gnollestatecountrypark.co.uk

Sizzle and Grill
http://www.sizzleandgrill.co.uk/MAN-v-FOOD.html

Mamhilad
http://www.visitblaenavon.co.uk/en/Homepage.aspx
http://oldpontypool.wordpress.com
http://moviemaps.org/locations/1ju

MoD Caerwent
http://billiepiedpiper.tumblr.com/post/48353352518/louisee
astell-on-twitter-has-posted-and
http://en.wikipedia.org/wiki/Royal_Navy_Propellant_Facto
ry,_Caerwent

Chepstow Castle
http://www.castlewales.com/chepstow.html
http://en.wikipedia.org/wiki/Chepstow_Castle

Thanks:

Sinead held everything together while I burnt the midnight oil on this one. She was, is and always will be a complete and utter star.

To everyone who took time out to accompany me, because the experiences would have been far poorer without them: Sinead (again), Dylan, Andy, Karl, Cecelia, Alex, Cath, Jack, Kate. Thank You.

To Tom and Lucy at Legend Press, and Robin, my agent.

To Paul at Diverse Music, for hospitality and the pics. (Speaking of which, that easter egg on my website – the internet-only chapter is set in Diverse Music, Newport, where *Blink* was also filmed. A clue: think Blondie's number one from February 1980. If you're stumped, email me.)

And, as ever, to my Mum and Dad. The two will always go together.

Lightning Source UK Ltd.
Milton Keynes UK
UKOW05f0346301113

222138UK00001B/1/P